Field and fern : or, Scottish flocks & herds (South)

Dixon, Henry Hall

BIBLIOLIFE

Engraved by Henry Walter from a Photograph by Beard.

HIS GRACE THE LATE DUKE OF RICHMOND. K.G.

PRESIDENT OF THE HIGHLAND & AGRICULTURAL SOCIETY 1831-1860.

DEDICATION.

TO ·

J A M E S   D O U G L A S,

OF ATHELSTANEFORD,

IN REMEMBRANCE OF THE TIME WHEN HE LED

THE "RED, WHITE, AND ROAN" TO VICTORY OVER THE BORDER,

THIS BOOK IS DEDICATED BY HIS FRIEND,

THE AUTHOR·

PREFACE.

THE object and the mode of my journey have been
so fully explained in the preface to part "North"
that I need not recount them here. It was my
original intention to have compressed the whole of
my notes into one book, but on further consideration it seemed that it would be for the interest
both of myself and my readers to make two parts,
which could be purchased separately. "Highlands"
and "Lowlands" were the natural divisions, but I
eventually decided to call them "North" and
"South," and take the Frith of Forth as nearly as
possible for my line of demarcation. Without en-
tering at any length into arable matters (which Mr.
Stephens in his "Book of the Farm," and other
writers, have handled so ably), I have endeavoured,
as far as lay in my power, to make these two parts
a reflex of that Scottish country life which I enjoyed
so heartily for three successive summers. There may
be errors, but still there is not a page in either part

but what has been submitted, not to one, but often to two or three men of the highest experience in that particular subject. That "doctors will disagree" is a truth which I have too often felt in the course of my labours, and I can only hope that in divers difficulties I have pinned my faith on the right "doctor" at last.

H. H. DIXON.

10, *Kensington Square,*
August 1, 1865.

CONTENTS.

c (s)

CHAPTER III.

EDINBURGH TO THE ROMAN CAMP.

CHAPTER IV.

ROMAN CAMP TO ATHELSTANEFORD.

CHAPTER V.

ATHELSTANEFORD TO COLDSTREAM.

CHAPTER IX.

FALDONSIDE TO DALGIG.

CHAPTER X.

DALGIG TO AYR.

CHAPTER XI.

AYR TO ARDROSSAN.

CHAPTER XII.

AYR TO DUMFRIES.

CHAPTER XIII.

TINWALD DOWNS TO HALLHEATHS.

CHAPTER XIV.

LOCKERBY TO MOODLAW.

CHAPTER XV.

MOODLAW TO ARKLETON.

CHAPTER XVI.

CANNOBIE TO KENSINGTON.

ENGRAVINGS.

(s)

FIELD AND FERN,

OR,

SCOTTISH
FLOCKS AND HERDS.

CHAPTER I.

GLASGOW TO CAPELLIE.

" An'l what a sweep of mountains grand,
From Goatfell, Arran's Pride,
To Northern ' Bens' and Eastern ' Tops,'
And your own ' Pad' beside !"

A. GRAHAM.

Mr. Harvey's Glasgow Dairy—The Easterhill Pigs—Merryton—The
Duke of Hamilton's Clydesdales and Ayrshires—The Prize Clydesdales
at the Highland Society—Mr. A. Graham of Capellie; his Farm,
Ventilation, and Coursing Career—Scottish Coursing Cracks and
Grounds—Barrator at Biggar—Waterloo—A Visit to the Renfrew-
shire Kennel.

"A TIRED man will struggle hard to get home."
Such was the reasoning of Captain Barclay's
father, when he began his planting at Ury as far
from the house as possible; and some such idea pos-
sessed us, when we made a special point of finishing
our journey North of the Frith of Forth before we

2 B

attempted the Lowlands We had done, to our
boundless joy, with "the deep-sea sailings" at last;
but there was nothing we specially cared for in
Glasgow, except the monster dairy. It lies among
a frowning forest of chimneys, and was reached
through mud and mire, now over a tram-road, now
across a canal, and finally past a manufactory where
horses are boiled into glue by the score.

Mr. Harvey's byres are distinguished by different
names—"The Parlour," "The Thistle," "The Hal-
low-een," "The Waterloo," "The Malakhoff," and
so on. There were some 1,700 cows and queys in
all, and about 1,000 of them in milk, and feeding on
turnip, cut straw, and distilled grains. The bulls,
which stand with them, are mostly shorthorns, and
so are 300 of the milch cows; the rest are Ayrshires,
with the exception of a few polls and recently a sprinkling of Dutch. They stand in long ranks tail to tail,
and the scourings fall into the gutters behind them,
which are duly flushed down. Hence each beast has
to be very accurately told off, on her arrival, into a
byre, whose stallage exactly suits her length. In
some of the byres there is only one line of cows, and
the calves are in small partitions opposite them.
About fifty of the queys are kept each year, and go
as yearlings and two-year-olds to Parks down the
Clyde, and the rest are dismissed as "slink veal" (to
adopt the term of the trade) to the butcher soon after
they are calved. Thirteen cows are allotted to each
milker, seven of whom live on the spot, and the rest

arrive at milking hours from Glasgow. The dairy
is under the Thistle emblem, and is furnished entirely
with wooden vessels. Turkeys were picking their
dainty way round the manure tank, and casting
longing eyes at the offal in the abyss, whose contents
are discharged through pipes for miles to the thirsty
meadows, and return to the fountain-head once more
in the shape of succulent grasses.

Easterhill, the Carrhead of Scotland, is reached
from Glasgow through Bridgetown, and lies about
four miles out on the road to the Clyde Iron Works.
The owner's tastes speak for themselves, as you drive
up the beech and oak avenue, and see "Nelly" and
four other sows routing in the meadow close up to
the iron railings. This has always been the Carrhead system, and it has been the fruitful mother of
many a litter. They are mostly tenderly waited on
at Easterhill when they do come; and we found a
woman with her fire and her bed in a small room
adjoining the piggery, and in attendance on two sows
which had just farrowed. Mr. Findlay began, about
nine years ago, with Windsors, two sows and a boar,
and got a Jonathan Brown boar from Cumberland
to cross the produce. The small breed was very
successful at local shows, and he consolidated it by
using Lord Wenlock's breed with its short broad
face, pointed ear, great jowl, and fine quality, upon
his Windsors and Windsor-Browns. His large breed
had their origin in a Harrison boar and sow, and in
a short time he came second with "Nelly" (the dam

2 B 2

of Sally, *alias* the Spotted Lady, and some other
capital sows) and "Bob" of his own breeding, in the
boar and sow classes at Kelso. Nelly has yielded
up her ham and bacon, and the only addition since
our visit is a boar of the large sort from Mr. Brown's
of Kirkbampton, near Carlisle. The middle breed is
a simple combination of the two others. Glasgow
Green in May (where Mr. Findlay won firsts
in the large and small classes this year) is the
great local pig show, and there the "Improved
Easterhill" pigs have done uniformly well. The
sows are generally ready to pig a fortnight after, so
as to be in nice trim for the Highland Society. Ten of
the small and large, and two of the middle breed compose the Easterhill breeding sow lot; and many
young pigs have gone to the West Indies and America, as well as all over Scotland, at very high prices,
from the teat.

Their owner rather enjoys "pig-racing," which, as
a country squire once said to us, "is quite as good
fun as shorthorn-racing, at one-fourth the expense."
The sister sport also profits, as another breeder made
it his boast "that he had three days a week hunting
out of two breeding sows.' The best pig joke we
heard in Scotland was at the expense of a man in
charge. His beloved sow had won, and some by-
standers would tell him that he had no right to the
prize, as she was not so good in her girth as the second. Through good report and evil report he was
bound to support her; and this he did most effec-

tually, after a fashion: " *Girth, indeed! we don't like
'em to girth ower much doon at our place*"—an expression which ran round the yard like wild-fire·
Except when the Society was at Newcastle, Mr.
Findlay has never sent any pigs to the English
Royal. He there took his stand on the small whites,
and was second with George 1st to Mr. Mangles's
Brutus, and third to Mr. Wainman's Silver Branch
and Mr. Stearn's Victoria 2nd, with his Lady Emily.
The latter and Silver Branch met again at Stirling,
and the Scottish Bench reversed the Royal decision.

Mr. Findlay and his brother Major Findlay breed
Clydesdales at their farm of Kenmuir, two miles
further on, from which their father sold Briton·to
the late Prince Consort, some nine years since, at
250 gs. We found there the three-year-old sire
which was second to Mr. Stirling's Baronet in a good
field at Kelso, the third-prize two-year-old filly at
Stirling, and some local winners, to say nothing of
Fabula (dam of Lord of Linne), an old Knockhill
acquaintance, with her Warlock foal.

Merryton, the home-farm of Hamilton Palace, was
the next on our list, and was reached by a walk of
two miles from Hamilton. Except when we chanced
to be toiling along, carpet-bag on back (and intended
to stand whisky to give it a ride, and follow on " the
cow and calf principle"), we didn't look much at the
carts, but here we were bound to note that they were
all green, with red wheels—a fashion which extends
from Tinto to Greenock, when the red and all

red begin again. The Clyde winds along to our
left, and the dome of the family mausoleum, where
the late Duke sleeps, just peeps above the Palace
woods. For many years his Grace took no great interest in stock; but when the Battersea Meeting
drew nigh, and many exhibitors grew faint-hearted
about the distance, he contracted a great wish to
see the Scottish ranks well filled, and Mr. Drew was
accordingly directed to get together a strong force
of Clydesdales and Ayrshires.

The task was exactly to his mind, and right well
executed, although he had only three days' notice
before the last day of entry. Sir Walter Scott was
bought from Mr. David Riddell of Kilbowie. He had
won at the Highland Society's Meeting at Dumfries,
and 400 gs. was the figure. It was his Grace's delight at his pony paces and the number of times he
had him trotted up the Battersea rows after his victory, which did much towards bringing about a
proper Royal parade at Worcester the next year.
Maggie, the second-prize brood mare, also came from
Mr. Park of Balquanharan, near Dalmuir. The
Ayrshire bull Sir Colin was bought from Mr. R.
M'Kean, and was first; and Brockie, the second-
prize cow in-calf, and Airblaes, the first-prize cow
in-calf, were selected with some seven other cows and
heifers, two of which were highly commended, out
of Mr. Drew's own Merryton herd. Merryton had
other collateral honours, as Colly Hill, who beat
Brockie, and had been sold out of its stalls, and Lord

Strathmore's second and third prize cows in-calf had also been bred there. The seven Hamilton Clydesdales made up a great array, and four firsts, two seconds, and a third were their spoils. This success worked his Grace up, and made him wish for the home-farm, and he accordingly bought all Mr. Drew's stock. His interest in them never faltered to the close; and during his last and very brief visit to the Palace in the May of '63, he hardly missed an afternoon among them.*

Sir Walter had forgotten none of his beautiful hock action; and Rosy, Jean, Jane, Sally, Maggy, and a number of other fine mares, were in the stalls. Rosy and Jean had been pitted three times against each other with the same result ; but still, at the sale Jean made 81 gs., or three guineas more, as being more durable and with better action, while Rosy had more size. There were 150 Ayrshires, young and old, and eighty or ninety of them in-calf. Brockie was there, as full of quality as ever, and so was Airblaes, who is much the bigger cow of the two. She has been first at Maryhill since her visit to Battersea, and she reversed her second at Hamilton when she and the winning cow met on Glasgow Green.

Mr. Marshall of Airblaes sold her to Mr. Drew originally for £60, and as one of her calves has made £30, and she has won £38 worth of prizes, her purchase-money has come back with interest.

* An account of the new farm buildings will be found in *The Scottish Farmer*, April, 1864.

The byre is 80 by 60 feet, and well papered with prize-tickets. Seven of them are Collyhill's, and all of those firsts; in fact, she never was beaten but once, and then almost immediately after calving. No butter or cheese is made here, but the cream goes to Glasgow with sweet and skim milk. The calves, of which his Grace rears 30 or 40 and seldom sells bulls, are always brought up with sweet milk for two or three months ; they then get on to oilcake and grass, and gradually to cut hay, steamed turnips, boiled barley, and barley-meal twice a day.

At one time the late Duke used to breed West Highlanders at Arran, but Mr. Allan Pollok so invariably beat him at the Highland Society that he did not persevere. His Grace began again in the heat of the Breadalbane sale, and bought four or five lots. They went, like the rest of his stock, to Kelso, in order that the wish of his life—never to see the West Highland, Ayrshire, or Clydesdale ranks bare at the Highland Society—might be fulfilled in his death, and were sold on the ground to his Breadalbane opponent, the late Duke of Athole.

We are quite in the county of Clydesdales here, but still there is no great stud of them, and some of the best have been bred by farmers keeping four or five work mares. The Clydesdale is well suited for the cold climate, and except for breeding milk ponies, the thorough-bred horse is very little used to cross them. Judging from the Barrhead Society prize-list, there is a distinction even in this class of dairy

labour. The prize drawer of the butter-milk cart is
to be a "horse not above fifteen hands," and of the
sweet-milk ditto a "pony not above fourteen-two."
Many farmers fancy that Clydesdales are getting too
lofty, but breeders will keep the high prices of
the lorry market in their eye. For this business the
buyers never look at anything under sixteen-two and
17 cwt., and they must have capital feet, "good
either for frost or fresh." Large ears, a fiddle-case
rather than a Roman or "Cheshire Cheese" head,
a good eye, broad flat legs, nicely feathered like a setter's, straight-away equal action, and a good mottled
bay or brown are all very cardinal points.*

The Glasgow meetings in 1826 and 1828 were the
first at which the Highland Society offered Clydesdale prizes, and since then they have gone on steadily.
With the exception of one year, the entries have of
course always been best in the Glasgow district, and
rose there in 1857 to 240. There were sixteen rare
mares at Perth in '29, when a black one of Mr.
Adam Curror's, and bought from "Sammel Graham,"
won; and the Kingcausie people, who were very con-
fident with one of their greys, had to take the second
card. Mr Fram of Bromfield, on the old road
from Edinburgh to Ayr, was soon well known
among Clydesdale men with his Glancer, who was
never beaten till he was twelve. The scene of his

* All the learning on the subject of Clydesdales is collected in the pam-
phlet published a few years ago by Mr Charles Stevenson, editor of the
"North British Agriculturist," in reply to the queries on the subject which
were sent to him from France

downfall was at Haddington, when he met Mr.
Steedman of Boghall's Lofty. They were led by two
brothers, and Glancer's arrival was so unexpected
that when Lofty's man heard of it, he soared into
the indignant latitudes, locked up his stable and
would not show his horse to his brother, and would
not in fact speak to him for years. At Aberdeen in
'34 the Clydesdale men had no high opinion of some
Lincolnshire horses which had been brought into the
neighbourhood, and thought them soft and greasy-
legged, and not likely to stand the climate; and in
the following year, the damp climate of Ayrshire was
given as the reason why the Ayrshire horses, old and
young, had bog-spavins and thorough-pins. The
judges were divided over the first-prize horse, and
the decision was so much canvassed that when one
of them who was in the minority gave effect to
his dissent at the dinner, and quoted one of his colleagues in confirmation, he was received with "loud
and long-continued cheering."

The greys were in the ascendant at Dumfries in
'37; but there was a good struggle between the winning one and Mr. Steedman's black Champion, for
which Professor Dick stood out manfully. The grey
mare had The Peacock at her foot, perhaps the
largest foal ever seen in Scotland, and the sire of a
very capital stock, many of them greys, in his time.
Champion beat everything quite easily at Glasgow
the next year; and no one was more delighted than
the Professor, as three or four times he had hobbled

him, and then begged him off. His owner was sorely
anxious to see the judging, but the rules did not
allow of more than one attendant. Accordingly he
bluffed his black, and took hold of one side of his
head, while his groom took the other, and, by met-
tling him up a bit, persuaded the policemen that he
had such a savage in charge that they fell back in
mortal terror. When he was once in his stall the
bandage was still left on, and "Boghall" slipped
down the ranks and "got a pig to wait on." With
such advantages he obtained as extensive and as accurate an insight into the judges' proceedings as he did
into Parisian life and customs, when he crossed the
Channel in 1856 as *chargé d'affaires* of the Scottish
stock under Mr. Hall Maxwell. At the right moment
he signalled the man to take off the bandage, and out
came the Champion, stepping like a pony, and well
might the Marquis of Tweeddale say "He wins in a
canter."

The Show at Aberdeen in '40 confirmed the an-
ticipations of six years before, that there would hardly
be a good horse, and they were well tried on the
granite. In '44 the show was again at Glasgow, not
in the cattle market, but on The Green. This was
the year of Loudon Tam, a very Blair Athol among
Clydesdales, with his beautiful bone and silky hair.
There was also a very good four-year-old mare, but
not equal to Mr. Fram's mare in '48. It is well
known that their coats are washed with butter-milk
till they look all glazed and painted ; but this mare

had been, it was said, in the fullest enjoyment of two
cows' milk for two months before. Cumberland furnished her grey Merry Tom to the Glasgow show of
'50, and the oldest judges agreed that they had never
seen a better for his age. Clyde, who was not
then Mr. Stirling's, won as a three-year-old, and four
very rare ones headed the old class. But for knuck-
ling over slightly, a Fife horse would have got it, and
even the one which was placed third was sold for
£350; but the amount of the luckpenny—sometimes
an enormous per-centage—did not transpire. An accident in his stable which prevented his showing so well
destroyed Clyde's chance against a " gay cocky little
horse" of Sam Clark's of Kilbarchan in '52 at Perth,
where Merry Tom was cast. He won at Glasgow
soon after, and a newspaper controversy raged as to the
Perth "why and wherefore." The judges were not men
to flinch when they had given an opinion; but
neither of them, although they corresponded on the
point, could remember why he was put aside. One
of them had "lost sight of him for two years;" but,
as "Boghall" happened to sit at dinner the day
before the show at Berwick-upon-Tweed, the grey
went past, and though he only saw him through
the wire blinds, he put down his knife and fork,
and exclaimed, without any preface, to the astonish-
ment of a crowded coffee-room : *"I see his fault
now ; his thighs are too light."* Clyde was against
him that year ; but though the bay was rather lame,
Mr. Gibson would not give him up, as he consi-

dered him a far truer type of a Clydesdale than the grey.

It was grey again at Inverness in '56, when Mr. Wilson showed Comet, and brought him to the show, not sheeted and by easy walking stages, but at a good swinging trot in his dog-cart forty miles from Durne. Since then he has won the gold cup three years in succession at Aberdeen, where in '58 an "oversman" was called in to decide between Black Leg and a grey. The bay was quite one of the Loudon Tam stamp, and no one could crab him, except to say that " *his leg's painted.*" Next year Mr. Steedman offered £400 for him, and he finally went to Melbourne, it was said, for another £100. The leaders both of the young and old ranks were remarkable at Dumfries in '60. Sir Walter Scott and his second exactly foreshadowed their Battersea places; and most of the younger horses left the country at about £300. At Battersea the young horses were bad, and the mares, of which four out of the first five were Mr. Stirling's of Keir, a remarkable lot. It was quite a Hamilton Palace year at Stirling, as the stud won three firsts, two seconds, and a third, against a strong competition; and the very clever first-prize mare in-foal had the first Sir Walter Scott of his Grace's breeding by her side. Still, Stirling, where Mr. Keir's Peggy was such a bay belle, had the best show of Clydesdale mares ever seen in Scotland; and " Boghall," who is quite the walking Peerage of the breed, was so smitten that he

bought a dozen mares and stallions at all prices from
£40 to £200 on the spot, for England and the Con-
tinent. Among the four or five greatest breeders of
Clydesdales are Mr. Samuel Clark of Manswrae,
Kilbarchan, and Mr. Peter Crauford of Dumgoyack,
Strathblane. The latter had Black Leg, and sold him
at £500, the greatest price that was ever given for a
Clydesdale stallion in Scotland.

From Glasgow we started for Capellie near Barrhead, to see Mr. A. Graham. We had a long climb
after " The Emperor of Coursers" over the Fereneze
range, and found him at last with Curds and Cream,
Analough, and General Bragg in the sheets, and the
smooth Editor and the rough Tassan in the slips.
Both of them strain back to Gilbertfield, who,
though rough himself, generally begot them smooth.
His own brindle was so peculiar, that, according to
the shade imparted to it by his condition, the judge,
on deciding for him, shouted *"Brindle!"* or *"Blue!"*
or *" Grey !"* It is now forty years since Mr. A. Graham began public coursing, and twenty-seven since
he became the annual chairman at the Waterloo
dinner. Farming has made him indifferent to
greyhound breeding and training, but not to the
business of the field. He is still there, as Mr.
Nightingale was wont to say of him in old days,
" with his eyes always open to make the most of the
game, and never wanting at the finish, so that I had
always some one to ride home with."

We kept beating away over Capellie heights, with

that glorious prospect of the Scottish hills in the distance, and the clear-bottomed surface drains at our feet. These are made with a plough constructed for the purpose, eighteen feet apart and five to ten inches in depth. A man with two horses can drain five acres a day; and the muirland bite has been improved not a little for the blackfaced ewes, which are crossed with Leicesters for early Glasgow lamb. Along the middle of the sheep-walk is an excellent rifle range of twelve hundred yards; and the sheep-walk itself is a great rural amphitheatre, where the West of Scotland sham-fight took place in '64, with 8,000 volunteers, in the valley, nearly 50,000 spectators on Capellie top and Killoch height, and the "Field Marshal of the Waterloo" in the double character of a Major of a Battalion and Lord of the Manor.

He is at pretty constant drill, both with rifle, tongue, and pen. As "A Public Courser," he first gave life and nerves to the dry bones of coursing literature. "*Sic itur ad astra*," said a rapturous lover of long-tails, when he read the beautiful scenery and character setting of his Cup victory in *The Life;* and in one sense the writer has now glided into "the milky-way," as he follows up sport with practice, as "A Renfrewshire Dairyman." Be it as chairman or lecturer, there is always the same eloquent flow and dainty choice of language, which might go from his lips to the press without altering a word, combined with the power of staying any distance, on any

subject, at any hour of the day or night. As Captain
Heys said, in proposing his health as chairman of
the Barrhead Agricultural Society, " whenever any
of the good boys of Barrhead attempted to enter the
ring, he had the happy tact of appealing to the
feelings of the model little man, who fled before the
Major could finish his address."

Much of the Capellie farm is from 600 to 700
feet above the sea-level, and many shook their
heads when Mr. A. Graham took to it. The green-
crop land is dressed, before it is drilled, with hot lime
mixed with kelp-salt, or common salt, which has been
found to be very efficacious against finger and toe,
as well as grubs, worms, and, as a matter of course,
moles. With this view, as well as to give strength
to the straw, the land sown with cereals is dressed
with salt at the rate of 4 cwt. per acre; and he
informs us that he has every reason to be satisfied with
the result, both in his corn, root, and grass crops.

The little farm steading, with its water-wheel
which is painted mail-coach colour and its ventilation
processes, has made many an agriculturist observe
that " Mr. Graham is all air and water." The stables
and cow houses are effectually ventilated, and abundance of water is laid on for drink, and for cleansing
within the byres, where a large number of Ayrshires contribute their quota, morning and evening,
to the voracious Glasgow milk-cans.

The very hay-slides are so managed as to prevent the stable being cold or warm just as

the rack is empty or full; and the ventilators arc remarkably simple. Every three yards along the ridge the roof is cut out, and one of them is inserted, rising two feet in the air with openings on the two opposite sides, protected from rain and snow by boards which overhang at an angle of 45 degrees. It is divided in the middle within by a thin board which descends six inches lower than the line of the ridge, and a horizontal board is fixed three inches below like a tray, to spread the descending air, and intercept it from falling directly on the cattle. According to the direction from which it blows, the wind enters at one side or the other, strikes the internal dividing-board, and descends, thus supplying fresh air, and pressing—one might say pumping—the used or heated air up the other or sheltered side of the dividing-board into the outer air. Mr. A. Graham considers it most efficacious against smells or draughts, or, as he puts it in his terse way, "no cough heard in the stable, no pleuro-pneumonia seen in the byre." The thrashing of cereals, the cutting of hay and straw, and the sawing of wood, are all done by water power, which is supplied by a long canal across a hill-side, fed by the drainage of some hundreds of acres. His irrigated meadows yield from three to five tons of hay per acre to one cutting; and when not cut a second time, they are pastured without injury, as the land has been thoroughly drained, and is perfectly firm.

Amid all his improvements and experiments at

2 c

Capellie, the love of the leash will peep out. There is an open heart in the centre of the book-case in his farm-office, and *of course* a greyhound, and not a ventilator, is embossed on it. He wears greyhound (rough or smooth we conclude, as they come) skins in the shape of waistcoats; and at Fereneze House, where he has latterly resided with his elder brother John, the old white horse, on which for well nigh twenty years he led the coursing-field, is buried under a sycamore. He was by Caleb Quotem, fifteen hands sharp, and not a very pleasant one to ride till he was seven or eight years old. A statue of the greyhound Oscar, from which envious Time has stolen the tail (which was turned round, and carried high in life), is over the front-door. It is the work of Greenshields, the self-taught sculptor, not from measurement, but simply from looking at the animal of which it is a perfect image. Mr. A. Graham took Oscar over himself to that little, quiet cottage by the side of the Clyde, and let him play about while "the fine hale mason, with a countenance like a book," noted every attitude, and then "fixed" him in stone from the self-same rock from which he had hewn the stone for his Sir Walter Scott.

Oscar always went from a loose slip, and used to roll his tongue strangely from side to side, while the beaters were looking for a hare. "Studying Oscar," said a great judge, "is studying coursing." He placed himself right in his hare's line, and realized the old saying that "a cunning dog will throw you over, but

that it takes some sense to win a great cup." Thus
Mr. Nightingale was wont to say of Ladylike that she
"had just sense enough not to be cunning; if the
hare went down hill, she would follow her just far
enough, and not too far, so as to stop herself; but if
she did miscalculate, she went like a shot." Mr. A.
Graham's British Lion had this faculty to a nicety,
as he would stop in two yards on the side of a hill.
He and Greenwich Time were both Fereneze cracks,
but British Lion was the best of them all. He was,
according to Mr. Nightingale, "a dog who would
run every day, and with a constitution against the
world—fine smooth action : even his failings were
respectable ; and if he was beaten, he ran well and
worked hard. Still, as a killer there was nothing
like Cerito for safety and science. Her measure was
perfection. She would never make a flying kill, but
draw herself back and be ready for the turns, and
kill them just on the bend or the broadside. Mocking
Bird threw herself at her hare farther off than any
greyhound I ever saw. Riot's was a very straight
and steady style. Both she and Wicked Eye were
wonderfully full of pluck; but, like Judge, they
would throw out a wild turn now and then."

Mr. A. Graham has several greyhound pictures.
There hang on his walls (although the greater part
of them and the coursing cups are at Limekilns), the
companions of many a proud and happy day—Gilbertfield and Black-eyed Susan (the sire and the dam
of Goth and Vandal), and Oh Yes! Oh Yes!!

2 c 2

O Yes ! ! ! with his brother Cacciatore, who ran
up with Empress for the Caledonian Cup. It was a
very memorable cup, from the fact that the winner
and Lord Douglas's black dog Kent were so exhausted in one of the ties that they were obliged to
lie down ; but there were not nearly so many dogs
as in Camarine's year, when more than a hundred
were in it, and it took above a week to run it off.
Screw was another of Mr. A. Graham's early champions, and he put the screw on with her to some purpose, as she won the Altcar Purse in England one
week, the Caledonian Cup in Scotland the next, and
the Prince Albert Stakes in the South of Ireland,
the one after that, long before there was easy transport by railway.

Mr. A. Graham began as a young man at Dirleton
and Danskine, East Lothian, and then extended his
circuit to the Lanarkshire, Renfrewshire, and Ayrshire Clubs. Sandy Robinson, so well known in
every coursing field by his enormous hat, quite a
covering from the heat by day and the dews by night,
was his trainer at first ; and when his trainer days
were over, he followed the meetings with a violin. As
a walker Sandy had few peers in his prime, and he
thought nothing of the 87 miles to Danskine and
home again with his dogs. After some days' rest, he
would go to Dirleton, which was nearly the same distance.

The dogs were collected, each from the farmhouse
where it was reared, and these walks were almost

the only artificial training they got.* Gilbertfield
or "the dog with the rough beard," was still the one
to which, in coursing phrase, Mr. A. Graham always
"belonged", and it was on his great rival Major
that he wrote the epitaph, at Lord Eglinton's request, "*Major quo non Mrjor.*" They ran in the
same thirteen public prizes, and each of them
won six. Gilbertfield was a very fast turner
going down-hill, and, as is the manner of rough-
haired dogs, closed with his hare at the fences. His
son Stewartfield was a finer dog to look at, and rough
like himself, and he never had an opponent more
worthy of him than Mr. Geddes's "Go," who made
with Glory, one rough and the other smooth, the
fastest dog and bitch brace in any Scottish kennel.
Their owner was as good a courser as he was a shot.
He always wore a shawl handkerchief, white bird's-
eye on a green ground, and walked all day wet-shod
with a pair of low thin shoes.

To a Lowlander the spots where great coursing
cups have been run off are invested with as deep a

* "Sandy was in the Graham family at Limekilns-House, in Lanarkshire
for the last sixty years of his life, teaching boy after boy of them to fish, shoot,
and curl—a model of unpledged temperance, tea his beverage and a Cremona
his evening companion In Scotch reel-playing he handled his bow after the
manner of his instructor, Neil Gow, so as to enchant the late Duke of Hamilton, then Marquis of Douglas who was the best reel-dancer of the North, and
at whose request it was that the old man's figure and broad-brim were im-
mortalized in the Caledonian Coursing Picture A great humorist, full of
anecdote, and an utterer of no end of shrewd sayings or maxims—such as,
"Maister Alexander, whatever you lose in the dancing be sure to make up in
the turnin' aboot"—he would have been worth thousands to the Great Unknown as the backbone of a novel And then the world would have been
fascinated with descriptions of coursing such as the graphic one of foxhunting by Dr. Chalmers in his sermon on "Cruelty to Animals," wherein he
defended the sporting spirit of "the assembled chivalry of half a county"
—A G.

significance as Doncaster Moor or Ascot Heath to an Englishman. The watch-towers yet stand on the hill from which Sir John Maxwell of Pollok used to watch the coursing, and enjoy the sport, all the more if "half Glasgow" shared it. Once he was ready mounted on Ambush, with his gamekeeper, slipper, beaters, and his own stud of greyhounds behind him to receive all comers at 12; and wherever the fixture was to be, the hares had been carefully netted out of the adjoining covers. Neil Cairnie was there on his sheltie, enthusiastic about "Susan"; James Crum on foot, with his constant friend "The Dock," in chronic raptures about Charles James Fox; and so was the indefatigable quaker, who took charge of the cards on prize days, and was sure to have them headed, "*He who runs may read.*" Never was there such patronage of coursing. But the old baronet is dead and gone, and no greyhound now twists and twines over those fine old pastures, except when Mr. A. Graham and a few others wake the old echoes with the So Ho! and the Halloo! Then there is Ardrossan, with its nice ten to twenty acre enclosures. Biggar has a great variety of ground, much of it near Abington rough and chancy, and some very good, generally sloping sheep pasture deep in autumn, and with a Black Hill as great a choke jade as the Newmarket rise from the dip in the Two Thousand or the Beacon Hill at Amesbury. The old Biggar Club runs there no longer, but was merged with the Caledonian Club into the

Scottish National, when the C. C. lost the Pettir-
nane ground near Carstairs junction, which was
leased from Sir Wyndham Anstruther, and was
then one of the best coursing places in Scotland.
It furnished many a good trial from the meadows by the side of the Clyde, up-hill to cover, but
now it is intersected with wire fences, and no longer
available. Carnwath, the property of Sir Norman
Lockhart, is a combination of lowland and muirland,
and well adapted for testing the merits of the long-
tails.

The Scottish National Club flourishes under the
management of its honorary secretary, Mr. Blan-
shard, and is limited to sixty members. It has the
privilege of coursing over the extensive Douglas
estates, &c., of the Earl of Home in Lanarkshire,
which combine all sorts of ground, including Pepper
Knowes, always so celebrated for its stout, racing
hares. The iron fences are so constructed as to be
hooked up during the coursing, and the tenants vie
with his lordship in giving the Club a welcome, at
their three meetings in October, December, and
March. The last-named is the grand wind-up or
open champion meeting of England and Scotland,
at which old Rebe won the cup this year.

Carnwath has many spring and autumn memories of the Duke of Hamilton's Drift and
Driver, and (although Arran was painted in as the
background) the Great Caledonian Picture meeting,
for which Mr. A. Graham acted as honorary secre-

tary, was held there. It was open to one hundred
and twenty-eight dogs named by any member of a
coursing club in the United Kingdom. They were
first classed in eight sixteen-dog stakes, each of
which was named after a celebrated painter. The
Snyders Stake and the Landseer Stake had each
two representatives among the last four. In the
former the struggle was between two black dogs, the
Marquis of Douglas's Drift and Mr. Wardlaw Ramsay's Rector, and in the latter, between Mr. Gibson's Violet and Mr. G. Pollok's Hawthorn; and
then the blue Violet, "the small, the pretty, the
strong," who was bred by Mr. Adam Curror, beat
Drift in the decider. Nothing was thought of Violet
at first, and till she had beaten two English dogs
handsomely, Mr. Nightingale "never noticed her
much." Mr. Gibson bought the renowned Sam specially for her, but she died in pupping. "Muirland
Meg," the Chief Justice adds, "fell on some grass,
when she had quite the pace of Drift in the Boat
Holme."

In connexion with Abington, Mr. Nightingale has
always a good word for Mr. Patterson's Susan White-
head, when she won the Puppy Stakes against Bold
Enterprise; and it was also the scene of one of the
finest courses between Barrator and Ladylike, who
afterwards divided the stake. Still, Barrator's se-
verest Scottish course was run with one of Toll
Wife's pups, at Crawfurd John, close to the village,
through fold-yards and over walls, through gateways,

across the road and up the road, and finally up the
hill over some very deep ground.   "It was just the
one for him, as he was the cleverest dog in England."
Omniscience was his forte, and his owner, a veterinary surgeon at Selby, knew how to foster it.   In
fact, he trained him by taking a second-class ticket,
and making him follow the train.   A more serious-
looking dog was never whelped, and with head
enough for a litter.   He would play at leap-frog
with his owner, walk in a field with hares on every
side and not look at one, and stop at a word if he
was running a course.   He would lie on a dinner-
table, and ask for nothing, and he would have worried a man out of hand if he got the office.   In fact,
"Barrator at Biggar" was quite a character, and between the courses, if he was not distressed, he might
be generally seen with a ring round him going
through his various performances.   He did a very
clever thing at Lytham, so clever, in fact, that Mr.
Nightingale always goes to look at the place for his
sake.   He pressed his hare to a gate, jumped over
her, and went round as if on a pivot, turned her
back, and killed her in his second jump.   It was
done so instantaneously that the dog seemed to throw
a back somersault in the air, and he had her before
the other dog reached the gate.

   The great Eden and Dusty Miller match for 250
sovs. aside, the best of three, quite agitated the Glasgow Stock Exchange on the day it was run off near
Beattock.   It arose out of Gilbertfield defeating

Eden for the Eaglesham Gold Cup, and as Mr. A. Graham would not accept the challenge, Mr. Geddes took it up with Dusty Miller; and Mr. Nightingale, who first judged at Lyme in the November of '32, made his Scottish *début* in the scarlet that day. Eden the black dog was the fastest of the two, and led in the first course till they crossed the Great Northern Road; but he was out of form, and Dusty Miller did all the work when they reached the hill, and won still farther the next time.

Cambuslang has some very severe ground near Gilbertfield on the slope of Dechmount Hill, half way between Glasgow and Hamilton. It is famed for its big and good hares, but they are hardly equal to those at Eaglesham, which in point of antiquity is quite the Ashdown of the West. It has a great variety of ground and plenty of hill, and the big, red-legged hares, which have a long way to travel for food, played havoc with Waterloo, who was always a bad killer. It was here that he won his match with Young Carron, who led him over the grass. Then came a bit of stiff plough, which was the yellow-and-white's great forte; and Mr. Geddes, who made the match for Young Carron, threw up his hands, and said, "*It's all over now!*" The conqueror had a terrible course here, with the Marquis of Douglas's Driver, up and down one large field, Mr. Nightingale sitting on his horse in the centre. Driver was fairly beaten, and too glad to be picked up; and Waterloo just stumbled into the next field, and lay down. It was in the fourth ties, and Waterloo was drawn, and he never fairly got over it. The crowd stood just like a pillar of stone where the hare wanted to come, and no persuasion could get them back. Seeing Waterloo do his work right under their noses was a thing which the Caledonians, however right-minded generally on these matters, could not forego.

Malleny Moor, six miles from Edinburgh on the Lanark road, was another great Scottish meet. Many of the courses were run off on the arable, and the hares were driven for it out of the field at the back of the Kirk of Curry. The severe hill behind the farm of Kinleath was what the coursers most dreaded, and it was accordingly a great thing to be drawn low down on the card. If the hare raced across the flat and put her head for the hill, it was death to the dogs, as when they did reach the top they were pretty certain to divide on a fresh hare in the whins. It was here that Neville won a great hundred-dog stake, and Leven Water ran up. "Neville," says Mr. Nightingale, "was very smooth and fast, and opened the pace from the slips, and, for a big dog, a good worker. Bennett's Rocket was the fastest I ever saw; Judge, who had magnificent forelegs, and Neville next, but perhaps Neville was the fastest of the two." Jamie Forrest also won a stake of equal amount over The Moor, and he too was "a rare dog, and the best of his day."

But a truce to old leash times. We slipped down from Fereneze past Paisley, which alone keeps

up the custom of racing for "The Silver Bells," to
have an afternoon with John Squires at the Lanarkshire and Renfrewshire Kennels, which are three
miles from the Houston station on the Greenock railway. The country is very open and nearly all grass
and moor, intersected with stone walls about five feet
high. Bogs are especially plentiful round Duchal,
but Squires has "kept pretty well out of them so
far." There are a few good gorses, and five or six
have been planted, one of them at Fereneze, but the
covers are generally small and thin for plantations,
and foxes do not dwell a minute after the hounds
are in. The cub-hunting is generally done in the
great Lanarkshire glens about the Duke of Hamilton's, where rocks and trees and underwood abound.
A large burn runs at the bottom of each, and it is
often as much as the hounds can do to hear one another,
besides which they frequently fall over the cliffs and get
terribly lamed. The foxes lay up their cubs in rocks or
old coal and limestone mines, and therefore a find is
often very doubtful, and earth-stopping a very heavy
item in the accounts. Every meeting involves eight
or nine stops, and Houston still more. In his first
season of 1862-63, Squires had seventeen blank days,
hunting twice a week, but last season there were only
two days without a challenge. "Weeping skies" are
the rule; and he told us, in quite a martyred tone, that
during his first eight weeks he had only two dry days.
It is also a hilly, heavy country, and "horses up to
their hocks and knees the greater part of their time."

Colonel Buchanan has been the master for fifteen
seasons, and succeeded Mr. Merry, who in his turn
succeeded Lord Glasgow. There are from fifty to
sixty in the field generally, and nearly half of them in
pink, and some very hard riders amongst them.
Saturday is the great day on the Caldwell and Lochwinnoch side of the county, as it is within reach of
the Eglinton Hunt men, and the Glasgow men are
at leisure.

The greatest difficulty that a huntsman has to contend with are the bogs and the roe deer. The hounds
enjoy the scent so much that they will change from
fox and go off for a mile or two, and the bogs
make it very difficult riding to head them. Old
hounds are nearly as bad as the one-season hounds
under this temptation, but they are more easily
stopped. Left to themselves they would cut up a
roe deer in about twenty minutes. There were about
31½ couple of hounds in kennel, principally drafts
from the South Oxfordshire, the Pytchley, and the
Cheshire. About twelve to fifteen couple of puppies
are sent out each year, and Squires has now 5½ couple
in kennel of his own breeding. Governor, Streamer,
and Diligence among the five-season, Pytchley Fear-
less among the four, and Chaser, Amazon, Welcome,
and Lictor, the last-named by North Staffordshire
Comus, are leaders among the three-season hounds,
while a one-season entry of five by Pytchley Marplot
from Nightshade have "taken to it like old ones."
The kennels were rather humble-looking; but a new

house has been built for Squires, who concluded a
fresh engagement, at a considerably increased salary,
for three seasons, at the end of his first—no slight
testimony to his talent and popularity with the
hunt. The hounds come to Houston on May 4th,
and stop till September 19th; then they go to Drum-
pellier, the master's seat, for five weeks; then back
to Houston till the middle of February, and then to
Lanarkshire, to wind up. " November 1st,—
The Kennels" opens the season either in Mr.
Spiers's woods or Barrachan Wood and Gorse, the
property of Miss Fleming, one of the strictest preservers in the Hunt. The half-dozen horses are all
Irish, and a very useful lot they seemed. White-
nose is Squires' Tuesday horse; and a white nose
poked over a loose-box to greet him, told that
Return had been confederate with him on many a
hard-fought Saturday.

CHAPTER II.

FALKIRK TO EDINBURGH.

"The sheep farmer thought a little, snuffed, sipped his toddy, and replied : 'The Duke of Wellington was, na doot, a varra clever man—varra clever, I believe They tell me he was a good soger; but then d'ye see, he had reasonable men to deal with—captains, and majors and generals that could understand him every yen o' them—both officers and men; but I'm no so sure, after all, if he could manage, say 20,000 sheep, to say nout of black cattle, that could na understand one word he said, Gaelic or English, and bring every hoof of them to Fa'kirk Tryst ' I doot it But I ha' done that ' "

AT was ten o'clock on the second day of the Falkirk Tryst. Whole lines of trucks were already laden with beasts, the shorthorn crosses bound to the North, and the West Highlanders South. The road to the moor was one struggling mass of Norlands and Irish calves, and ankle deep in mud ; and Mr. Adderley and Mr. Stirling, as they tucked up their trouser-bottoms, and trudged sturdily along, were a type of those " Faithful Commons," who had once to leave their coaches and walk half their time, through still more deep and miry ways from Scotland to St. Stephen's.

The sheep had come, and more than two-thirds of

them had departed on the Monday; and "*Yes !*
they're tarring 'em," was the constant response, when
we asked if certain lots of cattle were sold. The
sheep sales had been very large, and, in fact, for the
last five-and-twenty years, many proprietors and farmers, who were wont to sell by character at Inverness, have been gradually changing their tactics, and
sending ewes and wedders direct to the September
and October Falkirks. Mr. John Murray, who was
in early life a sheep manager for six years on the
estate of Glengarry, had sold on this occasion forty-
three lots from twenty-two different farms in his
wonted strongholds of Inverness-shire, Ross-shire,
and Sutherlandshire. At times he will pass some
24,000 through his hands at these two trysts; and
being always employed by farmers and proprietors,
who are breeders of stock, and do not buy on speculation, he confines himself here, as at Inverness,
strictly to selling. From 1843 to 1860 he bought
very largely at Inverness, principally for the late Mr.
James Scott, of Hawick, who did by far the largest
business on the "plane stones." He has few cattle
transactions; and the chief occasion of his buying
largely is at Melrose, where he selects Cheviot
wedder lambs on commissions for his clients in the
North, who send them back to him at Falkirk after
three years' keep. The great majority of his Falkirk
lots are Cheviot ewes and wedders; about a tenth
of them are crosses, and a still smaller proportion
black-faced. No sheep come to the August tryst,

and he very often sells twice as many at the October one as he does at the September. Last October his three largest consignments were from "Lochiel's" farm of Locharkaig in Lochaber, Captain Donald Colin Cameron of Talisker, Isle of Skye, and Messrs. Elliot and Scott of Drynoch in the same island. No less than 3,679 of Lochiel's were divided between the two trysts, and 2,378 of them were sold in the October, with 2,437 from Captain Cameron, and 1,673 from the Drynoch farm.

The Swans, father and two sons, are flitting about not in white swan's-down, but white linen coats, and note-book and pencil in hand. One son makes sheep, and the other cattle, his specialty. They had nigh ten thousand sheep on sale yesterday, and many thousand pounds' worth of cattle will have passed through their note-books before the sun goes down. Then we are told that Daniel Kennedy has sold the Corrynafarm wedders at 38s., and that Walter Smith has shaken hands with Kerr of Liverpool, who never saw Falkirk more, for 650 black-faced wedders at one-and-thirty. Buist had also been busy with his auction; and they told of Walter Brydon of Burncastle's black-faced tups fetching from £16 downwards.

The larger money transfers are generally managed by the bankers, who pitch their little "green-back" tents, and deal in more sterling currency. Liverpool, Yorkshire, and Cumberland men are their leading customers, and if any hitch arises about a cheque or

a banker's letter, a messenger slips away from the
muir, and telegraphs to head quarters for information. A Union Jack generally waves over the
Union Bank; the Royal glories in the white and
blue Prince's Feather; the National goes in for blue
and yellow; but the Clydesdale makes no sign.
Horse dealers also come out strongly with their
Clydesdales, whose tails they plait with an art which
Dunstable might envy. Ropes, straw, and tape are
all in vogue for such adornments, and so are ribbons
of every hue. A mule is pressed upon us in vain for
£3 10s., with an assurance that he is "varra corney,"
which he illustrates in one sense by backing into
corners among tents and potato-kettles, and stead-
fastly refusing to leave them. There are ponies, too,
of divers kinds, fat and unshoed, or standing in
melancholy-eyed Shetland droves, from one of which a
purchaser took five at haphazard for £17, luck-penny
unknown.

A donkey from the Bridge of Allan was always on
parade, and announced for sale "because the season
is over, ye ken." There was no lack of conjurors. One
of them said, "*I'll swelly the sword, if I fa' down deed
on the spot;*" but as we were quite proof against his
appeal to us to enter the ring and stand by him for
the honour of pulling it up when it was swallowed,
he winked at us pleasantly, worked "the West Riding
telegraph," as a relief to his feelings, and proceeded to
business. For a really brisk trade there was nothing
to equal the merchant who sells his packets for "a

shilling and a bawbee," and warrants his gingerbread to "drive a nail in the dark." In the tents, whisky and mashed potatoes were the great circulating media; and with meat and mustard to aid it, a stomach must be cynical indeed which cannot break its Falkirk fast. As you sit waiting for your turn, you hear hard bargains and harder slaps all round you, and see piles of greasy one-pound notes pulled out of breast-pockets and paid away by the smaller men, to whom a cheque-book is only a dream of the future.

There was a time when no shorthorns were seen on the muir, and Aberdeen runts and West Highlanders, and a few Ayrshire stots, formed its sole army of occupation. Robert M'Turk was a mighty buyer in old days, and was known to strike hands for seventy score of West Highland stirks at £8 each one Michaelmas tryst before he got off his pony. The Williamsons and the Thoms were also very comprehensive in their dealings, and so was old M'Combie, whose family mark below the near hock was known at Falkirk for sixty long years. It was only for the runts, as the West Highlanders were burnt with gustrils in the horns. Big Paterson was a mighty sheep seller from Caithness, and would sometimes bring nine thousand Cheviots. It was the boast of Cameron of Corrychoillie that he was the greatest stock owner in the world except Prince Esterhazy. He won the prize for buck goats when the Highland Society met at Inverness in '31, and he was not

averse to hair on his own face. None knew better
than himself and his retainers how to punish all candidates for the high ground at Falkirk. He had
most wonderful ponies, and would ride six or seven
times a year from Skye, a journey which he did not
shorten by his circuits to save the turnpike—"not
for pence, but for principle." "Boghall" once
bought a Highland grey pony, not highly fed, from
him for thirty shillings; and passed everything on
the road with it when he drove a friend from Edinburgh to the Berwick show.

"A sharpish bit of work" on the part of another
old dealer was long remembered on the moor.
He could not get rid of sixty beasts the first
day; and the next morning found him hard at it
with Robert Nichol of Fife, who offered him £8
12s. 6d., and was then within half-a-crown of
him. At this juncture, a little red-faced man on
a white pony rode up, and asked the price. "*I'ze
come doon to thirteen guineas*," was the reply. "*What
will you give?*" "*Eleven*," said the man, thinking
he had done a very clever thing; but the re-
joinder of "*They're yours, sir!*" and the hard clap
of the hand came so quick that he began to smell a
rat. The case was referred to a leading dealer, who
thus delivered judgment: "*They're good growers—
you'll soon mak them worth it—you just need to tak
them.*" And so he did, as the seller was not the man to
pass him. Another of this helpless stamp once came
for draft ewes, and fell in with a dealer who furnished

him with double-milled ones at 27s. a head. Some one overheard them winding up the bargain in a tent, and the colloquy was on this wise : " *Come awa, man, I'se had bad wark to keep them nice fowre year old yows for ye ; there was so mony customers, they wad hae them on me.*" Thus encouraged, the buyer consented, and paid. The seller then rose to the occasion. *There's a sovereign for you,*" he said, " *because you're a gentleman ; and there's another sovereign for you because I'se a gentleman.*" And so they parted, the one to have his laugh out, and the other to hear from his neighbours that he'd " better tak a sheep dentist to t'Muir next year."

There were some wonderful night scenes at the grieve of Carron's, and for many a long year the dealers sat round the fire, and talked of their mysterious visitor. He wore top-boots, a long blue coat, and buckskins, and was as clean as a new pin. The Man in the Iron Mask could not have created more speculation. He appeared about nine o'clock, and said that he had been looking at the cattle in the fields, that he was an ex-major in the army, and that he wouldn't stir a peg that night. All further attempts to " draw" him he parried, by simply saying : " *My nephew has more money than brains. I've come to buy a few things for him.*" Before lying down for the night, he became a trifle more talkative. " *I've never had a sick head or a sore breast ; I'm eighty-two, and when I go, I go at once.*" He repeated the " at once" so impressively, that they thought he was a

Warlock or deranged, and were glad to see him un-
dress and lie down in the middle of the floor to
sleep, with a blanket above him, and his waistcoat
folded under his head. At breakfast he was quite
lively upon hunting and racing topics, and then he
bought twenty score of the best middle horned beasts
with good judgment on the Moor. He did not want
to be asked for his money, but off came his coat and
waistcoat, and out came his pen-knife, and in a very
short space he had ripped Bank of England notes to
the amount of £4,400 out of his waistcoat-lining.
He did not breathe his name, and he was only seen
once more, at the next tryst, when he bought 120
more at rather a higher figure.

No men lead a more anxious life than the dealers.
If it is a dewy morning, and the cattle cannot eat and
come round and fresh on to the Moor, it is a certain
loss of ten shillings per head. Sometimes a whole
lot will get hoven with clover, and whisky or tur-
pentine and water have to be used, and perhaps they
have to be " stabbed" at last. Drawing and lotting
before the tryst is also a job of especial nicety, and
the great knack is to make the first lot the biggest
if you can. If an experienced grazier had 100 beasts
to sell, he would put 60 of the best and only 40 of the
worst together There are no drovers to be compared,
for natural talent, to the Irish, either for drawing or
making cattle go sweetly along a road. A good
steady man goes with two or three in front, to stop
the pace; but the second man has the most respon-

-sible post, and it depends more upon him whether or
not the drove "goes weaving away as canny as possible." The drover's cry always tells an old crafts-
man down wind if anything is wrong, without ever
seeing the cattle. If they are going " sweetly," they
should be two or three deep, the same thickness all
along, and streaming away like a flock of wild geese.
If once they take a panic and run off, they might go
for miles, and never settle, and even the clatter of
a little burn might do it.

Some very good drovers come from the Western
Islands, and none were better known to fame at Falkirk than " *Willy Run-her-out*," but only three or
four of the true old sort are left. Willy got the name
from running down a quey at Aikey Fair of Old Deer;
but he was so weary after his performance, that a light
which was applied for a bet to the sole of his feet
quite failed to awaken him. The droves generally
travel about twelve miles a day, with a break of two
or three hours about noon. Once the drovers only
got 2s. or 1s. 6d. a day, and no watching-money, but
the better ones earn 3s., and 1s. for watching at night
till September, and 1s. 6d. when the nights are
longer.

Many used to buy meal, and carry it on their backs;
and an unpopular one, who was called "Talavera,"
from his constant allusions to that passage of his
soldier life, had his supply very freely salted by his
-comrades. Being of a penurious disposition, he would
not throw it away, and went through three remark-

able weeks of excruciating thirst and unlimited suction at every roadside spring.

The bullocks were generally shod on the inside of the fore-hoofs, but very rarely behind. Holding the leg was a science of itself; and only one man, a blacksmith at the Bow of Fife, ever made nails that suited them. No other man's seemed to "drive," and large dealers kept supplies of them at points, and sent a bag with each drove. When the roads broke up after frost, it was terrible work for cattle, but shoes well put on might last for six months, though not as a rule. One "Rob," who was killed last year by the train, was a wonderful shoer, and once shod seventy cattle for Mr. M'Combie in a forenoon. He knew well, too, what people meant when they asked him if he had got any silk handkerchiefs or Hallow five-pound notes to spare, and when he dressed last like a minister.

Such were a few of the leading characters at Falkirk, whose season begins with the August tryst. It is principally for West Highlanders, of which from five to seven thousand are shown. Most of them are bought to go South into the Midland Counties, or to gentlemen's parks round London; but a few go to Cumberland, Northumberland, and Cheshire. Cross-bred cattle are sent from the neighbourhood; as well as Irish two years old and stirks which come over in the spring, and are sold off grass to put on turnips in Fife and East Lothian. The September tryst brings with it the first drafts of hill sheep from the

North of Scotland, and blackfaces and Cheviots
are pretty equally divided. Many of them have
been bought on speculation at the Inverness Character market, and forty thousand will sometimes be
pitched. It is principally a wedder market, as the
draft ewes do not come out in force before October.
The best Cheviot wedders go into Cumberland, and
the black-faced to Ayrshire, Wigtownshire, Edinburgh, and the West Lothian. The highest price that
the Messrs. Swan ever got for Cheviot wedders was
42s. 6d. for 758, bred by Mr. John Hall, of Seiber's Cross, and sold for Mr. Wallbank, who had
purchased them at Inverness. Within seven or eight
years they have risen 10s. a-piece, but they range
from 34s. to 40s., and blackfaced wedders which
have touched 33s., from 31s. to 27s. A lot of cast
Cheviot ewes from Mr. Mitchell's of Ribigill in
Sutherlandshire went as high recently as 31s. 6d.

The Kelso September fair has been very recently
established. It is made up principally of shorthorns
from Yorkshire and Cumberland, which are bought
to fatten in the district. The cast ewes are mostly
three-parts or half-bred, and are bought for Yorkshire and the East Lothian, the half-breds at from
35s. to 40s., and the three-parts at half-a-crown or
3s. more. East Linton, which is the centre of a
capital locality, comes between the two autumn Falkirks on the first Thursday in October; and although
it has only been established for six or seven years, it
averages higher per head than any lean market in

Scotland. Nearly all the cattle are English-bred, and the two and three year old shorthorns are generally of the best class, and readily picked up by the Fife and East Lothian farmers. The latter are very fond of "the Hempton beasts," which are sold at Carlisle at the " Three Hemptons" after the grass.

About fifteen to eighteen hundred head of cattle generally come to Falkirk October, and are bought up as straw treaders. At the September tryst several cattle are bought for early beef, and put into reeds or covertings, and get cut grass. Scarcely any Angus beasts come, and the best of the Galloways all go to Norwich fair. The great majority are West Highlanders from the Northern and Western counties and Skye, and, since so much land has been gradually given up to deer forests, they have risen very much in price. Three year old bullocks of the breed have fetched £14 10s., but they vary from £14 to £9, and two-year-olds from £10 to £6 10s., while queys may be generally quoted from 30s to £1 less; and stirks of both sexes from £5 to £3 10s. These figures apply to all the other markets where Highland cattle are sold, such as Dumbarton, Doune, &c. The shorthorn crosses have a sharp tussle to hold their own with the Irish, which are-quite as well bred, and come principally from Meath and Fermanagh by ship and steam to Glasgow. They have improved immensely of late years; and a half-bred poll, which was purchased in '63 by Mr. Crawfurd of Perth in a lot of twenty-two at £10 17s. 6d., came

out so completely from the rest, that, after being sent
along on cake and corn, it was sold for 76s. per cwt.,
and left £44 for eighteen months' keep. No sales
were more spoken of last year than this bullock's,
and the dozen three-year-old shorthorn crosses of Mr.
Harris's, which were lifted at £48 all round in Forres
Christmas market.

Calves also come to Falkirk in large lots from
Craven and the dairy districts of Yorkshire and Lancashire, and are purchased by feeders and graziers
north of the Forth, and principally from Forfarshire and Fife. Their horns are generally taken out
by the buyers, that they may take up less room, and
not be troublesome in the yards, and some of the
Dutch purchases have theirs extracted at a still riper
age. For cross-bred shorthorns, threes, twos, stirks,
and calves, £18 to £13, £15 to £11, £12 to £7, and
£6 to £4 are the general prices ; and the Irish-bred
ones range about £1 lower. Cast ewes come out in immense strength at this October tryst, and as many as
80,000 ewes and wedders, five-eighths of them Cheviots, will change hands, while blackfaced " Highland or Hill" wedders will muster 800 to 1,000 in
a lot.

The principal buyers at Falkirk are the Cumberland, Dumfries, and Wigtownshire men, many of
whom take large lots varying from 3,000 to 4,000,
and divide them with their brother farmers. In this way
some of the Cumberland .men will have as their portion 400 to 500 Cheviot wedders, and half as many

cast ewes. Young and Butterfield of Penrith bring
arge lots of cattle to the Falkirks, Dalkeith, Lanton,
Hallow Fair, and Big Wednesday markets. They
are also extensive buyers at the Falkirks of sheep,
which they either turnip on their own account,
or sell to the Cumberland farmers when the price
rises. They deal very largely in fat stock, attending the Manchester market weekly, and have very
considerable transactions as store cattle dealers.
Bowstead and Nelson, on the contrary, are entirely
sheep men, and take turnips. They are to be found
principally at Inverness, and the second and third
Falkirks. Nelson, perhaps, does more at Inverness,
and Bowstead at Falkirk, and the former has generally a show at the Bull's Head, Plumpton, near Penrith, where the Cumberland and Westmorland farmers
draw up and meet the lots. Maxwell of Carlisle attends
the Falkirks and Inverness, and turnips about 2,500
wedders, chiefly Cheviots, round Carlisle and up the
Vale of the Eden; and Richard Pattinson, another of
the Cumberland " grey-coats," goes to Falkirk with
a large commission from his brother farmers for Cheviot wedders, and divides them at home.

John Martindale, of Manchester, unites the grazier
and butcher business, buying up the best cast Cheviot
and blackfaced ewes at the September and October
Falkirks, and taking a lamb off them at his farms near
Manchester. John Gibbons has been well known
for these thirty years at Inverness, where he takes
many of the best lots, principally wedders, for his

customers in Cumberland and Dumfries-shire; and Yorkshire has no greater buyer than Jonas Walbank of Keighley. In fat stock, sheep, and store cattle, he does a great trade from February to June, and sends them all over England. After the Falkirk trysts, he takes very large supplies of cast Cheviot ewes to the York market, and Berwickshire and Roxburgh-shire have also a strong levy made on them for half-bred ewes, which he brings down to Yorkshire and the Midlands. Joseph Ruddock of Berwick not only buys up stores about Durham for Falkirk, and fat cattle in Roxburghshire and Berwickshire, but does a very large sheep-carcase trade with London. The Swans do nothing on their own account, but simply as salesmen, and guarantee the money for their commission. They have sold in one year as many as 65,000 Scotch and English sheep, as well as 12,000 Foreign ones. To this we may add about 20,000 cattle, of which a fourth are foreign and Irish. At one October Falkirk they passed through their hands 10,000 sheep, and 1,400 cattle.

Despite these large supplies, farmers have of late years found it so much more profitable to make their corn-sacks walk to market in the shape of beef and mutton, that they have often hardly known where to look for store beasts. Time has, indeed, verified what Mr. Aitchison of Linhope said in one of those glowing periods which used to "bring down the house," when he returned thanks for "The Tenant Farmers" at the Highland Society's banquet—

" Steam is your Highland drover." And so it was,
in verity, a few months since, when a dealer, finding
himself left short for Ellon, set off from Aberdeen on
a Wednesday, and returned with a large lot of Here-
fords from England on the Saturday.

A Denmark beast trade is being opened up with
the direct steam navigation from Copenhagen to
Leith, and fully 5,000 "Dutchmen" are passed
through the hands of the Swans between May and
October, and sold to the Forfarshire, Fife, and Lothian farmers at £5 to £8. They are small blacks
and whites, and very like the Ayrshires in size and
marks. The Holstein cattle, on the contrary, which
are poured in from Hamburg and Oldenburg are
not unlike the Fife breed, and of all colours, black,
spotted, and red and white. Mr. Smith, of Ley
Shade, near Dundee, imports about 500 or 600 of
them annually, and puts them into the farmers, and
then buys them back at a profit of from 25s. to 30s.
a month for a few months' keep. The smaller
butchers buy them up very readily, but the leading
men do not take kindly to anything but British-fed
beef and mutton. Still when the beasts have been
judiciously selected off ship-board, and fed for a time
in the country, they come out well, and command a
ready sale, as they carry both flesh and fat, and are
generally good killers. Between the middle of
March and the first of November, Hamburg ships
fully two thousand of these cattle, and fifteen
thousand sheep to Leith. Some of the cattle are

"as old as a man," and with strong marks of the collar; and many of the Merinoes are most venerable wool producers. They are generally four and five years old wedders, and suit the second-class Glasgow butchers, at all figures from 22s. to 30s., while the Holsteiners will fetch from £18 to £23. These sheep are the incarnation of ugliness, with long tails and white noses, and most of them with a strong dash of Merino blood. When they do not come over clipped, as a large proportion do, their skins make 7s. Plenty kill at only 7lbs. to 8lbs. per quarter, but the better class scale twice as much.

The Dalkeith fair is on the Tuesday after the last Falkirk tryst. No Highland cattle attend it, and from 5,000 to 7,000 shorthorn crosses, Irish, and Galloways, several of which have been grazed in the district, are the staple of its supplies. Mr. Dudgeon, of Almond Hill, gave £600 for a prime lot of thirty Galloways, but the general run of prices for the three kinds is for threes, from £17 to £13, for twos from £13 to £10, and for stirks from £8 to £6; and these quotations apply to all markets at that time of the year. Cumberland (more especially its Penrith district) and the country round Yarm send shorthorns, with a good sprinkling of calves; and the supply is strengthened by home-grazed beasts, some of which are bought here or at Hallow fair the previous year, and are now replaced.

The first Doune market, which begins on the first Tuesday in November, is principally devoted to

blackfaced ewes, two years old wedders, and double-
milled ewes. Some of the blackfaces from Argyleshire and Perthshire are very good indeed; cast ewes
have made as high as twenty-two shillings, and the
two-year-old wedders are picked up principally for
the coarser hill land in Cumberland and Yorkshire.
The blackfaced ewes go to Derbyshire and Lanarkshire, and many of them to West Lothian, to
be crossed with a Leicester. The cattle come on
the Wednesday; and what with small West Highlanders and country-cross breds, there will some
years be little short of twenty thousand. They are
mostly yearlings and two-year-olds, and are spread
all over Scotland (more especially Dumfriesshire),
Yorkshire, and the Midlands. The second fair, or
" Snowy Doune," comes off on the last Wednesday
of November, and is simply for cattle culls and sheep
shots, which go to Perthshire and the North.

Sheep are very seldom shown at Hallow Fair, except when business has been slack at the first Doune,
but the show of cattle will sometimes range from 14,000
to 12,000, nearly all shorthorns. Once upon a time,
the Angus men used to sell here; but now they, as
well as other farmers south of Aberdeen, are fain to
come and make up their winter lots from the two-
year-olds and stirks, for which this fair rather enjoys
a specialty. The trade at the Big Wednesday is very
much governed by the Hallow. This fair was formerly held at Gorgie farm, near Edinburgh, but last
year it was on the Fat Cattle Stance. It is not

attended by more than a sixth of the cattle which come to Hallow (and these are rather of the cull order), and scarcely any sheep whatever. By this time the farmers' yards are full, and only a few stores are required for the poorer land in the higher districts.

The blackfaced wedder mutton is specially sought after for the higher Edinburgh tables ; and the specimens which come up for the Christmas market are so good that a Kincardineshire pen of five, which won Messrs. Swan's Sheep Cup in 1863, sold for £6 10s. each, and one of them made 34¼ lbs. per quarter clean weight. The Glasgow market is of course much larger than the Edinburgh, and is very freely supplied by the Fife feeders from March to June; while the inferior mutton of the Hamburgh sheep meets with a ready sale.

The regular Scottish sheep markets of the year may be said to begin with the House of Muir, near Penicuick, on the first and second Monday of April. Rough half-bred and three-parts-bred, Cheviot, and cross-bred hoggs are brought out, with Cheviot and blackfaced ewes in-lamb. Those with the Leicester blood go mostly to the Lothians and Fife for fattening off grass, and the Cheviot hoggs to the higher districts for turnips; the Cheviot ewes are principally bought for the Lothians, and the blackfaced for Lanarkshire and the West. The St. Boswell's lamb fair begins about July 18th, and at times 10,000 to 25,000* feeders and breeders in

* We find the greatest difference of opinion as to the number.

2 E

the shape of half and three-parts bred lambs are
gathered there from all the Lowland districts. Fifty
years ago only rough Cheviot hoggs and black-faced
three-year-old wedders and wedder lambs came;
but time has wrought wonders in this respect. The
ewe and wedder lambs are generally sold mixed at
from 21s. to 29s.; but one lot of six or seven
score, three-parts bred, was quoted last year at
35s. 6d.

The clipped ewe and wedder hoggs are all similarly
bred, but they seldom muster above two thousand.
Northumberland, Fifeshire, and Berwickshire men
are all great buyers both here and at Melrose, which
is nearly a month later, and brings out Cheviot as
well as half-bred lambs. Many of the latter have
trenched on the high lands once used for Cheviots,
and it is these higher lands which furnish the chief
Melrose supplies. Once it was only a mart for
the shots of the St. Boswell's lambs, and there were
not more than two or three thousand of them. Now
70,000 to 80,000 Cheviot, half-bred, and three-parts
bred may sometimes be found there, besides Leicester
shots, whose tops, as well as those of the three-parts
bred, have been sold at St. Boswell's. Both it and
Melrose are early markets, and the lambs are on the
ground by six o'clock. St. Boswell's is more of a
mixed fair, and a great place for settling guano and
other accounts. The lambs have generally left the
ground by ten o'clock, and a horse, cattle, and wool
fair fills up the day till four o'clock. Of Lockerby,

Lanark, Callow, as well as some minor fairs, we have spoken in their places.

And so we leave Falkirk, and all the fair lore of which it is the natural text, and taking our mare once more from her snug Keir quarters, we passed on through Linlithgowshire towards Edinburgh. This county is not an especially interesting one, and, with the exception of the high farms, is mostly under tillage. Bare fallows are quite given up, and what turnip land there is generally grows yellow globes, and the Fosterton hybrid or big yellows along with swedes for spring. As a county it is rich in old grass parks, and none of them richer than Hope-toun and Dalmeny. The farmers go for feeding rather than breeding, except in the West, about Bathgate and Linlithgow, where they princi-pally keep Ayrshires, and do a little in the cheese, and very largely in the butter and milk line for Edinburgh. Falkirk is their great cattle mart, and if they have a leaning it is rather for Irish, and occa-sionally Galloway stores, which are bought as two-year-olds, and kept for six or twelve months in yards.

Mr. Melvin of Bonnington is the top Leicester breeder, and his tups are generally sold to cross with Cheviots and a few Southdown ewes for the fat-lamb market. Mr. Hill of Carlowie has 100 Leicester ewes, and sold two score of his tup hoggs for good prices in March; while Mr. Melvin parts with his at the Edin-burgh sales. Mr. Peter M'Lagan of Pumpherstown

2 E 2

has done well with his Dorset ewes; but Mr. Dudgeon of Almond Hill (who was the first to introduce furrow draining into Sutherland and Caithness-shire, where he held large farms in succession) did not succeed with his merinoes, as the ewes were too delicate, and although he sold some 40lb. lambs at a shilling per pound live weight, he did not care to renew the experiment.

The system of blackfaced Ochil ewe drafts on the higher ground is rather going out, and instead of breeding the greyfaced mules, the farmers are nearly all turning to half-bred ewes and Cheviots. They sometimes keep the lambs for sixteen or eighteen months, but they are generally sold off before clipping. Mr. Dudgeon of Dalmeny, near Kirkliston, got 56s. last year for 100 highly-corned and caked ewe and wedder hoggs; but this was in the golden-fleece era, and in ordinary seasons 46s. to 48s. was not to be despised. Those farmers who do not breed, buy half-bred lambs, generally tops, at Melrose and Lockerby, and sell them off fat about home out of the fleece in June. They will buy these lambs at 28s., and pay 38s. for Cheviot wedders the next month, and with eight months' high feeding they can bring the one up as high as 52s. to 56s., and the others to 56s. or £3, and hence the balance is against the wedders, which some also consider to require more food. With such a heavy opposition from young mutton, it seems more than probable that the Cheviot wedders will have shortly to sink a

year, as five to six shillings for a fleece on a hill farm
will not pay the year's rent and risk. Very few
hunters are kept, and hardly any farmer has bred
more than a couple of foals a-year since the horse
prices became low.

Tom Rintoul bade us welcome when we reached
the hostel at Linlithgow. His career began in the
racing stable along with Tom Dawson, under Dawson, senior, about the time when John Osborne was
hunting groom to Mr. Taylor of Kirton. Tom was
never "put up," and therefore his life was not like
that of the well-known Scottish rider about that
time, whose difficulties in wasting were so great that
he travelled from Ayr to Carlisle, leading a mare, on
four half-penny biscuits and two-pennyworth of
Epsom salts. His career with hounds began in
1817, and he came to Linlithgow in 1826 as first
whip to Kit Scott. Mr. Ramsay was true to his
family tastes, and kept stag-hounds at nineteen, as
his father had done at Golf Hall. The latter had
also hunted the Linlithgowshire and Stirlingshire
country along with Lord Elphinstone and Colonel
Murray of Polmaise; and he was wont to ride from
Barnton to Hamilton, hunt all day, and back again
at night, by changing hacks at Cumbernaud. His
son's country extended at one time over Lanarkshire,
Carnwath, Linlithgowshire, Stirlingshire, and the
West of Fife and Forfarshire as well. Once they
had eleven weeks in Forfarshire, and killed twenty-
one brace, hunting four days a week, and accounted

for nine brace more to ground. From one end of
the country to the other was fully eighty miles, and
it is a precious memory with Tom that one week
they "hunted it down" and killed four brace. The
hounds were generally of Beaufort and Lonsdale
blood; Bracer by Bedford, by Beaufort Brusher
from a Nichol bitch, was quite one of the best; and
Chalon, who once lived nearly a year at Barnton,
made him one of his chief hound studies. Lonsdale
blood was Mr. Ramsay's delight, and he bought 17½
couple of them at the Cottesmore sale. He had sixteen horses for his men, and as many for himself, and
yet some seasons he was not out five times.

His heart was in the Defiance and the Tallyho;
but when he did get a lead over a strong country, he
was very bad to beat. "Sim" Templeman would be
down occasionally after the Caledonian meeting, and
rode some of his hunters for him; and so did Harry
Edwards in '37, a few months after he had won two
Liverpool Cups in one week on Inheritor in his very
finest style. Will Noble would also help to whip in,
and William I'Anson bore a hand when he had
brought the race-horses from Gullane to Barnton for
the winter. Tom Cleghorn's old horse Davie was a
permanent resident at Barnton. The grooms might
well say that he had seen a vast of sport, as he began
when he was about three, and died at 35, quite white
on his head, but still "able to enjoy himself with
hounds." Tom rode in shoes and black stockings
and a mealy-brown suit, and whatever his hat might

have been in the morning it was invariably " a cocket
one" at the finish. If there had been a very good
run, he would stop at Winchborough with David
Brown for two days to discuss it. When the two
days were out, his attendants came with a cart and
blankets, and took him peacefully to his farm, with
his hunter tied behind the cart. Dr. Liston was a
capital sportsman, both on this and the Buccleuch
side of the country, and " knew Tom fine." Tinker
was his best horse, but he turned a roarer, and the
operation on his windpipe availed him nothing. For
nine seasons the Rocket horse was Tom Rintoul's
crack, and he rode him three times in one day over
the Lead Hills near Tinto, and killed three foxes.
He had one of his finest runs from West Craigs, beyond Bathgate, eighteen miles straight, and killed
in a wash-house near Denney. Craigie Hill and
Barr Hill were once grand places to work up the
young'uns; but never a whimper is heard among
their gorse and whins now. Lee Castle had also
strong covers in those days ; but now, as Stracey
says, " _you might as well run through this room ; you
can see every rabbit in it._" Once on a time, Tom
gave fourteen couple of the entry such a lesson in it
for twelve hours that they required no more teaching.
There had been some disagreement between the
keepers and one of them as a safety-valve for his
wrath, opened the earths as fast as the other stopped
them, and upwards of seven brace of foxes were
about.

Now there is no cub-hunting, except they have a turn or two at the Corstorphine Hills, which are all rocks and braes and brambles. They generally began there, and the gardeners and keepers light fires and net the rocks in some places, and even then the foxes will not be forced away, but make wild dashes at the nets. There are generally a litter or two in the rocks, but cubs are very seldom found in the country, and on the south side the chief dependence is on hill foxes. Macbie Hill is a great rendezvous for old Peebleshire foxes, which go back at the lambing time, and generally faster than they come. Morton covert is a capital cover, about three miles from Midcalder, and gives many a fine run over the Cairn Hill. It is almost always a sure find, and the fox is as surely a stout one. There is another famous whin half-way between Uphall and Midcalder, whose owner, Mr. Peter M'Clagan, is a most staunch game-preserver. Houston Gorse was also a favourite find in the late Mr. Ramsay's time, but now, alas! it is almost a desert.

There are miles of moss both about Cairn Hill and in the Carnwath country, and a huntsman has to *"pick and creep and screw"* to keep near his hounds at all, and even when Stracey is on North Briton he is often in sad tribulation. In fact, it is a regular choker over such country, and the hounds do it pretty much by themselves. As Stracey graphically puts it, "they have a turn at the Pentland Hills from Malleny, and face the hills up wind a mile as hard as they can

rattle; then they sink the wind: they never care
which way the wind blows, and I'm blowed if you
can tell what to do with them, it would puzzle mortal man, up hills four or five miles from the bottom,
and you tearing after them—that's the way they
work you, and so they nail us."

East to west, from Corstorphine Hill to Lee Castle,
the country runs about forty miles. The Carnwath
covers are all fir plantations on the hills, and the best
of them belong to the Earl of Home, at Stone-
hill, near the Tinto boundary. The covers are
very middling, the fir plantations are scarce and
grown out, and there are very few gorses. The best
are round Wall House, nice and dry fir plantings on
the side of a hill, with heather and rock. Near
Wall House the country is generally old grass, and
mostly plough near home. The home country is not
spoilt by wire, which is a perfect pest in Carnwath
without the alleviation of telegraph-posts to the
hunting-gates, as in the Buccleuch country. In the
Dechmount country, about nine miles from the kennels, the ground is sound and good, and all on old
grass. The crack gorse of the country is Riccarton
Hill, and Champflurie laurels have had a great re-
pute. Ever since Mr. Ramsay's death "the white
collars" have been under the mastership of his brother-
in-law, the Hon. James Sandilands, with a subscription
which was very nominal. His nephew has taken to
them on coming of age, and the subscription has been
fixed for the present at £900 a year. The land-

owners generally hunt elsewhere, but they are very
fair preservers of foxes, of which twenty brace are
generally brought to hand in a season. On the
Edinburgh side, a prospect of something good over
the grass from Dechmount, Champflurie, and Bangour will bring out the Edinburgh, and Glasgow gentlemen as well, and swell the field to fifty. Potts,
Purslow, Nason, and Jack Jones followed Tom Rintoul as huntsmen; and then Stracey, who had two
seasons as first whip with Jones (to whom he also
whipped in with the Warwickshire), went up, and
has now held the horn for five seasons, which makes
his twenty-third with hounds.

There are generally about 45½ couple of hounds in
kennel, and two dozen couple of puppies are put out
among the Barnton tenants. The strength of the
kennel comes from the Yarborough and Fitzhardinge
drafts, of which some ten couple have been sent from
England for four seasons past. The Yarborough dogs
and the Fitzhardinge bitches have done them most
service, and Bedford and Auditor among the former,
and Bertha and Songstress among the latter have been
the mainstay. The Fitzhardinge (late Morrell's) Baja-
zets have "proved themselves good workers and fine
constitutions," and the old dog was put away in his
eleventh season at the kennels, which are at Golf Hall,
five miles from Edinburgh. The Cromwell nose, which
helped Harry Ayris over many a dry fallow, also bids
fair to be perpetuated in his son Waterloo. In his
very first season he was the only one that would

speak to it through a dry fir planting, in a capital thing of fifteen· miles straight from Macbie, in fact " *such a nipper that it could never have been one fox.*" Mr. Sandilands does not care for a heavy-boned hound, as they get quite beat at the hills, and the leader at present is Yarborough Bedford, a spayed dog, light and narrow and high on the leg, but he finds "no country too heavy and no hills too high." On Tuesday they take the east side by Dalmahoy and Ormiston, on Thursday they generally train it towards Linlithgow, and Saturday finds them on the Wall House side, which holds, with Dechmount and Bangour, the best scent. The Carnwath time is from the 15th or 16th of March till about the end of April. They have killed a May fox there, and an eight-and-twenty miles trot finds them again in this hill country for nearly as long in the autumn.

When the West Lothian are not at work, the men of Edinburgh and the Lothians have had many a good river run with Mr. Waldron Hill's otter hounds. They are kept at his residence at Murrayfield House, about two miles out of Edinburgh, on the West Lothian side. Their owner never rides, but always runs with foxhounds, and sees as many foxes broken up as any man in the Hunt. Some years ago he had a pack of otter hounds in Monmouthshire of the Welsh breed, smooth and white with yellow ears; for the last five years he has had black and tans, a cross between the bloodhound and rough Lancashire hound, which is used in that county for otter and

foulmart. Their nose is nearly equal to the Lancashire hound, who are unrivalled in this respect, and
never disposed to be · tonguy. The bloodhound
cross also makes them more savage in their worry,
but they are often very unpleasant to manage in
kennel. Mr. Hill has found the foxhound fail in
working up to his otter in a cold drag, but excellent
on the line when the game is fairly started. With
him the southern hound has only failed from lack
of constitution, which is injured by too much
swimming.

The Murrayfield terriers are descended from the
pure Welsh breed of Mr. Ramsay Williams, who lived
near Carnarvon. He died eight years since, and his
hunting journal testifies to a most wondrous medley
of sport with fox, otter, marten, foulmart, and hedge-
hog. For twenty-five years did Mr. Hill long for
his terriers, but never succeeded in getting any
until the old man's death. They weigh about 15lbs.,
and have no cross of the bull-dog in them; their
length of leg enables them to scramble out of
any rocky cairn, where a fox can climb; and they
are always bred as flatsided as possible, so as to
squeeze into the smallest compass. To looks they
have no pretensions, but they stick to the water
most resolutely, and one of the best of them died
last October, after swimming an otter for hours on
the Lyne, near Drochil Castle, in Peebleshire. She
sternly refused to leave it, and foiled every effort
to get at her, till she sank fairly frozen by cold.

They worry and teaze the otter, but do not fasten on him and kill him in the earth; and Mr. Hill has found that half-a-dozen of them will go into an earth and never quarrel, but that if two of a bull-dog cross get together, there is sure to be a row directly. Winifred and her daughter Dinah are the flower of the terrier stock; and among the hounds Bangor, who "never tells a lie," and his sister Brenda are great on the drag, and Fairfax is unequalled as a marker to ground.

Mr. Hill's principal river is the Tyne, which runs through Haddingtonshire. It is well preserved for him, but far too full of drains, which are being gradually grated, especially in the town of Haddington, which is a great resort and stronghold of game. In some places the Tyne is deep, but there are very few rocks, it is more like an English river, and but for the drains one of the best he has. The Avon in Linlithgowshire has furnished great sport, and, strange to say, although the paraffin-oil works are situated on a tributary of it, and have effectually driven away the fish, it is always a sure otter find, and there have been more kills on it than any other river. Mr. Hill also hunts the North and South Esk, which rise in Peebleshire, join at Dalkeith, and run into the sea at Musselburgh. On the South Esk the sport has been first-rate. It is not deep, but very rapid and rocky; its banks are well lined with wood, and there is not a drain on it. Last August it was the scene of a very remarkable run, as the otter only touched

the water twice for a few minutes throughout a run
of eight or nine miles, and was eventually pulled
down in the heart of one of the East Lothian fox-
whins. Bangor distinguished himself greatly in this
run, and so did Dinah, a small but very fast terrier.

The Water Company's reservoirs on the Pentlands
sometimes furnish a good otter. In '62 the hounds
hit upon one at the Clutby Dam reservoir on the
north side of the Pentlands, and hunted him through
the sheep-drains right over the Pentlands, down to
the reservoir at St. Catherine's. He had gone
through it on the north side, and from there down
the Glencorn burn, nearly to the North Esk. Leaving
this for another burn across the country, he headed
back to the reservoir at St. Catherine's, where, on
account of the water being too high, he could not be
moved. This otter must have travelled nearly twenty
miles during the night, and it was well for Mr.
Hill that his terriers were longlegged, and that he
himself is always in condition summer or winter, or
he would have seen nothing of the fun on that hot
and very wet September morning.

A fortnight after, they went back for their revenge,
found him at the old spot, and, after three hours
without a check, fairly swam him down. In putting
him out from the rock under which he was lying,
one of the terriers (Caroline) had one side of her
face, from the eye to the nose, completely scalped,
and the otter came out holding her fast; but still,
when he was run into on the public road, she

attacked him as if she had never had a bite in her life.

On the Lyne and Forth in Peebleshire there has been good sport; but the first is small, and both are uncertain. The upper part of the Clyde is good, and also the South Medwyn in Lanarkshire, which runs into it. Mr. Hope Vere of Craigie Hill, on the Almond, is a staunch preserver of the animal, although he is very fond of fishing. He kept otters very strictly for the late Duke of Athole, and his part is still the surest find on the whole river. It was there that a large dog otter cut up Dinah and the terriers so fearfully in a drain last year, that they had to be carried home. In Fife the Eden is the best river, and has always otters upon it; but the numerous drains render it very difficult to kill, except by a mere chance. On the Leven, which is very deep and very dirty, owing to the mills, there has been good sport, and especially with a vixen otter, which lived before the hounds for 5 h. 10 m. without any intermission, and then saved herself under an oak tree, which must have been cut down for blood. The upper part of the Whiteadder in Berwickshire furnished a fine run last year; but its rough and rocky banks make it very difficult to keep up with the dogs, when they are running a fresh drag. Winifred, the terrier, backed up Bangor, Fairfax, and Potiphar last October in a run which Lord Wemyss, the owner of much of the property on its banks, would have rejoiced to see. There was a capital scent, such as is rarely met with previous to such a storm of rain as came rattling down almost at the very moment the otter was killed. In all these forays Mr. Hill has never got heavily bitten himself; but many years ago, when he was hunting on the Kenvy near Abergavenny, the otter came out of the water just before it was killed, made straight at the whip, who was a few yards off his master, shook him savagely by the trousers, and then passed on.

CHAPTER III.

EDINBURGH TO THE ROMAN CAMP.

" A hoary ridge of ancient town
Smoke-wreathed, picturesque and still,
Cirque of crag, and temple hill,
And Arthur's lion couching down
In watch, as if the news of Flodden
Stirred him yet—my fancy flies
To level wastes and moors untrodden,
Purpling 'neath the low-hung skies.
I see the burdened orchards, mute and mellow,
I see the sheaves, and girt by reaper trains,
And blurred by breath of horses, through a yellow
September moonlight roll the swaggering wanes."

ALEXANDER SMITH.

Arrival in Edinburgh—Professor Dick's "Constitution Hill"—Messrs.
Girdwood's Wool Stores—Origin of the Highland Society—Its En-
couragement of Gaelic—Its Early Aims—Original Members—Its
Agricultural Education—Gradual Development—Bagpipe Contests—
Cheese, Cured Meat, and Ploughing Prizes—Résumé of the princi-
pal Cattle Shows—Present Competition Rules—Agricultural Statistics
Inquiry—The Council Chamber of the Society—Pictures of Winners
The Museum—White Crop Samples.

IT seemed quite strange to be in Edinburgh at last,
with the mare quietly drinking at the Sinclair
fountain; but our reverie was broken rudely enough by
the boom of the one o'clock gun, and away she went,
best pace, down Prince's-street, and it took " a long
pull and a strong pull" to stop her. " Dick's Constitution Hill," as it is called by all the sporting men
and the faculty, would have been most opportune,
and we passed down it later in the day when we
went on our way to Tanfield. It is fully a quarter

2 F

of a mile on a very steep incline from the bottom of
Dublin-street up Duke-street, to St. Andrew's-square.
Professor Dick, whose first connexion with the Highland Society dates back to '24, tries horses there,
which are sent to him under suspicion of roaring or
disease of the heart. "They seldom require a second
turn, except it is on a windy day, or people are particular," and the Professor is often glad to get the
man off their backs, when they have come through
at a sharp canter. "*Run him against the hill, gentlemen, and you'll find him a roarer!*" was the trenchant
phrase in which he once opposed a public appointment; and the candidate merely observed, in reply,
that he was open to run the Professor. The Veterinary College in Clyde-street, over which the Professor
has presided for eight-and-forty years, is close by;
and we found him in the lecture-room with the skele-
ton of the blood mare Miss Foote at his side, the
hind leg of a horse fresh from the Grass Market in
his hand, and seven dozen students in front of him.

Edinburgh has gradually become a great empo-
rium for wool. In 1853, the system of public sales
for home-grown wools in Edinburgh was established
by Mr. Robert Girdwood, and after combatting for
three years the prejudices both of growers and consumers, it was accepted as "a great fact," and he opened
stores in Glasgow as well. Adams and Macgregor,
Crauford and Cree, and one or two other firms in Leith
and Granton have followed suit, and a very large
business is done. Mr. Girdwood has his Edinburgh

stores at Tanfield, which has gone through many different phases in its day. The premises were originally built by the Portable Gas Company, which sent out its gas compressed into malleable-iron bottles, but the speculation was a losing one, and the firm was very soon wound up. Sir Walter Scott was the designer of the original building, with its two gasometer towers, its halls, and large apartments, after the style of a Moorish fort.

The towers of five flats (of which one flat serves for the luncheon-room on sale-days, and the others for skin stores) are still left to tell of the strange scheme which gave birth to that building. It was afterwards sold to some wholesale grocers and wine merchants; and it was there that the Free Kirk ministers, with Chalmers, Candlish, and Cunningham at their head, first marched, after the disruption of 1843, from St. Andrew's Church, and held their meetings for fourteen years. What is now the "West Hall" had acquired before that a political renown. Those walls had echoed back the voice of O'Connell, as, with all that " action which completes speech," he talked to Edinburgh of Erin. He had canny Scots to hear him; but it held them in a spell.

> "To the last verge of that wide audience sent,
> It played with each wild passion as it went;
> Now stirred the uproar, now the murmur stilled,
> And sighs and laughter answered as it willed."

An East Hall has now sprung up where "once a garden smiled;" in 1861 the North Hall, covering a space of from 1,500 to 2,000 yards, was added, and

2 F 2

in 1864 a large three-storeyed building. There are thus about 10,000 yards of floorage, which are capable of storing 20,000 to 30,000 bales of wool for the sales.

When you have passed through the office, and perhaps paused to look at the photograph of one of Mr. Girdwood's earliest supporters, the late Mr. Gunn of Glendhu, you enter the room, where sheets and bags stand in piles all ready to send out. Above £2,000 is invested in them alone. A few are of Dundee manufacture, but they principally come from Jameson of Hull, and are made of hemp, as being most profitable, and very seldom of jute. The bags begin to go out in April, and so on till the very end of the year. Ten to forty sheets are sent out for clips in the Lothians, &c., &c.; but for big High-land clips from ten to two hundred bags are re-quired. A sheet generally carries 300 to 500lbs., but English and Irish ones will go as high as 6 cwt., when intended for exportation. A bag will carry ten to twelve Scotch stones (24lbs. to the stone) of laid wool, and eight stone of white wool, in fleeces ; and the Highland wool generally comes this way. It was once a very common practice with the Scottish farmers to weigh in lots of 2 stone, and thus in a bag of 10 stone the turn of the beam was against them five times, and they perhaps lost 5 to 10 lbs.; but to obviate this, 1 lb. per cwt. of draft is allowed. Sutherlandshire, Ross-shire, Inverness-shire, Argyll-shire, and Perthshire generally send their clips in bags, which carry 2 cwt. for the facility of carrying and shipping, while the south country Cheviot and half-bred wools mostly arrive in sheets.

The centre building has a great variety of home and foreign skins, principally from Buenos Ayres, in bales bound with steel hoops. The wools pulled from them are classed into three sorts, according to the part of the sheep they belong to. The fellmongers get the skins, and pull them after sweating, and sell the wool, and the skin is converted into parchment or leather. About 100 bales of New Zealand wool were lying there. It is very pure and white in its colour, finer than Cheviot, and shorter, although some is long and suitable for combing, and it is in demand both for tweeds and hosiery. The contents of the Round Towers of five flats are more various. Lamb skins figure as "morts," and sell from 1½d. to 2d.; and Shetland pickings lie cheek by jowl with German flipes, seal skins from Orkney, otter skins from Mull, and calf skins from everywhere.

The North Hall is full of the finest specimens of bred and half-bred* wools, from Caithness, the Lothians, Berwickshire, Roxburghshire, Peebleshire, Morayshire, and Fifeshire. Early in 1864, one sample fetched 2s. 5½d. per lb., the highest price known since 1818; but since then one or two others have reached as high as 2s. 7½d. The wools are all reclassed after examination by the buyers,

* Bred = Leicester; Half-bred = Leicester and Cheviot, Half-bred Cross = Blackface and Leicester; Cross = Blackface and Cheviot

who come to look over them two days before the
sale, and the men refill the bags, which are hung
from the roofs during the process The red clay of
the East Lothian, like that of Gala water, slightly
colours its wool, and one clip retained an oil-dip so
much that it might as well have been smeared.   Mr.
Girdwood stands on his "Melossoon dip," and several
tin jars and casks of it, hermetically sealed and
marked with the Highland ram's head, occupy the
floor of the East Room.   Butterate and White Smear
are his other preparations ; the latter is intended to
supersede tar and butter, but Time, " who knows
nor friend nor foe," will be the judge.

The public sales were announced in April, 1853,
and the first was held on July 14th of that year.
There were 320 bales, principally half-bred wools ;
and by the end of the first decade we find 7,000
bales or 1,364 lots in the catalogue of the corres-
ponding sale.   The first supply was principally from
the Lothians and Fife, with part from Perth and
Argyllshire; and the Highland and Highland-district
wools came later in the season.   There was a
large assembly that day, and the absence of the
Halifax men was made up by a strong body of the
Bradford for the half-bred and other combing* wools,
of which Mr. Baines especially was a large buyer.
Charles Fox from Dewsbury was also there for
clothing wools; the Wilsons of Hawick, and Paton

---

* Combing wools = breds, half-breds, blackface, and highly-fed Cheviot
hoggs, Clothing wools = hill-fed Cheviots, crosses, and Southdowns.

and Son of Alloa, for half-breds and Cheviots for hosiery and Alloa stocking yarn; Abercromby and Co. of Stowe Mills, near Galashiels, for Southdown and Cheviot for tartan shawls; Charles Wilson and Sons of Earlston were looking after Cheviot, crosses, and blackfaced for blankets; and local dealers for all sorts, and a bargain if it could be had.

"*Lot* 1, 3 *sheets, first pick, mark j b —Skin Wool C.,*" was the opening entry of the maiden catalogue. The first biddings were not up to the reserve price, and the lot was withdrawn, and sold that afternoon at 1s. 4d. to Mr. Joshua Hall. For Lot 2, "*Fliped Hogg C,*" Mr. Baines of Bradford drew first blood, and at the same price. At the second sale, Mr. Varley of Stanningley bought largely of all kinds, and the result convinced Mr. Girdwood that half-bred crosses, which had been sold hitherto at a price half way between Cheviot and Blackfaced wool, would come close up to the half-bred, as they have done.

To master that catalogue and all its phrases is no light effort. "*Smyrna Britch*" speaks, in a measure, for itself as skirts, or the coarse hairy parts of Smyrna fleece, and "*B A Bonnet*" as fine dark Buenos Ayres; while "*Capes*" are from the Cape of Good Hope. There is more significance in "*Brokes,*" or broken wools of all kinds; "*Fallen*" are fleeces gathered on the hills from dead sheep; and "*Burrs*" are wool-balls adhering to that prickle. After that our troubles begin, and it does require some effort of pencil or memory to master that "*Noils*" signify short wool

left in the teeth of wool-combs, and that it goes to
the blanket manufacturer; that " *Cotts*" are cotted
or matted fleeces; that " *Picklocks*" are divided into
best and second, or fine and coarse pick, from the
skin, by fellmongers; that " *Haslock* " is subject to
the same classification, but applies generally to the
coarse skirts of Cheviots, half-breds, &c., and the best
part of blackface; that "*Fine Grey*" is equal to Haslock of that colour, and taken principally from blackface for carpet yarns and blankets, and that " *Coarse
White*" comes from the shanks of the sheep, and
ranks in the social wool scale along with " *Coarse
Grey*," and even below " *Common Haslock.*"

The sales take place eight times a year, beginning
in May; and in September, which is the height
of the season, they last from four to six days.   Shetland sends very little native wool to public sales,
but, like Orkney, contributes some Cheviot.   The half-
bred wool from Caithness is of a beautiful quality and
fine fibre, with a peculiarly pure colour, all of which
delight the Halifax men.   The judges saw this at
the International Show, and both Sir George Dunbar's bred and Mr. Swainson's half-bred fleeces had
certificates of merit.   In fact, it is a hard race for supre-
macy between them and the East Lothian men, among
whom Major Hunter of Thurston, who farms about
five miles from Dunbar, stands very high with his
half-breds, Southdowns, and Southdown crosses.   The
east-coast have an advantage over the west-coast men,
owing to the feeding, which causes the wool to be

rather brighter and stronger in the staple. Sutherland
wools, which principally come up in July, are excellent for stockings, tweeds, pilot-cloths, blankets,
and blue flannels. Ross-shire sends good laid Cheviot and blackface, and the sheep-farms of Easter
Ross some of the best bred and half-bred wools.

The Highland smearing system extends through Inverness, Argyllshire, Ross-shire, and Perthshire (except in the agricultural parts); and these counties, with
Morayshire, parts of Banffshire and Aberdeenshire,
Forfarshire, Fife, Kinross, and the agricultural parts
of Stirlingshire, nearly all send white wool. Skye is
faithful to laid, which is principally Cheviot, and very
fine in the staple. South of the Forth, the public
feeling has gone against smearing for some years past,
and the flock-masters chiefly apply dressing which will
not stain the wool. Peebleshire is great both in Cheviot and Blackfaced, and the pastures of Ayrshire bor-
dering on Galloway, and Galloway itself, produce a
closer and finer growth of wool, which the clothiers
love. Wool is sold at character fairs, Inverness, Fort
William, Oban, Inverary, Crieff, and Tyndrum, which
are all held in July. St. Boswells unites a wool character and pitched sheep fair, and so does George-
mas; Jedburgh, Peebles, Biggar, and Kelso sell, but
never pitch ; and Hawick has regular pitched wool
sales of its own.

The Highland Society was formed in 1784, at a
small meeting in the Cowgate. Lord Kames had
given the times a wrench by his writings, and " Sir

John of projects rife" was beginning to "stand
forth" and make his voice heard from John o'Groat's
to Gretna. It was not, however, until July 30th, 1787,
that the Society was incorporated by royal charter, and
was known, "per nomen et titulum in vulgari," as
"The Highland Society of Scotland at Edinburgh."
John Duke of Argyll (its first President) and the
Right Honourable Elizabeth Countess of Sutherland
were the first and second "original constituent members" under the charter; William Macdonald of St.
Martin's was its first secretary, and David Maclean
its first piper.

It proposed to examine into the Highlands and
Islands, to establish towns, villages, and harbours
therein—to open communication by roads and bridges,
to extend and promote fisheries, to encourage agriculture, and to introduce manufactures. The preservation
of the language, poetry, and music of the Highlands
was also its care. It was to this end that it paid
teachers of Gaelic, that it gave prizes for the best performers on the bagpipes, and instituted "inquiries into
the authenticity and history of the poems of Ossian."
Henry Mackenzie, "*The Man of Feeling,*" was quite
the knight of the Gael in council. Year after year
he kept the subject alive, and never bated one jot of
heart and hope during that weary delay, which arose
out of the difficulty of finding an editor really fit
to cope with Gaelic manuscripts. It was long before
he could fairly report progress, and his last sickness
was on him when the completion of the Gaelic dic-

tionary, in two volumes of 776 and 1,015 pages each, was officially announced by the lips of another.

With the new century the Society extended its care in a measure to the Lowlands, and laid great stress on essays and reports. In 1824, its original hundred members had swelled to 1,461, and when the jubilee dinner was held in '34, with the Duke of Buccleuch, who was then President, in the chair, they numbered 1,900. The Duke of Wellington had been made an honorary member, and wrote his thanks from Cambray in the spring of '16, and a letter in acknowledgment of the same honour was received from Marshal Blucher at Carlsbad the next July. Sir Walter Scott took no very active part in its proceedings, and the last mention that we find of his name was at a half-yearly meeting in 1824, when he proposed that the ballot should be dispensed with in the case of Lady Gwydir and Baroness Keith. Fifty years had reduced the original members to four on the day of the jubilee—the Earl of Glasgow (who survived them all), Sir William M'Leod of Bannatyne, Sir John Sinclair of Ulbster, and General Campbell of Lochnell. They were all there to support the Duke, and were welcomed with the old, favourite strain of " *Owre the muir amang the heather.*"

New ones sprung up as they went down ; and beteen '45 and '65, which represents the secretaryship of Mr. Hall Maxwell, the numbers have increased from 2,569 to 4,055. Independently of the national feeling, which makes every young farmer anxious to

see his name on this great Scottish bede-roll of agriculture, the terms* upon which he can enter do not
encourage that mere membership for a year, when the
Society comes to his own locality, which is fostered by
the roving English pound. His Majesty Napoleon III.
heads the list, and the oldest member on the books
is "Mr. Robert Campbell of Sonachan, Inverary,
1802", and the Marquis of Tweeddale, K.T., who
was a constant judge at the earlier shows, dates from
1809. The Presidency has been held by sixteen
dukes. John fifth Duke of Argyll was elected in 1785,
and died when he had held office for two-and-twenty
years. All the others, with the exception of the late
Duke of Gordon, who also died during his term of
office, have presided for four years, and none of
them but the late Duke of Hamilton (who went on
for another year by virtue of a bye-law) have been
elected twice.

The cardinal object of the Society is, by means
of district competitions under committees and con-
veners, to throw out its fibres all over the country,
and to keep all the local societies in communion with
head-quarters at Edinburgh. Hence there were at
least 211 districts during '64 in the receipt of money
or medals under the Society's conditions, quite irre-

---

* New members are admitted at the annual meeting in January, and the
summer general meeting in June or July The ordinary subscription is
£1 3s 6d annually, which may be redeemed by one payment, varying from
£12 12s to £7 1s , and regulated by the number of previous annual payments
Tenant-farmers, secretaries, and treasurers of local Agricultural Associations,
resident agricultural factors, and proprietors farming the whole of their own
lands, whose assessment on the valuation-roll does not exceed £500, are admitted on a subscription of 10s annually or £5 5s for life

spective of those which were comprehended in the August Show district of the year. Agricultural education was provided for by a supplementary charter of 1856, by which diplomas were granted, and £100 is laid out annually in prizes according to the report of the Board of Examiners, which comprises, along with Professors John Wilson, Balfour, Anderson, Allman, Dick, &c., the well-known agricultural names of George Hope of Fenton Barns, Robert Russell of Pilmuir, John Wilson of Edgington Mains, and Peter M'Lagan of Pumpherston. As far back as 1824, we find Professor Dick's name as lecturer to the Society on " the diseases of black cattle ;" and money was then voted to set up a forge at his Veterinary College, in order to teach the young farmers shoeing. In 1849, Dr. Anderson was appointed Consulting Chemist, and gives his advice from " complete analysis of a soil, including determination of Alkalies and Phosphates, £3," down to " letters asking advice on subjects within the department of the chemist, 5s.," on a regular scale sanctioned by the Society.

From the first, the Society's intellectual activities have been boundless, and have extended even to bee husbandry. Was it locomotion? They were looking after the improvement of the Highland ferry-boats; they were resisting the attempt to get rid of the ancient drove-roads, and confine the cattle to turnpikes; and as far back as 1818 they proposed a 50-guinea prize essay on railroads. Was it cropping?

They were giving prizes for barley or bigg of the greatest weight; they were guarding against smut in wheat, and encouraging turnips in Orkney and Shetland, as well as sowing arable land with red clover and rye-grass; and Mr. Boswell of Balmuto was their Holker ambassador to see the drill system as practised by Mr. Coke, and to report whether it or broadcast answered best with barley, after a bare, and a turnip fallow.   Was it the reclaiming of land? Sheep-drains were fostered, and prizes given for the effective execution of not less than 6,000 roods, and attention was drawn to the extirpation of ferns from hill pastures.   The blowing sand was combatted in all the Northern Isles, and one of the first gold medals was given to Mr. Drummond of Blair Drummond, for "floating an extreme track of moss in Perthshire, and settling one hundred people on it, who in '92 had been compelled to leave the Highlands on account of sheep-farming."

Was it the improvement of implements or machinery?   They were offering a premium for a steam plough in 1837, which was competed for by Mr. Heathcot, and they awarded it to Mr. John Fowler, in 1857. Mr. Smith of Deanston was always secure of a trial from the Society, when something new in earth-tormenting was evolved from that teeming brain, and so was Bell's reaping machine.   Thanks to their bounty, Andrew Meikle, the inventor of a thrashing machine, was enabled to pass his later years in comfort; but when watches and a revolving battery were pressed upon them, they were fain to admit that they were not just in their line. Mr. Blackie, the "Armourer to the Lanarkshire Militia," seems to have read the meaning of the Society better, when he entered their temple of industrious peace, not with a new buckler or a helmet, but with a model of a reaping machine; and in 1825, two young Flemish farmers were brought over, with an amateur interpreter, to instruct the districts in the use of the Hainault scythe.

Still, the Society never lost sight of their earliest mission, and the newspapers were specially requested to take notes of the probable ripening time of the Lowland harvest, so as to prevent miscalculations on the part of the Highland shearers and the public begging which followed. The social questions which it grappled with were not always strictly agricultural, as the state of the Friendly Societies was looked into, and the average was struck of health and sickness specially dividing bedfast and walking sickness. Indoor labour was not passed over; and spinning hemp, making herring-nets, knitting worsted stockings not less than twenty-four pairs, and worsted, not less than twenty-four spindles and spun in the Highlands, all formed subjects of competition. Raising the pile of wool on cloths, and spinning the greatest quantity of Merino wool into broad-cloth not less than 600 lbs. weight, originated with Sir John Sinclair, who had a flock of them within five miles of John o'Groat's, and once held quite a shepherd and shepherdess *fête* in costume on a shearing-day. Not content with " an abstract of all that is known in woolstapling," the directors proceeded in after-years to give practical effect to the essay they proposed, by offering 100 gs. to any woolstapler who would settle by a certain day in a situation approved of by the Board. Besides their general researches into the larch and other Scottish trees, they inquired into the causes of the difficulty of raising trees at all on the eastern coast, and drew attention to the uses of brushwood and other underwood, which had been " unduly neglected by owners and the public." They encouraged the growth of osiers for baskets, and willows for barrel-hoops, under restrictions as to age and acreage ; and, aided by Mr. Boswell's report of his Italian tour, they strove to introduce a strawplait imitation of Leghorn, from common rye sown thick on sandy gravelly soil, and cut when it came into ear.

The marine portion of the earliest charter was never overlooked, and they took the breeding of salmon fry under their charge. " The adventurers in the herring fishery at Greenock" had every facility for " communing with the Society," when they repaired to Edinburgh to beg them to persuade Parliament to put the fishing bounties on a better footing, and to prevent foreign herrings from coming in. They laboured the point as to whether the "sea-grass" might not become a good proxy for horse-hair in stuffing mattresses, and more especially fostered the production of kelp as a substitute for barilla, as "the earlier stages of the process were calculated to encourage a seafaring life, and breed up seamen for the navy." Any attempt on the part of the Chancellor of the Exchequer to increase the duties on soap was therefore watched with an especially jealous eye; but beyond an attitude of defiance on herrings and barilla we find hardly any trace of political action.

The contests for the prize pipe took place in the Theatre Royal at Edinburgh each July, "immediately after the race." The judges wore their national garb; and on one occasion, when Mr. James Moray's piper won the prize pipe and forty merks to boot, there were forty-five competitors, and upwards of £150 was taken at the doors. The notation of pipe music was carefully attended to, and it was a cardinal rule that each candidate should deposit six ancient pipe tunes with the Society. Those, too, who could "produce tunes set to music by themselves, and sing or recite ancient Gaelic poetry or lines not generally known or published," were informed that they would "meet with due encouragement." Sometimes Strathspey or "Twasome" was danced as an interlude; and both it and the playing were so keenly relished, that more than once Sir John Sinclair had to warn the company that if they encored the performers so often the dinner-hour would find them only half through their work. Sir John quite gloried in being chairman of the musical jury, and the Peninsular war gave him great scope when he distributed the

2 G

prizes. IIis eye glistened when he told them that
Wellington heard no sound with more delight, or
Napoleon with more dismay, than that of a Highland pibroch; or when he pointed out that, as the
waists of Brussells belles were tied with Scottish ribbons, " such an example should not be *wasted* on the
belles of our own country." He could tell the
pipers, too, how one gold medallist had, since their
last merry meeting, forgotten all about the surgeon,
and continued to play on his pipe, when he was
severely wounded at Vimeira, and how one who had
gained a second pipe had been wounded four times.
The 42nd, the 71st, the 79th, and the 92nd regi-
ments had all a magic sound for his audience; but
still, the Scots Greys were first favourites, and the
roof rang longest and loudest at the mention of their
name.

The dairy claims were substantially recognized in
'24, when the expediency of sending sweet milk to
market in spring-carts and locked vessels was insisted
on, and prizes were proposed for Dunlop or " Mild
Ayrshire," and imitations of Double Glo'ster. No
competitor was to send in less than 10 stone of
16lbs and 16oz. to the pound. Fifty-two cheeses
competed at the first show, which was held in Edinburgh on December 22nd, and Mr. Sanderson of the
Black Castle, Lanarkshire, was first with Dunlop,
and Mr. Bell of Woodhouse Lees, Dumfriesshire, with
the Double Glo'ster. Prizes for North Wiltshire
cheeses were given the next Christmas; but the

judges observed that their pine-apple shape was not accurate, owing to the faulty nets, and advised that better patterns should be got. From the statement of Mr. Sanderson, who seems to have been with Mr. Nichol of Easterhouse quite the cheese champion of the day, the only difference between them and the Double Glo'ster was in the shape and size. In '27, Mr. Sanderson won with Stilton, but the imitations of Cheshire failed. Prizes were also given for the curing of butter, no competitor to send in less than 10 firkins, and in due time Sir John Sinclair (who was as enthusiastic upon this point as he was upon salting beef or salving sheep, to say nothing of his Vienna cabbage) was enabled to report that the butter from Aberdeen no longer classed with the fourth-class Irish, and that the difference of 30s. per cwt. between it and the best Dutch had been gradually reduced five-sixths.

Deacon Milne of that town seems to have had a monopoly of the salting prizes. Sometimes we read of him curing 262 tierces of 300lbs. each of beef, and 38 tierces of pork, with rock or bay salt; and later on he shipped his 90,000lbs. weight of beef at Aberdeen, drawn solely from Aberdeenshire, Banffshire, and Kincardineshire. Veal, too, was not overlooked, and there was a prize for the breeder who brought the greatest weight of calves to market, which had been fed on milk for not less than six weeks, and had been carried to the fleshers on spring-carts or by canal.

The ploughing matches formed no small local

feature in the earlier history of the Society, and in a report of one held in 1819, in the Kincardineshire district, where twenty-four ploughs were drawn by a pair of horses, and three by oxen, " a small sum of money was allotted to each unsuccessful candidate." Gradually the system was given up, or confined to a silver medal to the best ploughman " on the report of one or more members of the Society;" and competitive implement trials were annexed to the programme at each of the meetings. These were abandoned after '61, and the implements are not now arrayed in sections as they once were, but exhibitors group exactly what they like at their stands. A committee send in a report, and select new inventions or important implements for trial, and at Athelstaneford last year some reaping machines were tested. The withdrawal of the prizes has rather increased the number of implements exhibited. The Kelso entry was very much larger than the Perth one, and stood at 1,101 as against 11 at Edinburgh in 1827.

Their earliest premiums were given for "black cattle," or rather Argyllshires, and the expression still lingered out of courtesy at the head of the list long after the other breeds were acknowledged, and had distinct classes. The maiden show seems to have been one for bulls at Connel Kilmore in Argyllshire, on October 20th, 1784; and the directions to the judges were "to attend to the shape of bulls, and not to the size, as we encourage the true breed of

Highland cattle." For a time, the favoured bull-
districts were Lorn, Mull, with the Island of Coll,
Morven, with Ardnamurchan, Kingerloch, and Ardgower. Then three-year-old queys received prizes as
well as bulls; and when Argyllshire ceased to have
a monopoly of the Society's cattle attentions, a prize
of £5 was given to the man, either in that county,
Inverness-shire, Perthshire, or Ross-shire, "who
spaves most queys with success." In 1816, there
were prizes for the improvement of work-horses,
and by degrees a distinction was drawn between
Clydesdales for heavy and Clevelands for lighter land.
An attempt to encourage the breeding of chariot
horses ended in one pair being shown, and one of
them being disqualified for over age. At Kelso the
£50 blood-horse competition was nearly as un-
satisfactory; Captain Anstruther Thomson and
Captain Percy Williams threaded the ranks in vain
for anything worthy of the name of a hunter, and
so the Clydesdale has slowly and surely swallowed
up every other breed.

Short-wools as well as long-wools were recognized
soon after '16; and the Duke of Athole, Lord Lyne-
doch, and Mr. Smith of Methven judged them in
Perthshire, with instructions to "have regard both
to wool and carcase." Things had ripened by '21
into twelve district competitions for "black cattle,"
two for horses, and three for sheep; and Donald
Horne of Langwell and John Hall of Seiber's Cross
were showing their hands as Cheviot winners.

The first show was held at Queensberry Barracks
in 1822, the very year that England began her
Shorthorn Herd-Book. Fifty-nine oxen and eight
sheep were entered, and it was expressly stipulated
that the oxen were not to be fed on "oilcake or distillery wash and grains," and that particulars as to
the distance they had travelled and the time they
had been put up to fatten should be specified in the
certificate. The "Teeswaters or Shorthorns were the
favourites with the Border agents," says a local
chronicler, who adds that "Baillie Gordon, his Majesty's carpenter, put up the sheds." The show was
kept open for 2½ days, and sixty-five new members
were added to the Society. Rennie, the younger,
showed twenty-two shorthorns, and was first of all
with one, which was sold for 60 guineas. This
success routed up the champions of the national
breeds. *The Dumfries Courier* as the time again drew
near, exhorted the Galloway men to send "your hairy
representatives to the great annual congress of
beeves;" but Rennie was first again, and again when the
show-yard had been removed next year to the Portable
Gas premises at Tanfield, and "9s. and 10s. per stone
was the ordinary rate of agreement for cattle." One
of them, "Fat Charlie," bred at Monreith, fetched
the highest of the twain; and it is recorded that
"more would have been got, if the show-man who
exhibited him had not wanted to sell the caravan as
well." All the oxen were shown in pairs, and Shorthorn, Fife, and then Aberdeen was the order, when

the winning pairs were drawn and placed for the
Plate. Both cattle and sheep mustered stronger
than ever in '24, when a West Highland ox made
11s. per stone, and an 160-stone ox arrived in a van.
Well might an Edinburgh paper "not wish to boast";
"*but* yet we have no hesitation in expressing our wil-
lingness to compare notes with our friends at Smithfield."

Store cattle had been admitted the previous year,
but even that advance and the opening of the classes
to England and Ireland did not help the show in '25
(at which Mr. Stirling's Shorthorn-West-Highland
played first part), and in the following year it
was determined to take it to Glasgow, and have
classes for horses as well. Change of scene brought
with it a complete revival. The Duke of Montrose
kept up the honour of the district with his oxen
Romulus and Riva, and nineteen Clydesdale brood
mares were in the ranks. Glasgow has always stood
highest in the entries. In its '44 show there were 558
cattle, in its '57 show 240 horses and 112 swine, and
it has only been beaten by Berwick-on-Tweed in
'54, and Edinburgh in '48, for top place with the
sheep.

The first decided symptom of the impetus which
had been given might be seen in the announce-
ment that the Highland Society were directing
their attention to the habit of letting bulls and
rams, and that "all who had paid attention to
the selection of individual animals, native or im-

ported, were requested to communicate with the Secretary." The straw had begun to stir at last; and
when Edinburgh had held another poor meeting, and
Glasgow a good one, it was decided to give up the
biennial rotation of Edinburgh and Glasgow, to
erase the conventional term "black cattle" from the
list, and to accept the invitation to *Perth* on the first
October Wednesday of '29. Gradually the Society
has fallen on to regular circuit towns, Inverness in
the North, Aberdeen in the North-east, Perth in the
centre, Edinburgh as the capitol, Glasgow in the
West, Dumfries in the South-west, and Kelso in the
South-east. Dundee was once the venue in '43, and
Stirling in '64, after an interval of one-and-thirty
years, while Ayr has been given up by common consent for very nearly as long.

The second *Glasgow* was another success, only
marred by the rule that Clydesdales should be "bay,
black, or brown bay all over," which prevented any of
the forty-two from claiming a prize, and made the
Society tolerant of white-legs and blazes for the
future. Then the regular country meetings began at
Perth, with £357 worth of premiums, and among the
192 in the cattle ranks nothing was more looked at
than the West Highlander, which was said to be the
fattest that had ever been fed at Keir. Thirty shorthorn bulls came to *Dumfries* in '30, and "Old Moodlaw" began his prize raid with the "five best Cheviot
gimmers." For many years the winning history of
these classes was interwoven with his name, as well as

Young and Craig's, Aitchison's, and Donald Horne's,
and then his nephew young Moodlaw took up the
running with Elliot, Borthwick, and Patterson of
Tereggles. Among the blackfaced classes, on the
other hand, we meet with Blacklock of Minnygap,
Dryfe, Watson, Alexander Denholm, Murray of
Eastside, Wilson of Crosshouse, and Aitken of Liston-
sheils.

The Caithness and Sutherland men with Hous-
toun of Kintradwell, amongst them, brought their
forces well up at *Inverness* in '31, when Mac-
pherson of Belville swept four blackfaced prizes,
and Corryhoylie descended from the mountains with
his buck goats. Mr. Blamire, who had just been
elected as the colleague of Sir James Graham in East
Cumberland, and whose white horse " Cappy" had
carried him to all the fairs and markets of Scotland
for many a year, when he slept in the saddle and
never dreamt of St. Stephen's or the Tithe Office,
judged his beloved shorthorns with the Marquis
of Tweeddale, at *Kelso*. *Stirling* in '33 witnessed
the intellectual activity of Mr. Smith of Deanston
in every detail down to the arrangement of the hall
for dinner, a ceremony which was so well observed at
Aberdeen in '34, that deputations kept moving between the three rooms, to inform the respective chair-
men that their healths had been drunk, and the
chairman who sat the longest proposed " the health
of the departed." Captain Barclay was in force with
his cows, and so was Lord Kintore with his " ox ;"

and Mr. Guerrier, the London salesman, was received
most cheerily when he said he had been the first to
receive an ox consigned by water to London. Ellman
sent Southdowns to *Perth* in '36, and Hugh Watson
refused £100 for a Leicester tup, one of those celebrated three from Keillor, of which, as we have before mentioned, each judge got one. Sir John
Campbell confessed himself fairly beaten over cattle
and sheep points, and told his audience, when he
spoke at the dinner, that "he should not have much
chance of being raised to the (show-yard) bench."
Next year the steam plough succeeded once in
moving three hundred yards in 3½ minutes, and then
it stuck fast in Lochar Moss, although Mr. Parkes
and his men had been in strict attendance on it for
three weeks before. Sir James Graham worked up
his audience with one of his finest speeches, which he
concluded by repeating, in reference to "The Buccleuch"—

"Constant still in danger's hour",

and the battle between Aitchison and Brydon waxed
hot over the Cheviots, the one winning with his tups
and the other with his ewes. *Glasgow* had one of its
great meetings in '38, when Sergeant Talfourd
spoke to a toast, and 16,920 people paid to go
on The Green. *Inverness* in '39 was marked by a
crusade in the discussions against the shorthorn
crosses, which were fast creeping in and making the
Highlanders very jealous; but the voice of Mr.
Wetherell was heard on the other side, and he met

the assertion that Earl Spencer's cattle were "fed, groomed, and clothed like race-horses," with a flat negative, and another English breeder indorsed him. The Buccleuch Shorthorns and the Richmond Southdowns were very distinguished at *Aberdeen* the next year, and M'Combie won his maiden prize with an ox, and showed two four-year-olds of " great merit." Booth with Bracelet, Bates with his Oxford cow, and Crofton's heifers were in the shorthorn ranks in '41 at *Berwick-on-Tweed;* and Elliot of Hind-hope fairly vanquished Sutherlandshire on his own ground. At *Edinburgh,* Crofton's Provost was first for the fifty-sovereign prize in a field of twenty-four bulls; and the Duke of Buccleuch's were first, second, and third in the cow class; while the blood horses In-heritor and Little Known were among the extra stock, as Dardanelles and Patron had been at Berwick. Jonas Webb's shearlings, which had been prevented by stress of weather from coming to Berwick, were winners at *Dundee,* where Watson of Keillor and Aitchison of Linhope made a brilliant finish to a great show career. *Glasgow* had one of its monster meetings in August, but the time was not steadily fixed yet, and the Society were at *Dumfries* in the October of the following year, and fell in for the fes-tivities of the southern race meeting. " The Belville year" of '46 (of which we spoke " in another place") preceded the *Aberdeen* year, when M'Combie began in earnest with four firsts, the Brothers Cruickshank and Hay of Shethin kept the head of the Shorthorn classes pretty well against all comers, and the laird of Langwell swept every premium offered for Cheviots.

At Glasgow, in '50, Maynard's Crusade was the Voltigeur of the Shorthorns ; and Belville reappeared with four more years on his head, and very little patchiness in proportion, as the winner of a sweep-stakes with twenty entries. Booth, Wilson, and Towne-ley fought hard in the female classes, and even Fife sent forty-three of its blacks. It seemed an expiring county effort, as only fourteen came to *Perth* in '52, and they were seen in the lists no more. Booth's Windsor was at *Berwick-upon-Tweed,* and Douglas was there with his Captain Balco and Rose of Sum-mer to meet Booth and all comers. With *Inverness,* in '56, the biennial system, which had gone on ever since '48, gave way once more to the annual. At *Glasgow,* the next year, it is well remembered how the Duke of Athole mustered his clan, and marched to meet the Queen of the Netherlands ; how closely Elliot and Brydon contested the Cheviot classes ; and how John o'Groat, the first of Mr. Stirling's three Royal roans, came from Keir with his Salis-bury honours on his head. In '58 the Granite City had its fourth visit. It was a grand sheep year at *Edin-burgh* when the Richmond Southdowns were in front, and Cockburn beat Wiley in the Leicester tups, and then had to go down before those rare Brandsby gim-mers. "The Duchess twins" came to *Dumfries* in '60, to be beaten by Douglas's Clarionet, and thus, through *Perth, Battersea, Kelso,* and *Stirling* we reach our own times.

The winter show of fat stock was renewed at Edinburgh in the off year of '53, with £300 of prizes, but with entries not much greater in extent than they had been thirty years before. A West Highlander kept up the old Keir charter, and both Mr. Stirling and Mr. Knowles had rare oxen at Glasgow the next year. With these two efforts, which entailed a heavy loss on the Society, it fell through once more, but was taken up again by the Messrs. Swan on their own account at Edinburgh in 1855. Last Christmas there were twelve well-filled classes for cattle, and five for sheep, the winner in each receiving two-thirds of the entrance-money, and the second one-third. The Cattle Cup of 10 gs. was won by Messrs. Martin of Aberdeen with their cross-bred ox, and the five-guinea Sheep Cup by Mr. Thorburn of Juniper Bank, Inverlethen, for his pen of Cheviot wedders, which sold at 95s. all round. There were also classes for dairy cows fed in Edinburgh, some of which made £25 each; while M'Combie's blacks, and not his best, went for 75s. the hundred-weight.

The whole framework of the Society is condensed into its annual book of premiums. Taking that for 1865, we find Class I. given up to reports. These are subdivided again into sections "On Subjects connected with the Science and Practice of Agriculture," "Woods and Plantations," "Land Improvements," and "Agricultural Machinery," *i.e.,* "Invention or Improvement of Implements of Husbandry." The reports in the last section are rewarded by medals or sums of money not exceeding fifty sovereigns; and in the former, the prizes range from thirty sovereigns to a "gold medium medal or five sovereigns." Class II. is devoted to District Competitions. All grants in aid for any year must be applied for by the 1st of November previous, and on the '65 list fourteen districts were down for cattle, two for draught horses, three for entire colts, three for Leicester sheep, two for swine, and five each for Cheviots and blackfaced. "The Society's premiums are granted to each district for three alternate years, on condition that the district shall, in the two intermediate years, continue the competitions by offering for the same description of stock a sum not less than one half of that given by the Society; and at the intermediate competitions a silver medal is placed at the disposal of the committee, to be awarded to the best lot exhibited." The money premiums are restricted to tenants, factors, and small proprietors, farming the whole of their own lands. Proprietors generally can only compete for silver medals; and a bull or tup, for instance, belonging to a tenant, factor, or small proprietor cannot enter into competition for these medals, unless it has gained a first money premium at a previous show. The competitions take place between April 1st and October 10th, and are open to all parties within the district, whether members of the local Association or not. In some

districts a silver medal is given to the best sheep
shearer, provided the district gives £2 in premiums,
and there are three competitors.

Class III. takes in Dairy Produce, and allots, under
similar distinctions as to proprietors, silver medals and
money prizes for the best couple of sweet-milk cheeses,
and cured butter in samples not less than 14lbs., but
for three consecutive years, from dairies which have
produced not less than 1 cwt. of butter and 2 cwt. of
cheese during the season. The Ayrshire Association
is specially marked out for honour, and two gold
medium medals are annually given at its Kilmarnock
Show—one for the best lot of Cheddar, and the other
for the best sweet-milk cheese of any other variety—
but in either case the cheeses must have been made
in Scotland.

Exhibitors of seeds—not less than three-quarters
of each variety of grain, or two quarters of
beans or grass seeds—and the best ploughman at
ploughing competitions of not less than fifteen
ploughs, and the best servant manager where there
are four reaping machines at work, are the principal
medal claimants under Class IV., or "Crops and
Culture." It, however, includes a number of silver
medals in aid of local societies not on the list of the
district competitions; and stock, wool, the best-
managed farm, dairy, green crop and hay crop, the
best sweet-milk cheese and cured butter, the best-
kept fences, and the best collections of roots and
seeds, all share its favours.

The most expert hedge-cutter can be a medallist,
if the club in his district apply for such a decoration,
and so can the labourer most expert and efficient in
opening, laying, and filling drains, and otherwise
executing the works necessary in thorough draining.
Tenants of well-kept cottages and gardens are
also rewarded by money as well as medals; and the
soc'eties or individuals who establish such premiums
at their own expense receive a silver-medal acknowledgment. The improvement of the greatest number
of existing cottages, the erection of the greatest
number of improved cottages of not more than £5
rent, inclusive of the garden, by any proprietor,
within a certain number of years, and the erection
of the most approved farm buildings in reference to
the proper accommodation of farm servants, are all
acknowledged by gold medals.

In short, the energies of this venerable octogena-
rian Society have only ripened with its years, till
it may well be said to hold Scotland in one universal network. Shorthorns, West Highlanders, Polls
(Angus, Aberdeen, and Galloway), and Ayrshires are
the four pure cattle breeds at the August Show;
and the Galloways have generally separate classes
and premiums. Fat stock, either pure or cross,
have seven classes to themselves, with £63 and
seven bronze medals. All cows must have had
calves previous to the show; if in-milk the birth
of the calf must have been certified within nine
months of the show, and if in-calf, within four

months after. The shorthorn bull no longer gets his fifty sovereigns; but the aged Clydesdale stallion is in the post of honour with thirty sovereigns and a silver medal for the breeder. Leicester, Southdown, Cheviot, and Blackfaced are the four acknowledged sheep breeds; but "other" long, and short wool classes let in the Cotswold and Shrop. All the ewes must have reared lambs that year; and the pen of five ewes not above four-shear in the Cheviot and Blackfaced classes must be in-milk, and have lambs at their foot—a plan which greatly adds to the difficulty of sending up a level pen and of judging. Shepherds' dogs of both sexes, and not above six years old, have their place at last; and the artificial colouring of fleeces, in which all exhibitors were beginning to follow the lead, in self-defence, of a great Cheviot winning flock, have been abolished at last by an order in council. In the swine classes there is no colour distinction, and the middle breed is not recognized; and capons are not forgotten in the poultry list, which also gives the black Norfolk turkey a class of its own.

The Agricultural Statistics Inquiry for Scotland was commenced in 1853 by an experimental trial in three counties at an estimated cost of £900, which exceeded the outlay by £228. It was undertaken for the Government by the Highland Society, and conducted by its Secretary, Mr. Hall Maxwell, and enumerators in the different counties. The enumerators and members of committee were all practical

2 H

farmers of high standing, the former receiving a small fee for their superintendence, and the latter no payment whatever except for their travelling expenses, and no further acknowledgment but a dinner when they met to strike the "Estimates of Produce." In 1854 the Inquiry was extended to the whole of Scotland, and annual returns were made for 1855, 1856, and 1857. It was managed with such tact and economy, that the total outlay fell short of the £14,900 estimate by £2,778. Owing to difficulties with the Commissioners of Audit, whose requirements were considered by the Directors as "inconsistent with the voluntary character of the Inquiry, and of the machinery employed, as well as Mr. Hall Maxwell's position as Secretary of the Society," it was not continued after 1857 and the rank of C.B. was given by the Government to Mr. Maxwell for the services he had rendered.

The returns were so accurate, that when the head of the Ordnance survey, wishing to try how far Ordnance maps might be made available for statistical purposes, caused the area of the grain and green crops in Linlithgowshire to be ascertained, the estimates of acreage in the two returns were only found to differ by 316 acres on 29,599. This variation was quite accounted for by the minute official allowance for roads and fences.

The Society's return gave 43,432 as the number of occupants, and 3,556,572 as the total acreage under rotation of cropping in the thirty-two counties

of Scotland, ranking Bute and Arran as one, and
Orkney and Shetland as another.

In wheat (of which Shetland had 3 acres), Fife and
Perth were a long way a-head, and Forfarshire third;
and in barley the same counties came to the fore,
but Forfarshire had second place. Aberdeenshire
was an easy first in oats (165,275 acres), Perthshire
and Ayrshire close together, while Lanarkshire well
up. In rye, Fife was first, and Elgin second; and
in bere the struggle was a close one between Aberdeen
and Orkney, while Caithness and Argyllshire were far
behind. Stirlingshire, Perthshire, Fifeshire, and
Ayrshire, in order, were the only ones which exceeded
3,000 acres in beans, and Berwickshire and Aberdeenshire had it respectively in peas and tares. The latter
county was some 50,000 acres a-head, in turnips, of
Forfarshire and Perthshire, which made a very close
race of it for second, while Berwickshire, Roxburghshire, and Dumfriesshire finished well up. Perthshire
and Fifeshire had nothing near them for potatoes;
Ayrshire beat Wigtownshire in mangolds; and Wigtownshire returned the compliment in carrots. Ayrshire (1), Lanarkshire (2) was the cabbage return;
Dumfriesshire was first for rape, and Fifeshire for
summer fallow; and for grass and hay under rotation,
"the Ayes had it," or rather Aberdeenshire and Ayrshire. These returns were, of course, subject to the
absolute acreage; and when the proportional acreage
is taken into account, Haddingtonshire is first for
wheat and barley, Caithness for oats, Orkney for rye

and bere, Clackmannanshire for beans and peas, and Roxburghshire for turnips.

Aberdeenshire leads in horses, calves, and other cattle, but Ayrshire beats it in cows ; and in the cattle total it is a sharp thing between Ayrshire and Perthshire. Both in the sheep total, as well as in sheep for breeding and feeding, the order of Argyleshire, Inverness-shire, and Perthshire is maintained; but Dumfriesshire, which is fourth as regards the two first, resigns its place to Ross-shire, and comes very low in the last. In lambs, Argyllshire is still ahead, but Dumfriesshire gets the better both of Roxburghshire, Perthshire, and Inverness-shire, and beats every county, save Ayrshire, clean out of the field for pigs. Sutherlandshire is tenth in the sheep total, but in sheep for feeding it stands fifth.

Having thus investigated the earlier history of the Society, we refreshed ourselves with a stroll through the Museum and the Council Chamber. The old museum was once a little room at the bottom of the Secretary's garden in Albyn-place, but this very different building arose in 1840 in the old town, and combines in itself a museum, a council-chamber, and committee-rooms. The first picture that we read of, in our ransacking the Society's files, was presented by the present Mr. Ramsay of Barnton's grandfather, but we could not identify it in the collection. In the committee-room, where we worked for four days (with occasional visitors in the shape of Mr Gourlay Steell, Mr. Duncan,

and the beadle), two Argyll blacks, Rhyneberg
and Cruib, bred by Colin Campbell of Jura, and of
" 115st tron each, sinking offals," represent the Society's earliest " black cattle" love; and a group of
Alpacas served to recal the show at Glasgow in 1840,
and made us think, every time we looked up at them,
of the Poll Herd Book, and its Grey-Breasted
Jock.

William M'Donald, the earliest secretary, in
buckles and powder, with the charter in his hand,
by Raeburn, faces you as you enter the Council
Chamber. John fifth Duke of Argyll in his robes as
a peer hangs behind the President's chair; and
opposite him is the bust of another secretary, Gilbert
Innes of Stow. Much of the remaining wall space
is taken up by portraits of early stock winners, but,
one by one, the venerable antiques, both in breed
and drawing, disappear and a Gourlay Steell
succeeds. One of the Duke of Buccleuch's Leicester tups is there, and quaintly described as " A full
Thomson." There, too, are Cheviots, black-faced,
and an old breed from Brae Moray, with roan face
and legs, hairy wool, and as wild as a roe-deer, and
with lambs which are always yeaned with a red spot
on the shoulder and the tip of the tail. Jonas Webb's
Southdown does not lack a place, neither do white
Berkshires, or a Western boar with a nose like an
ant-eater. The Hereford is leggy enough; the Fife
bull, with his white black-tipped horns, looks ready
either for the knife or the plough-share; Walker's

Angus cow is white on the shoulder and sparky below, and Belville and Bracelet represent the Shorthorn interest. Duntroon and Whitestockings have gone up as king and queen of the West Highlanders, and Sir Colin Campbell and Colly Hill of the Ayrshires. A dark Suffolk chesnut still lingers on the walls, and so does Splendour, the most beautiful of Clevelands, although his breed is not in honour; and Sir William Wallace and the Perth mare stand boldly out as the Clydesdales of the present.

In the Museum every Scottish root and vegetable is modelled in wax, from the mangel-wurzel down to the tiniest pods. Disease has its specimens as well as health. One turnip has borne out the "loves of the plants," and though it cannot exactly be said to

> " Eye with mute tenderness its distant dam,
> And seem to bleat a vegetable lamb,"

it bears a strange affinity to a ram's head. Finger-and-toe has converted a potato into such a natural hand, that you begin to think that man may throw back to a vegetable as well as to an ape. A kohlrabi has taken the more airy form of a purple butterfly. There is also a section of the bole of every Scottish tree, and a case of worsteds to illustrate vegetable dyes. In the gallery there hangs a portrait of the Dunearn ox, a spotted shapeless mountain, half Fife and half Shorthorn, with some West-Highlanders flanking it; but the stuffer's aid has not been invoked, save in the case of one huge horned head of the " Ovis Ammon." A sheep-

washing apparatus lies on the floor, with some
model-cottage sections; and in one corner rests
the "old original" plough, which might have
been used in the days of Hilpah and Shalum,
and is still said to be seen in Skye. Eight models
of modern ploughs are in array on the window-seat,
the East Lothian swing, Howard's, Ransome's, the
turnwrest, the subsoil, and the Cunningham, with its
long mould-board. Of wheat there are upwards of
200 specimens, one of them the "Fenton," just fresh
from Fenton Barns. Thirteen or fourteen specimens
of the blithe and lusty barley belong to the Chevalier
sort. Clover boasts of its nine varieties, and oats of
its forty at least. There is the Fly-oat, more suggestive of the fish-kettle than the kail-pot; the Sandy,
which ripens four or five days before the Potato;
Tartarian (white and black), Early Angus, Tam
Finlay, Blainslie, and Kildrummie, all of which the
beadle has " *heard most highly spoken of.*"

Mr. Hope, of Fenton Barns, has kindly furnished
us with the following synopsis of these specimens :—

"There is a numerous collection of the various grains. The specimens of
wheat in straw, in the upper gallery, number upwards of 200, and there are
60 more in cases below, besides numerous varieties, of which only two or three
heads are shown, with a small sample of the grain of each   The varieties
now generally cultivated in Scotland are Hunter's, Fenton, and Hopetoun
The first of these has long been a great favourite with the Lothian farmers.
Of late years the Fenton has rivalled it, and perhaps now exceeds it in the
quantity sown   This arises from its wonderful productiveness, where the soil
is in high condition, though the quality is barely equal to that of Hunter's.
The Fenton, being short and stiff in the straw, is not easily lodged, and it has
been known to yield eight quarters per imperial acre, which is a great crop
for white wheat   The Hopetoun wheat is tall in the straw, and has a beautiful appearance when growing, as it has a large square head, and the crop is
perfectly level when it approaches maturity   The quality is also excellent,

and it generally fetches 1s. per quarter more than Hunter or Fenton. There are several specimens of woolly-eared wheats, some of which stand unrivalled for milling purposes, and are often successfully cultivated on soft soils, but in untoward seasons they suffer more than some other varieties. Gregorian, Brodie's, Archer's Prolific, and Chidham are kinds all more or less sown. The last is often of great weight per bushel, and invariably sells well, but from the smallness of its produce it is not generally a favourite Both Gregorian and Brodie's are also noted for quality, and are found to be suitable for spring sowing. Red-strawed white is always in demand for seed in autumn, and is sent in considerable quantities both to England and Ireland; but though frequently highly productive and a fine sample, it has not increased in popular favour. Amongst the red wheats, Spalding's and Lammas Red are those most extensively cultivated the first is one of the most productive wheats known, while the last produces flour of the finest quality.

" There are upwards of 40 different specimens of oats in straw, besides those merely showing the heads with small samples of grain. In the best districts the Potato oat is the most extensively cultivated, as under favourable circumstances it stands unrivalled for produce and quality combined It has been known to yield 12 quarters per imperial acre, weighing upwards of 44lbs per bushel. Its greatest drawback is its liability to shake as it approaches maturity, and there is always a loss in harvesting it, even before it is quite ripe Of late years the Sandy oat has greatly increased in favour in all high and late districts, from its earliness, the superiority of its straw, the excellent mealing properties of its grain in proportion to the weight per bushel, and its being much less liable to suffer from wind than any other variety. The Early Angus oat possesses some of the qualities of the Sandy, but the straw is shorter and comparatively inferior The Late Angus is suitable for stiff and second-rate soils in tolerably early districts, as it grows freely, and is not liable to tulip-root and other diseases, which sometimes overtake the Potato and finer varieties when sown under such circumstances. It was a great favourite in the Lothians, when the land was undrained and the use of artificial manures unknown. The Shirreff oat is the earliest oat known; the produce is frequently large, but from the weight per bushel being very light it is not extensively sown. The Hopetoun oat—another excellent variety, which agriculturists owe to that indefatigable improver of the cereals, Mr. Patrick Shirreff, Haddington—is extensively cultivated; its quality is about equal to Potato oats, while it is much taller in the straw. The Black Tartarian is growing in favour, from its enormous produce, and being suitable for horse feed; but it is light in weight, and very easily shaken , and the colour is also against it

"There are some 36 or 38 samples of barley in straw, but of these the Chevalier is the only variety extensively cultivated. It was not until some time after the introduction of this barley that the Edinburgh brewers would purchase it, but now they will have nothing to do with any other kind."

CHAPTER IV.

ROMAN CAMP TO ATHELSTANEFORD.

" Yonder the coast of Fife you saw,
There Preston Bay and Berwick Law ;
And broad between them rolled,
The gallant Frith the eye might note,
Whose islets on its bosom float,
Like emeralds chased in gold."

SCOTT.

Coursing at the Roman Camp—Woolmet—Dirleton Common—The
Lothian Ram Sales—Camptown—Wood Pigeons—Stock in East
Lothian—The Grave of Phantassie—Whittingham—The Athelstane-
ford Herd—The East Lothian Hounds.

"IT made no matter if the coursing was a little
dull at times, there was always the view,"
said "Will Nightingale," when he spoke to us of the
days when he went judging at the Roman Camp.
You reach this fine hanging slope of plough, grass,
and seeds, which faces the Pentland range, on one
side, by the road behind Dalkeith. It lies only
two miles from the town, and rather less from the
Duke's kennels; and yet not once within the memory of man was Will Williamson seen on the
field. The village of New Battle lies at the foot
of the coursing ground. Many of the best courses
began near the present site of the coal-pits; and
the hare would make through Mayfield Farm to the
firs of the Roman Camp (that favourite Runnymede

of colliers on the strike), and away by Camp Mcg's cottage.

The Mid-Lothian Club, which was quite an upperhouse among Scottish coursing clubs, held its meetings here. No betting was allowed, under divers pains and penalties. Every member who purposed attending sent his own dish to the ordinary at the Cross Keys. The Duke of Buccleuch furnished venison, Sir Graham Montgomery a haunch of blackface, Major Hamilton Dundas black puddings and haggis, Mr. Sharpe ducks of eight or nine pounds weight, Lord Melville pork, Mr. Callender beef, Mr. George Wauchope perigord pie, and so on; so that it was no Barmecide business. In fact, many of the members kept no dogs, never saw a course, and only appeared at dinner-time. The meeting came off, frost permitting, on the first Tuesday and Wednesday in November, and again in February; and Mr. Nightingale judged at twentynine in succession. He was so fond of the place that even when the meeting clashed with the Waterloo he gave it the preference. Of course, the Waterloo card came down, and the Chief Justice was requested to advise upon it. He ran it over, and gave, we believe, the result of all the first courses correctly, save that between the brother and sister, War Eagle and Wicked Eye, on which he would not hazard a guess. His summing-up was still more remarkable. "The ground should suit Cerito and Neville best"; and they were the winner and the

runner-up.   On another occasion frost came on, and
Mr. Gibson initiated him into the natural mysteries
of curling.   Johnny Rogers, the livery-stable keeper,
always horsed him ; and " the Chief Justice" remem-
bers well how a boy galloped up to him on his first
appearance, with some sort of confused message in
his head that " Mr. Wauchope has sent me to tell
you, sir, which way the hares go"; and how that
green courier stared at the reply, " I shall soon find
that out for myself."

Mr. Sharpe, with Will Carfrae as his man-at-
arms, was always in great force with his jokes ; and
it was remembered for many a long day how he and
his pony were bogged at Crichton.   The hares were
very good, and on the occasion when Mr. John
Wauchope's Claret won the Tureen, there were
more than ninety dogs, with Monarch among them.
The meetings were given up on the death of Mr.
George Wauchope, who had long officiated as honorary member ; and the Champion Cup, to which every
fresh holder added a little shield with an inscription, was presented to his widow.   The Club
died rich, and the members devoted themselves to
dining the funds away, and have not finished yet.
Many of the fields have been divided with double
rails, and hardly a " So-ho !" is heard there now.

After our tour of inspection which Mr. Sharpe,
ever loyal to old friends and old times, charged us to
make or never speak to him more, we harked back
to Woolmet, where Mr. Gibson is equally fond of

his farm, his poultry, his greyhounds, his flowers, his
Shropshire Downs, and his Cotswolds, let alone the
old sorrel mare and her line. Dorkings and Rouens
have always been his feathered favourites ; and it was
with the Woolmet, the Mellerstain and the Comiston
lots that the Edinburgh January poultry sales began.
He has bred Cotswolds to cross with half-bred ewes
for these eight or nine years past, and raised
his flock in the first instance from Lane, Hewer, and
Handy. The fat lambs have made high prices in the
Edinburgh market, and Mr. Gibson hopes ultimately
to see both them and the Shrops (which Mr. Randell
selected for him) holding their own with the Leicesters and the Southdowns. Lord Wemyss has also a
small Cotswold flock, and so has Mr. Scot Skirving ;
and a tup and twelve ewes of Mr. Beale Browne's have
come to Mr. Reed's of Drem ; but it is to his lordship, Mr. Skirving, and Mr. Gibson that the Highland Society competition has hitherto been confined.
At Woolmet there are one hundred and sixty
ewes in the Cotswold, and eighty in the Shropshire flock, which is of much more recent date ; and
so far Mr. Gibson has been enabled to get £3 or £4
for his tup lambs, and £6 to £14 for his shearling
tups.

He has been a courser for more than thirty
years ; and the Caledonian coursing picture by Ans-
dell, which hangs over his side-board bears its
silent record to many a good comrade passed
away. His trainer Robert Murray's talk is more

of dogs than of men. He is full of Violet, who
won that picture, and her sire Victor to boot ;
of Stanley of Dirleton and Malleny St. Leger
memory ; of Shepherdess, who ran a decider with
Blue Light ; of Grasper, who was never beaten in
his first season, and killed fifty-four out of his fifty-
six hares by *"just nipping 'em in the rump"* ; of
Lassie by Jacobite out of Sister to King Lear, and
the bitch which beat Clive in the run-up for the
great Caledonian St Leger the only time that
Waterloo crack ever was beaten ; of Barman, who
was carted back by mistake (when his leader had
been seized with a fit), instead of being brought out
for the deciding course at Amesbury ; and of Ayr
shire Laddie, Caledonian, and Nimrod, " all by old
Sam, and all much about it ! " Sam was after Mr.
Nightingale's own heart, " with a beautiful style of
running—so true that you might ride miles after him
without ever seeing his nob—and with quite a greyhound face like Sunbeam's" ; and the veteran
loves to tell how astonished Squire Osbaldeston
was when he ran clean away from his dog at
Amesbury. Robert's old bay, with some five-and-
thirty years on his head, still occupies the stall in the
kennel, where Snowflake, and old Oscar—both spotted
ones, and one of them suckled by a cat to begin with
—Golden Dream, the game old white, Coorooran, and
the black Agility, once first favourite for the Waterloo Cup kept him in company. The two blacks—Gun-
ner and Gunboat, by Jacobite from Cazzarina—were

only saplings then. The latter, a very racing-like,
strongbacked dog, was walked by Mr. Tom Welsh at
Ericstane, and he has proved himself a high-class one
by the style in which he has run forward in three or
four great stakes.   Manganese was rejoicing in
the paddock, and a lot of Beacon puppies, one
of them old Frolic to the life; while Mary Morton had ten rolling over her, all white, with brindled spots on the head and ear, and a double cross
of Wigan.

Next morning we were eighteen miles " from
Edinburgh town," among the great Lothian arables
—" good land," according to Carlyle, " now that the
plougher understands his trade," and, in fact, " fit,"
as Mr. Randell exclaimed, when he first saw it, " to
grow potatoes for all England."   In that grand district to the left of Drem, and stretching away towards
North Berwick Law and " Bass among the Waters,"
the well-filled stack-garths and chimneys of Hope of
Fenton Barns, Deans and Handyside of East and
West Fenton, Todd of Castlemains, Begbie of Queens-
ton Bank, Gray of Kingston, Hay of Chapel, and
Sadler of Ferrygate dot the landscape, and tell of the
richness and fatness of the land, in spite of wheat at
forty shillings a quarter.   Within that four-mile area
there are no less than five private steam ploughs,
none of them verifying their sarcastic welcome to the
district, that they " would require an engineer at one
end and a banker at the other."

But coursing, and not corn, was our mission ; and

crossing over the village green hard by the ivied ruins of Dirleton Castle, and so past the lodge gates of the lord of the soil, the Hon. Nisbet Hamilton (at whose steam-plough banquet in the Castle garden Richard Cobden, in the autumn of '62, made his last Scottish speech), we were on Dirleton Common with the dogs at last. It is a pleasant spot, almost within hail of Gullane, where Lanercost once cleared his pipes in good air, and Philip broke in verity the heart of Ballochmyle; but the green woods of Dirleton fringe it on the left, and lure many a hare to cover. There are sixty members of the Dirleton Club, to which there is a two-guinea entrance, and nothing more. Mr. Callender, the honorary secretary, who is ever constant to Lytham and the Waterloo and all the Scottish meetings, "has the happy knack of holding a meeting twice in the season, never asking for annual subscriptions, and yet having money in hand."

There are very few bad hares on the Barony, and the memory is still green of one of $11\frac{1}{4}$lbs. which was found on a stubble, and killed, by Mr. Gibson's Pruth, a daughter of Sam, and then carried in triumph to Mr. Begbie's to be weighed. The stubbles (whose hares pleased Mr. Nightingale best) are very good in October, but the common has fallen off, and become a prey to the rabbits and the moles; and the state of Coorooran's head after a trial, which decided that he and not Golden Dream would go for the Waterloo Cup, was a bleeding protest against the

wire fences round it. Kingwater only arrived from
Longtown in time to try a puppy in one of the large
Woolmet stubbles; and Clasper by Clansman, fresh
from running up to Dunoon at the Border meeting,
was the illustrious stranger. He had at least 6lbs.
too much flesh on him, and was led by a most enthusiastic boy, who was overjoyed when neither
Ivy nor Golden Horn was able to cope with his
red.

Leicesters, which are used for crossing half-bred and
Cheviot cast ewes from the upper and middle districts
of the Border counties, as well as Selkirkshire, and
the farms at the foot of the Lammermoors, are the
tups most in demand in East Lothian, though
Southdowns hold their own pretty well, and Cotswolds and Shrops are creeping gradually in. Once
there were a few Bakewells at George Weir's of
Scoughall, but the breed wore out. He once met with
old Bob Barford of Foscote, and there was a joke
that, after dining together and exchanging minds
upon "the original Bakewells," they embraced, and
agreed to share the philosopher's stone. The East
Lothian men go for the true Border type, high on
the leg and big in the lug, and lay against the blue-
faces and the bare-bellies as heavily in the Edinburgh as the Borderers do in the Kelso ring. Open
coats are also a great point with them, so as to keep
clear of the Cheviots. Blue-faces, they maintain, do
not travel so well, and are not so hardy; and in this
the Skipton men bear them out. Against bare-

bellies they may well wage war, as they have to fold their sheep on heavy clay land, which becomes so wet by the end of November that they are obliged to shift them to the stubbles or old grass (if they have any), and cart the turnips on. Unfortunately there is far too little old grass in Haddingtonshire; and independently of there not being a permanent bite on it for the stock, the seeds cannot resist the summer heat nearly so well.

Mr. Lees of Maringston, Mr. Smith of Stevenson Mains, Mr. Hope of Fenton Barns (the chairman of the Scottish Chamber of Agriculture), and Mr. Balfour of Whittingham, who bought Sam Wiley's first-prize pen of gimmers at Edinburgh, and won the second shearling prize when the Highland Society met at Kelso in '63, are the only Leicester tup breeders, so to speak, in East Lothian, though Mr. Ainslie of Costerton (the owner of Duke of Tyne, and a shorthorn winner of late years) may be said to "march" with it. The ram sales, which have been such a hit at Kelso, have been gradually extended to Edinburgh, under the auspices of the "Lothian Ram Society." Some even of the Kelso breeders prefer sending there, and the two rings of 1863 became four last September.

On that day there were twenty-four lots of Leicesters, and the highest average was £9 14s. for twenty-eight of the Duke of Buccleuch's. His Grace's prize shearling of the day was at the head of them, and was sold for £50. A score from Mr. Ain-

sie's, of Costerton, who had the second-prize shearling and the first-prize aged ram, averaged £7 18s.
9d.; but none of them made more than £22. Mr.
Watson of Esperston, who was second for aged tups,
stood third, with an average of £7 5s. 11d. for thirty.
Mr. Gibson beat the Earl of Wemyss in the Cotswold
competition, and his sixteen averaged £7 10s. 6d.
The highest-priced sheep in the Gosford and Woolmet
lots made £13 5s , and just one other lot of Cotswolds
was exposed.   There were only two lots of Southdowns, a class of sheep for which no prize was given,
and the prices ranged from £6 to £3.

Mr. Moffat of Kinleith was first and second for the
shearling Cheviots, and an average of £8 for twenty-
seven, with £14 10s. for the premier, was the signifi-
cant commentary upon his success. In the blackfaced
class, the first and second prizes were awarded to Mr.
Wilson of Crosshouse, whose average of £7 for twenty-
seven, with £20 15s. as the top price, was far beyond
any of the seven lots " with the curly horn."

The Duke of Buccleuch keeps from seventy to
eighty Border Leicesters, and for nine years past
has used Lord Polwarth's tups.   The shearling tups
are sold generally at Edinburgh, and the draft ewe
hoggs go to Ireland.   His Grace also keeps a large
flock of half-bred ewes, which he crosses with the
Leicesters, and sells the lambs.   The pure shorthorn
stock at Dalkeith numbers some five-and-twenty
head, and Booth blood is followed with the bulls.
At present the cows are in-calf to Royal Errant by

Mr. John Booth's Knight Errant, dam by Booth's Cardigan. This bull has rather revived the days when the Duke was wont to be so often in the van of the Highland Society's shorthorn classes, as he beat the second-prize Royal Newcastle bull at Stirling last August. It is also well worthy of notice that he and another first-prize winner, Mr. Mitchell's Blue Belle were both from Cardigan cows bred by Mr. Wood of Stanwick Park, near Darlington. A good many crosses of all sorts are also fed off in the Park, and a dairy of from twenty-five to thirty Ayrshires is kept to supply Dalkeith House. In and round it his Grace keeps about 500 acres of old grass and arable in his own hand. Mr. Black, who brought out so many Highland Society winners, is dead, and has been succeeded by Mr. James Deans, brother to Lord Polwarth's factor.

Mr. Aitchison of Alderson, Mr. Scot Skirving of Camptown, Mr. Sprot of Spot, Major Hunter of Thurston, and Mr. Nisbett Hamilton, all breed Southdowns; and Mr. Skirving has had a pretty fair share for some years past of the Highland Society prizes. Forty years ago, his late father began at Camptown with a small lot of Southdowns, selected by Mr. Giblett, the well-known London salesman. Then came a high-priced tup from Lord Jersey, for which his lordship had given £90, at a time when he had a flock of 1,100 ewes. In those days their wool was worth 2s. 6d. per lb., and was very much sought after by the makers of hats. Other tups succeeded

from Hugh Watson of Keillor, and for twenty years
past none have been used except from Jonas Webb's
and the Duke of Richmond's flocks. For a long time
the Camptown flock did not catch the judges' eye at
the Highland Society. Two seconds at Paris, where
Mr. Skirving had also a prize for wheat, were the pre-
cursor of better things; and at Aberdeen and Stirling alone his winnings were very little short of
£100. At the Royal Irish Belfast show, one year, he
had also all the first and second prizes. He bought
twenty-five ewes at the Babraham sale, and with
that exception the flock were bred at home. It
averages four score, and about three hundred half-
breds are kept to be crossed with Leicesters or Southdowns for early lambs or hogging. Each year he
sells about twenty-five Southdown tups, the majority
of which are bought at home for crossing or sent to
the colonies. The recent price of wool has not
helped the sale, but it has revived again of late

No one has spoken more effectively with his pen,
than he has done in the *Cornhill* and elsewhere, against
the abuses of the bothy system, or stated the real
position of the Scottish labourer, from more close
and searching observation. He has thrown himself with equal energy into the wood-pigeon crusade,
where, unlike the Christian Advocate at Cambridge,
he has not annually to beat the air and confute an
imaginary sceptic. The case for the wood-pigeon has
been stated as follows: "They cannot dig with their
beak and feet: they remove beans and other seeds

wasted by careless and slovenly farming : they eat
wild mustard, charlock, silver-weed, goose-grass, and
other seeds which would become weeds, as well as the
roots of tanzy in limestone; and they divert attention from the melancholy cry of the cuckoo."

Mr. Skirving considers that the "balance of power"
of which the wood-pigeon was said to be so conserva-
tive has been completely destroyed, and thus argues
the point : " In the first place, it is only since improved cultivation introduced its clovers and early
spring crops that the wood-pigeon has been attracted,
in such numbers from more northern districts; and,
in the second place, the ' balance of power' was destroyed when game preservators almost extirpated
our birds of prey, and in particular the magpie.
Those writers who think that because the wood-
pigeon feeds on wild seeds as well as grain it is therefore innoxious are entirely in error.   The bird is an
epicure as well as a glutton, and its weeds bear the
same proportion to its corn that Falstaff's half-penny
worth of bread did to his intolerable amount of sack.
As illustrating the wood-pigeon's powers of destruc-
tion in winter, I may mention that some years ago I
had twenty acres of rape-seed, which was attacked
by such multitudes that, though the man sent to
watch it killed twelve hundred in one week, yet the
pigeons won the battle, and ate up every particle of
the crop.   Then in summer, though each bird has his
crop crammed with corn till it resembles a cricket-
ball, the food consumed bears no proportion to the

food destroyed. They fix on a part of a wheat-field where the grain inclines to one side ; they trample it flat, and beat out the corn with their strong wings, and leave nothing but broken and blackened straw."

The rook he considers to be " quite an agricultural saint" by the side of the wood-pigeon, and thus points out the extenuating circumstances in favour of "the gentleman in black," whom the Ettrick Shepherd defended in mole shape : " The rooks, while following the plough, may, indeed, by some rare chance pick up a stray grub, but they are there for the purpose of feeding upon the earthworm, one of the best, if humblest, auxiliary cultivators we have ; while the presence of crows among the turnip-fields in early summer indicates the existence of grub; they are then never disturbed, as their operations are wholly for good."

The East-Lothian men, more especially those who farmed near the sea, were once very fond of using the Southdown tup, and selling early lamb. Then the Irish lamb competition was so strong in the Edinburgh market, that hogging seemed likely to pay best. Gradually the inferior quality of the Irish lamb has told against it, and some breeders are again resorting to the Southdown and half-bred cross. Mr. Peter M'Clagan's recent success with Southdown-Dorset lambs, which were dropped in December and sold well in January, one of them as high as 54s. for 50lb. live weight, is making the Dorset ewe fashionable, and Mr. Skirving, among others, has bought some.

Most East Lothian farmers hogg and shear their
lambs, and sell them fat in spring and early summer.
When the breeders do not hogg them, they sell them
for that purpose to feeders in the county about the time
of St. Boswell's fair; and the cross-bred lambs from
the Lammermoor farms go up then to the little East
Lothian fair of Oldhamstocks. On the low farms
cast half-bred ewes bought in from 38s. to 40s.,
from Gala Water and all the district through which
the North British runs from Edinburgh to Hawick,
are in a majority of ten to one over the Cheviot.
The cast Cheviot ewes at about 28s. greatly prepon-
derate on the higher farms. They come for the
most part from Peebleshire and the Lammermoors,
where they graze on the braes and the best of the
hill land, while the blackfaces hold the muir ground
on the summits ; and some farmers go to Falkirk for
them. Mr. Douglas speaks of them as good nurses,
not perhaps so prolific as the half-bred ewe, but
rearing their lambs to a greater weight when kept
till they are wedders, and feeding nearly as well. It is
always desirable that the lambs should be dropped in
April. If they are sold fat off grass, they are generally gone by Midsummer, and then the ewes get
cake and corn, and are turned off fat before the end of
July. If ewes stay on the farm for eleven months they
pay about eight-pence to nine-pence a week, including
the lamb, but the lack of young grass prevents their
being kept to any great extent. Efforts have been
made to supplement young grass by mangold, but,

to use the words of Mr. Sadler (who introduced the
first steam plough to East Lothian, and came second
with a capital sow at Stirling), "mangold is a perfect
hoax in our climate."*

Haddington—where the East Lothian Farmers'
Club hold such animated discussions, and differ so
widely on some points of sheep practice—is becoming
a great fat market, and on June 1st of last year a
lot of Southdown-Cheviot lambs made 34s. at the
weekly public auction. If farmers are short of lambs
they often buy rough hoggs or hill-tails at the House
of Muir. Near "the grim, old honey-combed Castle
of Dunbar," where the "red soil potatoes" have no
London market compeers, and along the higher districts of the country where the arables die away into
the Lammermoors, some of them keep blackfaced or
Cheviot wedders, which they buy or bring down from

* This gentleman gave the following in a recent speech at the Haddington
Farmers' Club, as his experience of the different kinds of sheep introduced into
East Lothian "In 1859 he was in the south of England, and he was very
much struck with the prices which they were getting for the Hampshire Down
sheep He bought thirty ewes at 50s , and a ram, but they rather disappointed
him Each ewe had not a lamb , and they had also less wool than his half-
breds He kept them as hoggs, and they had brought five shillings more than
his half-breds, but he was certain these beasts ate 10s more than the others.
They were very easily fattened, but they were tremendous consumers He
saw the ewes getting fat upon his pastures in the summer months, and he sent
them off He happened to meet his landlord at the Lincoln show, who told
him the immense prices that were got for Lincoln hoggs, and also for Lincoln
wool He bought forty Lincolns in 1861 at 51s , but he was disappointed with
them also They were long-necked, and the wool in wet weather seemed to
be like silk on their backs He took a notion that they were also great consumers, and not very ready fatteners, and he put them away because they did
not bring a higher price than his half-bred hoggs He had not had any experience as to the effects of crossing the Lincoln sheep with other breeds. He
also tried the Cotswolds, but he did not find them very prolific The Cotswold
had a lamb each, but were very bad milkers , but the Cotswolds might come
up in spring He thought these sheep required extra crops, and he could not
grow a crop of winter tares in consequence of the hares He thought that,
with their high rents, they could not afford to keep large breeding stocks of
sheep ; and if they were to increase the number of sheep, they must do so
merely by purchase."

their own hill-farms, and put on turnips. The latter
are also bought by the low-country farmers, and are
kept on turnips with cake and corn all winter. In
fact, all through the winter, feeding as in Fife goes
on to a great extent, and in 1853 Mr. George Hope
sold off a farm of 653 imperial acres, 1,200 sheep,
90 cattle, and 100 pigs. Major Hunter of Thurs-
tonfield farms on a large scale at Thurston, Thurston Mains, and Woodhall, at the edge of the Lammermoors, and breeds both pure Cheviots, Southdowns, Leicesters, and half-breds. His crosses are
Southdown tup with half-bred ewe, and Leicester
tup with Southdown ewe, and last year the return of
ewe and wedder hogg prices, at his annual fat and
store sale of cattle and sheep in June, showed an advantage in favour of the former cross.

Shorthorns, Polls, and Shetlanders are all on the
Major's sale-list, and some of the latter averaged at
the last sale £16 5s. a head. The cattle buyers in
East Lothian principally go to Jedburgh, Linton,
Dalkeith, Berwick, Hallow, and the Falkirks in
September and October, and to Hallow Fair in November for six-quarter and two-year-old stirks.
They give them turnips and oat-straw in the yards,
and finish them off with six weeks' cake and bean-
meal, for Newcastle and the Southern markets in the
spring. The younger ones are kept, and soiled with
clover, grass, and tares, and sold off after six weeks of
turnips. The more moderate beasts, as a general
rule, go to Edinburgh, and the heaviest to London,

Manchester, Wakefield, and Newcastle.   Many men
will feed from fifty to a hundred, all shorthorn
crosses.

A few West Highlanders and Shetlanders may creep
in, but scarcely any polls.   There is no inducement
to tie them up, as the climate is good, and they are
mostly kept in small open courts with good sheds,
and very seldom in boxes.   As regards oat-straw,
horses get the preference, and the cattle have to fall
back on barley, wheat, and bean straw as it is
thrashed out.   The straw is very seldom given
chopped and, if there is enough to spare from the
horses, the cows get next turn.

"Of the softer turnips, the white globe occupies
the largest space, but it has been to some extent displaced by the Greystone, a species recently introduced, which produces the heaviest crop of any
variety.   Being very soft, and liable to injury from
the frost, its use is restricted to the early part of the
season, a circumstance which must always tend to
circumscribe the extent of its cultivation.   Skirving's
purple-top succeeds the earlier turnips, whilst green
and yellow varieties follow as the food of the farm
till Christmas, when the Swede becomes the reliance
of the farmer for all animals, save breeding ewes, for
which white or yellow turnips are reserved.   An annual sweepstakes, which is held under the auspices
of the local agricultural society, shows the following
as the highest weights on the best five acres of
turnips of different sorts — Swedes 31 tons 18

cwt., yellow 36 tons 10 cwt., white 45 tons per acre."*

We were hardly likely to pass through East Lothian without visiting the resting-place of Rennie of Phantassie, the friend of Lord Leicester and Christian Curwen, and of all the first breeders of his time, and perhaps the man who did more than any other to encourage a pure shorthorn taste in Scotland. Two other noted men lie in Preston Kirk. Hugh Ramadge, the faithful servant of "Phantassie" for eight-and-fifty years, was the first to go. He died in '28, and only a few months after his old master had placed a stone " in testimony of respect to his memory," he himself had his summons on the verge of eighty. His hard-working Boswell, Brown of Markle soon followed him, and left behind him two very sombre-looking volumes, with mottoes from Pliny and Thomas à Kempis, and dedicated to Sir John Sinclair. The volumes are hardly such a record of the Northern Bates as we had hoped to find them; but they tell how, in 1811, he assured his incredulous countrymen that the beasts which would ere long become their beef staple " were wider and thicker in their form or mould" than the ones they cherished, "and consequently feeding to the most weight, and yielding the greatest quantity of tallow."

Young Phantassie was of a more dashing turn, and bought cows at high prices from Wetherell and

* "Ten Years of East Lothian Farming," by Mr. Soot Skirving (" Royal Agricultural Society's Journal," March, 1865).

Mason. His most noted feat was coming direct
North when wheat had risen 8s. in London, getting
off the mail at Belford, where the bags were shifted
and sent on in a mail gig, beating the post by two
hours into Edinburgh, and buying very largely for
the rise. His last speculation was to bring a ship
load of cattle from Shetland; but it sunk, with himself and all hands on board. Every trace of the
primitive steading at Phantassie has disappeared, but
the shorthorn spirit still thrives at Whittingham,
since Mr. Charles Smith came there in 1852 from
Hill Head, and Prince Loth and Great Seal have
been the leading evidences.

The King Loth of antiquity lived near North
Berwick, and had a daughter who "made sheep's
eyes" at a swineherd. Any little parental obstacle to
Gurth's happiness, on the score of blood or settlements,
was promptly overcome by his shooting the King in a
morass. The Dryasdusts cannot tell whether he
married the daughter, but they dug like ghouls for a
fortnight at the edge of the Whittingham property,
in the hope of discovering the royal sepulchre, and
didn't. A live bull proved better than a dead king to
Mr. Balfour, who did not care for the bones, but sold
his King Loth to New Zealand. Great Seal went to
a Sunderland butcher when his show days (during
which he beat Forth at Perth) were over, and his
216 stone of 14lbs. nearly rivalled the weight of the
Durham ox. One of the family, Lady Seal, was left,
and The Belle tribe, as well as the Lady tribe, were

all crossed by him ; while Rose of May by Sir James
the Rose, and Lady of the Manor were put to Royal
Standard.

Mr. Balfour, whose father died nine years since,.
in the very prime of life and usefulness, owns nearly
seven thousand acres round Whittingham, of which six
hundred belong to the home-farm. It is principally
on the red sandstone, and has taken many prizes for
grain and roots, more especially on its loam. At
the steading, where the turkeys and poultry betoken
a fancier's care, we found some Great Seal bullocks,
many of them from the dozen dairy cows. The calves
all get milk from the pail and a little oilcake the first
winter, they are grazed the next summer, and then
gradually carried on with turnips, cake, and corn till
they are shown at the United East Lothian or Haddington in the spring, where hitherto they have
had the first and second prizes for lots of five. Great
Seal left four crops of calves behind him, and the
last were just being dropped. Prince Loth, who was
second both at Newcastle and Stirling in his class
last year, is very much of the same lengthy, thick-
fleshed type as his father, and likely to be as good in
his generation as a steer-getter. His dam, Rose of
May by Sir James the Rose, a fine big cow, with
the regular family horn, stood side by side in the
byre, with Lady of the Manor opposite Northern
Belle and her calf, those relics of Hill Head ; and
Lady Blanche, a cow of no great pretensions herself, but the dam of the prize heifer Lady Windsor,

was with the dairy lot. This good heifer was highly commended at Newcastle, and third at Stirling, where she, at all events, beat all the Scottish lot; and a double cross of her Lady Blanche blood had told well on British Standard.

There are from 100 to 120 Leicester ewes, and 80 half-breds in the home flock. The former are principally bred from Cockburn of Sisterpath, Hardy of Harrietfield, and Simson of Courthill; and some of their own prize tups have been used as well. We found them in a glen of old grass of thirty years' standing, which has made many a shorthorn man's mouth water with honest envy. The Whittingham burn flows along it, among the elm and beechen shade for miles. Still, we hardly took in its real beauty till we had scaled the ruined tower of the old Whittingham Castle, and looked away to the vast arables, which no longer keep their "fallow sabbaths" round Traprain and Berwick Law.

Below were the Whittingham gardens, rich in the rarest trees, the dark shade of Bothwell's yew, with a still darker story annexed, and the grove in which a solitary monument stands to record that it was once the burial-ground of the Drumelzier family. The laurel and the bay wear the glossy sheen, which the red sandstone fosters, and which no frost can blight; and beyond, towards the Lammermoors, and towering above still lochs which we wot not of, are the oaks and larches on the hill which make up the

sure find of Presmennan. The eye wanders coastwards along the glen, over wooded masses, to
Tyningham and Newbyth, dear to old Meltonians
for Sir David's memory, and so away to Dunbar,
and the Pass of Dunglass, where Cromwell foiled
the foe on that fearful night, when the " sea and
the tempests are all abroad, all asleep but we, and
there is One who rides upon the wings of the
wind."

A drive of eight miles across country brought us
to Mr. Douglas's homestead at Athelstaneford. It
lies at the foot of the glen, down which the Cocktail
Burn—whose waters are connected, in Scottish history, with a bloody day between Athelstane and the
Picts—flows from the Garlton Hills. On the highest
point of the latter stands the Hopetoun Monument,
to tell of valour in a more glorious field. In modest
contrast to it is the obelisk, just rising from the
centre of the village green, which the zeal of the
present minister, Mr. Whitelaw, has reared to the
memory of Blair, who, like the author of "Douglas,"
was one of his predecessors at the manse, and sleeps
in the kirk-yard.

Traprain Law is on the right, and running gradually out near Dunbar is the bold range of the
Lammermoors, which Mr. Pusey skirted on his
second agricultural visit to East Lothian; while
below you is the deeply-wooded valley, which seems
to reach for miles, from Gilmerton House to that
"grim niched barrier of whinstone" which shelters

(s)

this fertile land from " the chafings and tumblings of the big, blue German Ocean."

Mr. Douglas occupies a farm of three hundred acres at Athelstaneford, belonging to Sir David Kinloch ; and he also holds Muirhouses, of two hundred and fifty acres, under Earl of Wemyss, about a mile and a-half from it.   The pure-bred short-horns were kept entirely at Athelstaneford, where Mr. Douglas resides, and the store-cattle at Muirhouses.   The whole is principally dry-field land, with, in some places, a large admixture of clay ; and, with the exception of six acres, there is no old grass.   The system is the six-break one : about seventy to eighty acres are annually sown in turnips, and from eight to ten in mangels, of which, in his prize-cattle days, he preferred the orange globe variety.

There is much to remind one of the old love.   The heads of Sir James the Rose and Rose of Summer are sculptured on the garden vases, among some scores of other roses of every kind and hue, and they live again from the head to the hocks in painted glass windows. Still, botany has quite supplanted bull-calves, and useful farm buildings with a clock replace those ancient tenements and the rocky fastness from which Sir James the Rose used to sally.

Lalla Rookh's, Ringlet's, and Rose of Summer's are the only heads preserved.   Lalla's wore the rosette at the Highland and the Yorkshire shows; but she was jammed against a wall by a cart, and died after breeding one calf.   "The Rose" is also in a picture with Captain Balco (12546), the sire of her calves Rose of Athelstane and Sir James the Rose; and Water Lily shares her canvas honours with Snip the Clydesdale mare who gained the Royal English prize at Carlisle. The silver medals are not to be sought for in a cloud of cases, but they have all been melted up, and form a tree, with the old downhorn family group at its base, and twenty-eight gold medals hanging like the apples of the Hesperides from its boughs.

The Provost (4846), from a daughter of Colonel Cradock's old Cherry, and Melrose by Gainford (2044), one of her sons, first attracted Mr. Douglas at the Highland Society's Show at Edinburgh in 1842, and his improved shorthorn impressions date from that day. Still, it was not until 1846, when the Royal Society met at Newcastle, that he made any extensive purchases. Belleville (6778) was then all the rage, and it was with two yearling heifers by him that he won the second and third prizes in their class at Aberdeen, the following summer. In that year he also bought Florence of the Booth's Farewell tribe, and Lalla Rookh at Mr. Carruthers of Dormont's sale, the former of which he parted with to Mr. Bolden, senior. His early prize winnings were not confined to females, as in 1848, when his name was fairly established in Scotland, he not only got the second cow prize at the Royal Irish, but won with his Red Rover in the yearling-bull class, beating the Hon. Mr. Nugent's celebrated Bamboo.

When he determined on having a sale in 1852, he hired Mr. Maynard's prize roan bull Crusade (7938), whom he still holds to have been far the best in England of his day, in order to have his cows all served by him. Among them was Rose of Autumn, which he bought at the sale of Mr. La Touche, in Ireland, into whose possession her dam Pelerine, and Polka, those celebrated Killerby twins by Buckingham (3239) from Mantalini had passed by private contract. Her first calf at Athelstaneford was Rose of Summer by Velvet Jacket (10998), which pleased Mr. Douglas so much, that he determined to reserve her along with her half-sister Lady Like by Stars and Stripes (12148), Scottish Blue Bell by Captain Shafto (6833), Marchioness by Belleville, Purity by Crusade, and Second Queen of Trumps by Belleville, which he purchased from Mr. Unthank of Netherscales for 120 guineas, as the nucleus of a second herd.

Up to the time of his sale, he had won fifty-nine premiums and eight commendations for cattle, and Rose of Summer and Scottish Blue Bell, who were on more than one occasion first and second to each other, "took up the running" right gaily in the new era, till the latter went to Mr. Corwin of Ohio. Rose of Autumn and Village Belle were parted with at the sale, with leave to exhibit them at the Highland Society the following week, where they won the prizes in their respective classes; and then the former, who was nursing Rose of Summer, went with Brenda (in-calf with Lord Raglan by Crusade) to

their new owner, Mr. Stewart of Southwick. Lord
Raglan was purchased back by Mr. Douglas, and
the produce of Rose of Autumn who broke to Crusade, and was served by Heir-at-Law (13005), came
back to Athelstaneford in Rose of Sharon.

With that admiration for the Booth blood, which
made him once bid Mr. Richard Booth 500 gs. in
vain for Charity, and 550 gs. in later years for Nectarine Blossom, Mr. Douglas went to the Killerby
sale in the autumn of '52, and bought Birthright, a
grand-daughter of Bracelet, in-calf to Hopewell
(10332), as well as Officious, a calf by the same bull,
and of the same tribe, which he dipped into still deeper
by the purchase of Spicey and Ringlet. Warlaby
also furnished him with Extasy from Isabella Exqui-
site, which was re-registered, with Mr. Booth's per-
mission, as Isabella Hopewell. Along with Rose of
Sharon, there came a 600-guinea lot, in the shape of
Hawthorn Blossom, Heather Bell, and Cherry Queen
from Cherry Blossom, a daughter of Old Cherry, and
Imperial Cherry (the dam of Lady Pigot's prize
winner Cherry Empress) from Cherry Blossom's
daughter Rose of Southwick. It was quite a case of

> "Cherry ripe! cherry ripe, cheap I cry,
> Full and fair ones—come and buy,"

and the yearnings which had sprung up in Mr.
Douglas's mind, as he conned his two favourites in
the yard at Edinburgh, fourteen years before, had at
last their fulfilment. Three out of the four were by

Col. Towneley's Hudibras (10339), an own brother to the famous Alice.

His greatest bull hit was made when he bought Mr. Ambler's Captain Balco (12546) by Balco (9918) from Cowslip, a shabby little cow, by Upstart. He considered "The Captain" to be the best Bates bull he had ever seen, and he had not only Rose of Summer's two calves by him, but the Third from the Second Queen of Trumps, which vied with Rose of Athelstane, in sweeping the three National prizes in one year, as Rose of Summer had done before them. Captain Balco, after winning several prizes as a yearling in 1854, was second at the Royal Dublin Show to Master Butterfly, the nearest thing that the "unbeaten one" ever had, and Richard Cœur de Lion (13590) and Cadet (12521) ranked next. The Society of Shakers, who farm 1,000 acres of the finest land in Ohio, gave 400 guineas for him, among the twenty which they purchased from Mr. Douglas in the course of two years, and his son Sir James the Rose (13290), whose very first calf was Maid of Athelstane from Ringlet, took his place, and was long the main prop of the herd.

In the same year (1855) that Captain Balco went abroad, Mr. Douglas bought Hymen (13058) by the Duke of Cambridge (12742) from Bridecake, as a calf at the Springfield Hall sale; but he scarcely used him, as his senior did not leave England till nearly the end of the season, and after winning the county prize with him against bulls of all ages, he

sold him for 200 guineas to M. de Trehonnais at the
Paris International Show, the following year. This
sale, which seemed a good one at the time, was a
source of some regret, when two out of the three
calves he left behind him appeared in the show
yard. One of them, The Lamp of Lothian, a strong,
fine-loined but rather short bull, from Isabella
Hopewell, beat 132 yearlings at the Royal Dublin
Show, besides getting the gold medal as the best
bull in the yard; after which he was sold to Mr.
Crosby of Ardfelt Abbey, Tralee, for 250 gs., and
proved himself one of the best prize-heifer getters in
Ireland. The other, Lady of Athelstane, from Playful, not only won well herself, but was the dam of
Pride of Athelstane, the second-prize calf at Battersea, and the first-prize heifer in-calf at Newcastle
last year.

Playful by Fourth Duke of York (10167), a cow
of considerable sweetness, nicely-covered huggins and
neat bone, introduced the pure Bates blood into the
herd, and Cambridge Rose and Britannia by Prince
George (12938), a Son of Lord George, are combina-
tions of it with Booth's. The Hawthorn Blossom tribe
also came from Warlaby, through Venus de Medicis by
Harbinger (10297), who goes back to that celebrated
dam of Nectarine Blossom, through Bloom; but
this beautiful white never bred, and died at Southwick.
The Princess tribe from Mr. Troutbeck's of Blen-
cowe included Polly Gwynne and her daughters, Prim
and Priscilla, and her bull-calf Omega; and it was

with Clarionet from Mr. Wood's in Ireland that the
Gunter twins, which had to give away a great deal
of age, were beaten at Dumfries.

In 1858 the herd was at its height. At the Yorkshire Show at Northallerton, Queen of Trumps,
Rose of Athelstane, and Maid of Athelstane, all took
firsts; and Lady of Athelstane and Venus de Medicis were honourably mentioned. It seems but yesterday that they were walking down the streets
of the quaint little town; and well might the shorthorn Yorkshiremen joke and call them "*Scott's
lot,*" as they were all stabled and fed below the Grand
Stand while waiting to be trucked. Others were not
so well up in the matter, but quite as free to communicate. "*Those belong to my friend Mr. Richard
Booth,*" said a fussy little man on the steps of the
inn, and he began checking them off on his fingers :
"*That's Queen Mab, or Nectarine Blossom!—I don't
exactly know which, but I've often seen them—That's
Queen of the Isles!*" while he was really indicating
Queen of Trumps and "The Rose," till at last a
Northumbrian struck in, and said he'd "*better shut
up,*" as they all belonged to a Scotchman, and
"*none of your grand Mr. Booths.*"

It was indeed a wonder how a plain tenant-
farmer could have brought such a lot to the post,
and fight single-handed against all the experience,
talent, and outlay that could be arrayed against
him in England. It was a fearfully hazardous business, under the present artificial show mode, as only

high feeding enabled him to put his animals along-
side such competitors, and pains and penalties duly
followed. In one year alone he lost two Cherries,
a calf from Playful, and the grandest calf he ever
had, a roan heifer by Sir James from Rose of Sharon.
Let another Scot go in and try to fight the English
breeders successfully at such fearful odds, and he
will find what " nights of weariness and weary days"
mean, when he has had a month of travelling in
steamers and railway trucks, of lingering in show-
yards and of waiting at stations with his cattle, to
say nothing of the expense, and the risk of accidents
or of feeble judges. A few prizes, and an assurance
on the part of the agricultural papers, while his mind
is racked with anxiety and his eyes bloodshot with
fatigue, that he is " taking the grand tour," prove
but a very small compensation. All this Mr. Douglas
went through, without flinching, for two-thirds of the
fifteen years, from the era of his first-prize bull Red
Rover down to Crown Prince of Athelstane, the last
he ever bred from Queen of Athelstane.

A few words upon his cracks. Rose of Autumn
had not the perfection and form of Rose of Summer,
but was rather light in her fore quarter. Her
daughter Rose of Summer was a perfect type of the
Athelstaneford mould, and was, in fact, a true square,
with her legs so well under her. Well might the
Herd-Book editor express his delight, when he saw
Mr. Douglas lead her, as fit and as ripe as a Derby
favourite, out of her truck at Lincoln! As a calf

she was small, but thick as a cow, and with one of
the finest fore quarters ever seen. Still, Mr.
Richard Booth's Bridesmaid, who had nearly a
year's pull, was too much for her at Carlisle in '55,
where she was obliged to meet her in the cow class.
Paris proved fatal to her, and when she was un-
trucked at Drem Station she could only crawl to a
shed near Muirhouses, and despite the highest care
and skill she died after a few days' illness. The loss
can hardly be estimated, as upwards of 500 guineas
had been refused for her at Paris, simply because
Mr. Douglas considered that the continued success
of the herd depended on her and her tribe.

Her calf Rose of Athelstane was able to get $1\frac{1}{2}$
miles further to Athelstaneford, and lay there for two
months, more dead than alive. Still, she took heart
of grace at last, and defeated Mr. Booth's Queen of
the May in the struggle at Salisbury. She travelled
about 5,000 miles by land and sea, and won some
twenty premiums; but she was not a lucky cow, as
all her calves were sadly delicate, and none of them
were reared. She had great substance, with hair
and quality, and was at least two sizes larger than
Rose of Summer. Third Queen of Trumps was a
dark roan, with all the Captain Balco marks, a rare
quarter, and loins as level as a table. There was
more gaiety about Rose of Summer, but she was
not nearly so deep-fleshed. " Third Queen's" end was
a tragical one, as, when a storm blew great guns,
seventy miles from New Orleans, the sailors threw

her overboard, with some Clydesdale horses, and the
400-guinea Royal winner rendered up her sirloin to
the sharks. Venus de Medicis had a lovely leg and snug
neck vein, and a wonderful tendency to lay on flesh.
In fact, save a slight contraction near the tail head,
there was hardly a blot to be found in her, and hence
once in their five public trials she was placed over
Third Queen of Trumps.   Lady of Athelstane was a
compact, buxom, little body, with very fine flesh, and
always a favourite with the English and Scottish
bench, and if she had been only a size larger she would
have been exceedingly dangerous.

The Maid's masculine head and upright horn
spoilt her, and as a calf she was a trifle weak in her
loins.   Mr. Douglas knew this so well, that when she
met Duchess 77th and the immense calf field at
Northallerton, his orders to his man were not to keep
her always in the judges' eye, as many clever showers
do, but to hold her head tight, and keep touching
her up perpetually with a little switch in the flank.
Mr. Robinson was not to be deceived even if the
judges were, and he slyly congratulated Mr. Douglas
on her being "shown so well." The Queen of
Athelstane from Ringlet was a perfect beauty, and
she and Rose of Cashmere were a rare pair of yearlings while they were doing the first and second
business at the Highland and Northern Shows.   In
his own mind Mr. Douglas could never whip her
apart from Rose of Summer, and bracketed her as
head of his red, white, and roan tripos, with Third

Queen of Trumps next, and then Rose of Athelstane. Lady Pigot could not resist her even at five hundred, and the Branches herd never had a heavier blow than when she died unbeaten and in preparation to meet The Duchesses at Leeds. Second Queen of Athelstane was also a good one, and in that wonderful box with the top-lights, and the walls papered with prize-cards, she looked, with the roan "Gem" as her lusty foil, pretty nearly invincible. Still, she was never a public favourite. Nothing improved more than Pride of Athelstane from "The Lady" as a yearling, and she was well worthy, as a two-year-old in-calf to win a first prize for Mr. Douglas at the Newcastle Royal, in a class where Rose of Summer, Third Queen of Trumps, and Rose of Athelstane had all showed the way.

Captain Balco, for form and style, fine quarters and loins, was quite the head bull at Athelstaneford, though he was hardly so deep-fleshed as Sir James the Rose, a bull of great sweetness, but a little slack behind the shoulders and a trifle soft in his handling. Hiawatha, another son of Playful, was not so good as Sir James, but he was a clever winner, and beat, among others, the great Lord Garlies; and two whites, Freemason, who was pretty nearly all Booth, and Next-of-Kin, who was second and then first at the Highland Society, closed with Lady of Athelstane the history of a very remarkable Shorthorn career.

The kennels of the East Lothian, of which Mr.

Kinloch is a joint master with Sir David Baird, are at East Saltoun, a mile from Pencaithland. Will Williamson was born a few miles from here, and they do say that in later years he carried the green collar out of the country. They hunt the whole of Haddington and Berwickshire up to Ayton Castle, and go as far as Dalkeith, White Hill, and Melville Castle in Edinburghshire. The Stone country, which is twenty miles away, has been recently given up to the Duke. Mr. Hope is the secretary, and they hunt three days a week, and about two-and-forty scarlets have been mustered at times. There are sometimes eight or ten officers, and the farmers are beginning to come out more and more every season, and well mounted to boot.

Arniston country holds the best scent, and is, in fact, the only grass country. The rest is nearly all under plough, and its drains, sheep, and manure militate sadly against scent; while the wild goats of many colours on the Lammer Law are often as tempting to the young hounds as roe deer. In the Gladsmuir country, which extends to Blackshiels, they get on to the Lammermoors for those fine wild runs which Williamson loved, and carry a great head over the heather. There are a few good gorse covers, Whitbury, 1½ miles from Saltoun, the Hopetown Monument, Shilling Hill, and Killduff, which consists of fifteen acres fenced in at one corner of this grand nursery for foxes. The seventy or eighty acres of Killduff Wood bear an immense amount of sifting during the season; but Saltoun, Long Yester, and Eckyside Hill have all become very hollow.

The hunting begins early in September, with "the whole fleet" at The Hopes, that great juniper cover of the Lammermoors, and goes on one day a week at Newbyth, Tyningham, and Coalston Wood. Newbyth and Tyningham often furnish four or five litters, but the greater part of the foxes are laid up in old coal mines near Elphinstone Tower and Ormiston Hall. Atkinson, the huntsman, who is now in his sixth season, has had an exploring journey for miles under them, and heard the cubs scampering in all directions.

The hill-jumping is entirely confined to walls; but in the low ground, it is hedge and ditch, and the ditches and burns are most unpromising about Drem Both the masters are hard riders, and the Hopes, Scot Skirving, Innes of Phantassie,* Tweedie of The Coates, Ford of Harding Green, and Primrose of Lauchland are also among the first flight. Sir David's well-known chesnut Crimea was shot last autumn, and Strand, Hope, a chesnut who had been extensively "repaired," and Purvis, whose ugliness does not interfere with his goodness, are Atkinson's best.

---

* An old friend has added the following to our previous remarks on the late Mr Rennie of Phantassie "He was an extremely shrewd man, and farmed Phantassie exceedingly well, but he never was a breeder of shorthorns, so to speak He had an extensive whisky distillery at Linton, close by Phantassie, and with 'the drough and dreg,' as the Scotchmen call it, he bred up and fed off in sheds from three to four hundred head of cattle all the year round He was an excellent judge of shorthorns, but his son, with whom I had many transactions, knew very little about them "

In kennel they have about 33½ couple, with eight couple of young ones, principally got by their own Harmattan of Rufford Helpmate, Wynnstay Romeo, and Rufford Dreadnought blood. They have had drafts these last five summers from Lord Middleton, the Bramham, and Brocklesby, and latterly from Lord Henry Bentinck. When the ten couple were destroyed by poison in Killduff, Sir Watkin, Lord Fitzhardinge, the Vale of White Horse, and Lord Doneraile all helped out. As usual, some of those died which could have been least spared, and among them 2½ brace of the best puppies, including Render, the cup puppy Roister, which had also entered so beautifully, and Yarboro' Handmaid, the best bitch in the pack. They are now running the dogs and bitches separate, and for choice they like to find at Bolton Muir, and go straight to the hills with a traveller. Seaton Gorse, near Gosford, some eighty yards from the sea, is a sure find, and the foxes run along the west to Archerfield, and are killed or more generally lost on the Law. Sometimes they get on the ledges of the rocks, and the hounds run great risks if they get a view, and if they go over near St. Abb's lighthouse, they are seen and heard of no more.

The puppies are judged every year in Mr. Hislop's coach manufactory at Haddington, and Primate and Priestess, brother and sister, one bred by Mr. Wood and the other by Mr. Kinloch, and both by Harmattan, won the cups in '64. The old dog, who has one eye cut clean out, and his brother were in kennel with their

great thoughtful heads. Herald has most pace, but
is too often silent when he is wanted. Funny, Laven-
der, and Comical are quite a little trio, and the
badger-pie Comical has many peculiarities about her.
She has never been in season, and she "can beat the
big ones through a hedge when they are thinking of
it," and she struggled through the poison. Nearly
thirty couple were out on the day of that fatal find,
and many of them show the effects yet, if they have
had a very severe day. Ranter and Raffle are both
of the Middleton brand, and although he has lost an
eye and is as deaf as a post, there is no guide-post
like Ranter when they come to a road, and no one
to carry it over a dry fallow like Raffle. Petulant is
another of the low-scented ones; and Banker, with his
rather bitchlike head, is generally seen some lengths
at the head of affairs. Helpmate and Hermit are
two trimmers of the big-headed Harmattan sort, but
they don't come to hand well after a hard day.

Hermit is a very savage breaker-up; and one of
the kennel curiosities (along with the head of the
Yester Fox, which the woodmen looked upon as a
sort of "Old Mortality") is the two-ounce shank-
bone of a fox, which he swallowed at Newbyth.
Ringwood has only one draw of it, and won't try
again till the fox is found, and then he will hold the
line like Fleecer, whose cocky stern and peculiar character soon tempted us to ask Atkinson, "Who's
your friend?" Lucifer was called up, and we heard
how he dared to cheer him his maiden morning at

Weatherham Steps, as he had done his dam Bracelet before him. Traveller, too, hunted his first day, and he is by Tonic, a name of Will Goodall's, who had to use all his skill to get him over the distemper. Bounty had nearly been put away for this cause, but Atkinson persevered, and kept her entirely on eggs. She rewarded him one day by stopping short at a wall, and hitting it down the dyke, in a fast thing over the muirs from Ealingshaw, when the body of the hounds flashed over it. Rallywood has also his good mark for picking it up in a dry furrow when the fox had lain down near Gladsmuir. The Burton old draft of 13½ couple were still dark, and what was contained in the sweet heads of Fashion, Phillis, and Proserpine was still a weighty and anxious problem, both for masters and men.

CHAPTER V.

ATHELSTANEFORD TO COLDSTREAM.

" MR. DONKIN, fully sensible of the especial favour that has been conferred
upon him, by having placed in his hands this commission of Sale, and no less
conscious of the responsibilities which such a trust imposes upon an Auctioneer, considers it his duty to avail himself of those Channels through which
tidings of deep interest are conveyed to the Agriculturists of the UNITED
KINGDOM, to call attention to an opportunity about to present itself for the
purchase of Farming Stock of SURPASSING EXCELLENCE and to the infusion of
the best blood of the Shorthorns, the Leicester Sheep, the Cart-horse, and
the Bacon Swine into districts now laudably emulous of an eminent niche in
the Temple dedicated to the manes of Bakewell and Collings, of Cully and
Bailey ; while to the Agricultural Student fresh from the Arcadian Acade-
mies, and about to commence on his own Account the tranquilizing pursuits
of a Farmer, the means are here placed within his grasp to lay the solid foundation of a breeding flock that will relieve him from the Sacrifices attendant
upon a correction of those deformities in Animals, which public opinion now
declares shall no longer be tolerated in our markets. Upon a closer inspection of the stock upon ―――― Farm, however well the Draught horses maintain
the character of the blood that has for generations run in their veins, and
though true to the texts of the Herd Book are the aristocratic portion of the
cattle, yet commentators must allow that the Leicesters will form the most
prominent feature of ―― sale."

Ride across the Lammermoors—The Highland Society's Show at Kelso
—A Sketch of it in 1833—Kelso Race-course—Kelso Ram Fair—
Scenes in the Sale Yard—Lord Polwarth's Sale—The Border Leices-
ters—The Yetholm Gipsies—The Earl of Wemyss's Hounds and
Hunters at Coldstream.

Two shirts and three pairs of stockings proved but a
slender ægis against 16 degrees of frost, as we set
our mare's head before daylight straight from Athelstaneford over the Lammermoors. We began the
ascent beyond Yester, the residence of the Marquis
of Tweedale, one of the very best farmers and " all
round" judges in Scotland. The wind cut us

to the cheek-bone like a knife, and we thought "the mules" or greyfaces happy in their thick-set fleece when we were descending by flinty ruts and ice-bound burns, on the welcome Kelso side. As their breeders say, "they come as big as you like, and the turnip comes out on the wool"; seeing that with extra feeding the best of the hoggs will often clip 8lbs. They are very fond of them in some parts of York-shire, and the farmers of the Askrigg district buy the shots of the blackfaced ewe hoggs solely to breed them.

The hill farmers burn their heather on a regular rotation, and Mr. Clapperton gave it as his opinion recently, at one of the East Lothian Farmers' Club meetings, that "when properly burned it would feed blackfaced sheep better than any young grass in East Lothian." Under a thousand feet, at least, Mr. George Hope considered that "more money had been made by converting heather into arable land than by any other system of farming in Scotland, potatoes and altogether," provided the land was taken at a heather rent, and landlords gave some assistance in fencing and draining.

Carfrae Mill had not the attraction for us which it has for the Duke's field two or three times in the season, and at Lauder, nearly every stall was full of horses whose riders had gone to the rink. It was a right cheery ride by Mellerstain and Smailholm, and Mr. Usher (as ardent a curler as he is a hunter) was just returning from the ice on Benvoirlich when we

2 L

reached Stodrig. He might well congratulate us on the punctuality with which we had done our two-and-forty miles, and promise us as our reward a night with "The Northern Angler," who was in his finest form, and, stirred by our host's good songs, delivered "the Gaelic sermon."

It was not just the season to realize the rich pastures and warm turnip soils of the Vale of Tweed, but we had seen them some months before. on a sunny August morning. Then, as we passed the ley where Howard was at work with his steam plough, and farmers were following the furrows like rooks, and saw for the first time "the ruined central tower" of St. Mary's Abbey, with Floors Castle amid its deep green setting in the distance, and the Tweed and its latest tributary rolling along past vale and cliff together, we could hardly wonder that the Duke of Argyll should have confessed that, looking back through the vista of a quarter of a century, he did not remember one foot of the road between Edinburgh and "merry Carlisle," save that view from the Bridge of Kelso. In his boyish rapture he visited it five or six times that night; and we, too, cherish our glimpse of the bridge, as the stately Clydesdales were filing over it from the showyard into the town, and little Hotspur was caracolling in the centre, as if the memory still stirred him of the days when he stretched the neck of the Eglinton crack through the mud at Epsom, and sent the heart of Scotland into its shoes.

The show-ground was by the river-side, and the Springwood Policy woods sheltered it south and east. Trees, too, occasionally broke the uniformity of the shed avenues, and between the Ayrshires and the busy horse-ring they clustered still closer within the low palisades of the ancient burial-ground of three parishes, where the grey headstones lay strewn in wild disorder among the rank nettle crop—a cherubim here and cross-bones there. Nine acres were devoted to the stock; and the great implement interest, which has grown so surely and so well, occupied seven. The horse-ring—not exactly our grand English oval, but still 140 feet in diameter—was there, for the morning and afternoon parade; and not unfrequently a goodly assembly of dukes and masters of hounds stood in the centre, watching the Clydesdales at their long steady trot, and looking out for hunting action among the blood sires and the half-bred geldings; while the poultry classes proved to sceptical henwives that a noble M.F.H. can take a delight in breeding foxes and first-prize coloured Dorkings as well.

There stood in one grand line a century of sturdy Clydesdales, most of them with white stockings almost to the hocks; the red-flecked Ayrshires, with their clean expressive heads and wedge-like figures; two first-prize roans from the Royal, "The Pride" victorious, and "The Duke" defeated; the sires and dams of "heavy blacks," round which the London butchers hold their earliest parleys with the salesmen, at the

great Christmas fat market; the West Highlanders, black, dun, and red, and fierce-eyed, even in
their subjection; the Border Leicesters, which can
keep both Cotswold and Lincoln at bay; the blackface
from whose three-year-old veins " the gravy runs out
like brandy"; and the ruddle-coated, game-headed
Cheviots, part of that great Clan Hornie which Brydon, like a Lowland Chieftain, will lead in due
season to the links of Inverness, and invite Sutherlandshire to the wager of battle.

The contrast between it and its humble prede-
cessor of '32 was brought most vividly before us in
a public-house ingle near Coldstream, where we
waited, deep in oatcake and ale, for the train. Our
informant had seen "baith Kelseys," and was all
for progress. "First one," he observed, "was like
a bit of a country tent pitten up; nothing round
aboot it—same kind of thing, bless your heart, but
not gitten up in the same style. Things are varra
much improved since you; feeding's gat up to a different pitch. I saw a lot of bad Ayrshire coos among
them, but varra nice pigs; I canna mind on whose
they were. It's drawn a deal of money noc doot.
He's a varra clever body, they tell me, that Mr. Hall
Maxwell."

Now that great congress had vanished, the park was
green once more, and the gateways built up. Hence
we strove to revive the memories of Lanercost and
Beeswing on Berry Moss to which " oval course of
exactly a mile and a quarter, with a straight run of

half-a-mile up a slight ascent," which General Chassé
would have loved, the Kelso meeting was removed
from Caverton Edge. Thanks to the Duke of Rox-
burghe, and the untiring clerk of the course, Mr.
Usher, the meeting has never faltered. The obelisk
monument of the poet of "The Seasons" faces you
above the turn for home, but it would puzzle the
gentle philosopher to define the length of the racing
season now. The middle of the course seems to be
quite a workshop for the moles ; and wild-ducks and
sea-gulls rise from its ditches. Along the back
stretch it is very deep going in autumn, and it is no
wonder that 9st. 11lbs. should have told on Beeswing, or that Sim Templeman should have found
Songstress tire to nothing. As for Benvoirlich or
Beef and Greens, half-brother to Blink Bonny on
his dam's side, his and Mr. Usher's appearance was
always as keenly looked for, in the Hunting Plate, as
Bob Johnson's and Dr. Syntax's on a Preston Cup day.
He won it three years running ; and if he did not
show in '62, he renewed his strength the next autumn
with his owner up in the yellow with green hoop and
cap, making all the running and hugging the rails at
the turn, to the old tune from the farm lads, of "*Had
awa', Ben!*" On the Turf he did not care to be
asked the question too often, but with the Buccleuch
hounds he was endless.

We do not advise a quietly-disposed person to be
in Kelso on the last night of December · for what with
the wake of the dying year, and the celebration of a

birthday, it is, for flags, music, and cheering, unequalled. The New-Year greetings in the Corn
Exchange next morning were a hushed whisper by
comparison, as we sauntered round its chocolate
stands, looked at samples, mouse-traps, oilcake, and
turnip-cutters, and pondered the thrilling query,
" *Have you tried Thorlieshope lime?*"

But we must go back to September and the rams,
which make visitors throng the borough, and gladden
the innkeepers' hearts. The small plant has slowly
and surely waxed into a great tree, and sheep-
breeders from Ireland, Yorkshire, and Wales now
come to sit under its shadow. Seventeen years ago
there was only a slight sprinkling of rams on The
Knowes, a small green near the Abbey, from one or
two breeders who let them for the season. Then
the show was commenced, which last year rose to the
dignity of six auctioneers, fifty-seven sellers, and
2,300 tups. The prizes of the Union and Highland
Societies had been given the day before, and Stark
of Mellendean, Simson of Courthill, and Purvis of
Burnfoot had been winning with Leicesters, and Elliot
of Hindhope, whose sheep have not exactly the
Brydon glint, but excel in fleece, as all the hill sheep
of the East Border do, had left but one Cheviot
prize for ten gimmers to Shortreed of Attonburn.
Mr. Oliver had also been busy among the half-bred
tups, and Mr. Gibson, from that most bleak-sounding
place Windydoors, had finished with £9 per head for
twenty-two, and £13 5s. for "the top yen."

It was, in fact, " the great autumnal assize of the
Union Agricultural Society, held at Kelso, before
the most profound bucolic jurists of the age,"
and Messrs. Donkin had "solicited the attention of the
élite of Border Society to this golden opportunity of
embellishing and enriching their Dairies with the
Poetry of Cream and Butter," from a consignment of
Alderney and Guernsey cows. When we add that
" symptomatical of superexcellence," " a jewel for
the lawn," " the Darling of the Dairy," were mere
" remarks" in the sale-bill, on the grey, smoky, and
mulberry fawns, we have given but a faint specimen
of the powerful stimulant which this Robins of the
North applies weekly to his clients in " the little kingdom of Scotland and Northumberland."

The ram sale has outgrown its doorway; but that
sturdy borderer, Tom Gibbons of Burnfoot, is a good
man to follow in a crowd, and joining sixpences we
shoved in together. The lots vary from a hundred
to five, and are divided among four rings. The
Messrs. Donkin have at present the lion's share of the
business; and Messrs. Fairbairn and Penny, Mr.
Oliver of Hawick, Mr. Shiel, and Mr. Embleton duly
take their turns with lots, whose precedence of sale is
decided by ballot. Up to two o'clock business is brisk
enough; but, except it be Lord Polwarth's, an
average will suffer severely if the lot is not put up
before that hour. Buyers begin to tire, and want to
be away, and some breeders from round Kelso have
sent their sheep to Edinburgh in consequence. The

sheep are duly ticketed, and the names of the flock
labelled on the pen. Some auctioneers can sell eighty
in an hour, but a ram a minute is the general calculation. It is very hard work to begin at ten
with only four rings, and to sell off by five. Biddings beyond £5 are all by five shillings, and they
quite reverse the line, " I'd rather have a guinea
than a one-pound note."

The different styles of the auctioneers are most
delightful to a stranger, and after we had been once
or twice among the pens, the spirit was ever moving us
to make tours of inspection, simply for comparison.
The dramatic, the impulsive, the crisp, the melancholy, and the homely styles, all had their interpreters.
We heard no home-thrust like that once delivered by
the late Mr. Fairbairn, when he had sold a topper :
" *Now, Sir ! your flock has been falling off for some
years · you've got the sheep to suit you.*" They did
not rise beyond, " *Look at that sheep, and waken
up !*" and some such antidotes to sloth, or assurances
that he was " *clipped in June as bare as a vegetable
board ; and look at him now !*" Then the word went
round that the Polwarth lot, which is as keenly
looked for here as Mr. Cookson's at Doncaster, was
going to be put up, and the audience at rings 2, 3,
and 4 begin to thin rapidly. The few remnants of
the preceding lot only acted as a whet. " *A £5 note
for a start of him,*" says the auctioneer, a sterling-
looking fellow, with a little switch for a hammer, and
a supply of good, sound Border Doric, which falls quite

pleasantly on our Cumbrian ear. *"There's a good un, there's noe doot of it;"* but even this eulogium is not quite to his mind, and he adds apologetically, *" I canna spak oot for this wind." " Here's a good skinned yen." " Sic a sheep again there, gentlemen, —£5 for a start of him sure-ly."*

Then comes the Polwarth prelude, but the speaker is equal to it, and no wind interferes with the glowing assurance that their *" heads, rumps, and skins are the wonder of the world."* The tall and limber-looking shepherd, Andrew Paterson, in drab leggings, and with a handkerchief in his hand for the final polish, brings the first of the thirty-five into the ring, and *" Ten pounds ten times over"* was the first auctioneer's remark on him. *" Look at him   Oh   dear !   I'll get £20 for him in a minit, I'm sure o't;"* and Mr. Wilson of Haymount drew first blood at twenty-four. Bidders went much sharper for No. 5, and it was *"36 ten times over,"* and when it was at 60, with a good round of Border music, the seller had only this dry eulogy for his audience, that they had *" taken a terrible deal of time."* One pound more, and it was Mr. Wilson's again. *" Here's a better yen,"* said *the shepherd,* mantling with delight ; but the bidders soon discounted his speech for him. As for No. 10, *" It's no use wasting any time. Come! twenty for a start,"* and he got it; and the £60 top finish of last year between Mr. Purvis and Sir George Dunbar's agent was converted into a £71 between Torrence of Sisterpath and Douglas of Ross-shire. As Mr. Usher

professionally observed, " *The home stable won again.*"
And so the average went steadily on, till it was only
3½d. short of £27, or £6 12s. 9d. beyond the average
for the same number in '63, no small rise on the
£10 8s. all round of '60. The ring cleared out after
the closing lot, 35, just like the House of Commons to
the smoking-room, when a great speaker is down, and
who shall we say gets up? and "£3 2s. 6d., *gie
us a bit stiffer than that, Mr. Swan,*" were the last
words that were audible in our reporter's gallery.

In the course of the day £57 (as well as £9 0s. 6d.
for 48) and £51 were made respectively by Mr.
Stark and Mr. Calder. "Sisterpath" kept up its old
prestige with £10 10s. 8½d. for 49, and Mr. Purvis
was there again with £9 7s. 9½d. for a hundred.
The Simsons were pretty close, "Blainslie" with £7
10s. 9d. for 80, and " Courthill" with £7 17s. 8d. for
70; but there is no fair comparison of averages unless
the time of putting up is stated as well.

Lord Polwarth has fine old grass and very beautiful shelter and climate for his flock at Mertoun, four
miles from St. Boswells, and he sets the fashion as
completely as Mr. Sanday did in England, and never
buys tups at Kelso. In fact, the other Border
breeders declare that it is a perfect Caucasian mystery
where he does get his tups from. The uniformity of
his lordship's sheep is very marked, from their gay looks,
flat backs, round ribs, and slight deficiency about the
scrag. In size and wool some of the other flocks
are their equals, and in the two-shear competition

his lordship was beaten by Mr. Stark of Mellendean, and has by no means always the best of it in
the show yards.   Only some six score ewes are kept
at Mertoun, but some of the very best go on to a
great age, and the greatest caution is used in ascer-
taining what sort of stock a tup gets before he is
dipped into.   The ewe and gimmer draft have been
sold for many years to the same farm in Fifeshire.
Nothing but the highest tact, combined with advantages of situation, could give them such a long lead.
They have been put up to auction for fifty-eight years,
and whereas in 1820 thirty-five of them only averaged £3 15s., in 1864 the same number reached
£27.   The Cotswold element, which was once fancied
on the Border, has never been introduced amongst
them.*

The Border can show its Leicester title almost as
far back as the beginning of the century, and Mr.
Robertson of Ladykirk and Mr. Cully of Wark
began it.   Mr. Purvis has been at it for full fifty
years, and has crossed with the flocks of Lord Polwarth, Compton of New Learmouth, Smith of

* "This celebrated flock, which has long commanded top prices at the
great Kelso sales, and whose strain is distinctly traceable in the flocks of
almost all the best breeders of pure Scotch Leicesters in the country, originated in 1802, when 80 ewes were purchased, at £2 15s each, from a well-
known Northumberland breeder, Mr. Jobson of Hidgley, near Chillingham,
and 140 ewes from Mr. Waddell (also, we believe, a Northumbrian breeder),
at £2 14s.   Where the rams were obtained from, it is now somewhat difficult
to ascertain.   At that time, however, the most reputed breeders did not care
to dispose of their rams, and it is probable that these were hired from the most
famous Border flockmasters, of whom Mr Robertson of Ladykirk was one.
Two years after Lord Polwarth had purchased the flock from Mr Jobson he
commenced a sale of rams at Mertoun, and from that time (1804) continued
them every year at that place until 1852, when he sent his rams down to Kelso,
where they have ever since been sold."—*Scottish Farmer.*

Marldown, Cockburn of Sisterpath (who was once quite at the top of the tree), Calder of Kelloe Mains (who gets Mr. Simpson's of Court Hill's ewes), Chrisp of Hawkhill, &c., and thus the perpetual interchange of blood with all the crack flocks goes on. The Highland Society, the Northumberland Society, and the Union are the only local shows the breeders attend, and the latter holds its spring show alternately at Kelso and Coldstream in March, for those who have young bulls and cart stallions, and two and three-year-old cart colts and fillies, in the district. Independently of their public sales, Yorkshire and Northumberland are great customers, but the latter county is falling into the radical English error of having their Leicesters a little too fine. The Border breeders contend that the big sheep are hardier than the small, and able to live and thrive at a great height ; that near the foot of the Cheviots the Leicester-Down and pure Leicester (particularly the former) cannot live in a storm, and require far more keeping up before lambing. The very high feeders calculate on five fleeces to the 2 stone or 48lbs. for tup hoggs. Some also dislike swedes for their tup hoggs, as they are too nutritive, and apt to crook the pasterns, and never give them to their ewes till after lambing, when they are off to the grass. They generally begin with Skirving's Purple Tops, and have their hoggs on them or Greystone and White Globe all the winter, and the breeding ewes are put on the same by the end of January. Australia is beginning to fancy the sort, and this year Mr. Purvis got £10 for ewe hoggs and £20 for tup hoggs out of the wool, to go over. These were not the pick of his lot, as he always takes care to have 100 of his best tup hoggs for Kelso, when they ought to weigh 50lbs. per quarter.

The farms, partly hill and arable, of Roxburgh-shire, Berwickshire, Selkirkshire, and Peebleshire are mostly farmed on the principle of bringing Che-viot ewes from the hill, keeping them to five or six years old, and taking half-bred lambs from them each year. This system generally obtains in every district not more than seven hundred feet above the sea; and the small half-bred ewe shots are made quite as good as top Cheviot wedder lambs. Those who follow it regularly buy from the hill farmers two-fifths of their Cheviot ewe lambs each year, in order to keep up their stock. It ascends Teviotdale, five miles above Hawick, up Kale and Bowmont Water, to the foot of the Cheviots, all along the banks of the "shallow brawling Tweed," Gala, and Leader beyond Peebles, and nearly to Lanark.

> " Drygrange with the milk-white ewes,
> 'Twixt Tweed and Leader standing,"

is faithful to it; and in the Vale of Yarrow every-one breeds half-breds, if his land is low enough, and he has winter keep. In the Bowmont Water district the farmers go a step further, and use Border Leices-ters to the four or five year old Cheviot ewes, which are then in the very height of their milk, in order to

breed Kelso half-bred sale tups, and so keep up the
Cheviot hardihood. Still, although half-bred on
half-bred has been a good deal tried, yet Leicester
on half-bred has done best. They are very particular about the dams of these tups, and some farmers
go to Sutherland for picked ewes. Regular breeders
will buy half-bred lambs from another hirsel, and pay
as high as 28s. 6d. for them. All who breed half-
breds give the ewes six to eight weeks of turnips in
winter, or they could never nurse their much-heavier
lambs. It is therefore no wonder that half-bred
lambs increase so much for Melrose. There have
been as many as 90,000 there, with ewes and
wedders always separated, whereas twenty years
since fully half of them were Cheviots.

We did not step aside to see the gipsy Scone at
Kirk Yetholm. King Charles Blyth slept with his
fathers on August 19th, 1861, and Queen Esther, or
Esther Faa Blyth (the widow of "Jeddart Jock"), who
reigns in his stead, holds levées daily in her neat
little cottage. We might have heard more from her
of Will Faa her kinsman, with his " eye as keen as
a hawk and as black as a sloe," and who handled his
leister on the Tweed with the eye of an Indian,* but

* We extract the following from an annual flysheet entitled " Present State
of the Gipsies in Yetholm " " It is noticed that their circumstances, humble
as they are, are somewhat declining ; their pottery wares are becoming less
abundant, and a greater number of individuals depend upon the making of
besoms, baskets, &c , than formerly Only two families regularly keep horses
and carts, the others who aspire to such a dignity being occasionally obliged
to sell theirs to relieve themselves from pressing difficulties During the last
two summers many have made a considerable amount (it would be impossible
to say how much) from wool They buy the offal of the folds from the farmers,
and, after much labour in cleaning, sell it at a high price ; yet winter finds
them, as usual, badly prepared for it, and at present several are miserably fed

we cared more for Coldstream and the Earl of
Wemyss's kennels.

His lordship first hunted Berwickshire and East
Lothian from '34 till '43 " beginning from all kennels." Transport, an eight-season hunter of Sutton
and Beilby blood, Alfred of Musters and Tavistock,
Chantress of Osbaldeston, Rainbow of Sutton, Vola-
tile of Belvoir, and Sensitive of Shropshire were his
leaders and counsellors. Out of eighty couple of
waifs and strays forty-nine were drafted, so that his
lordship and Joe Hogg, late of The Four Burrows
and now of Calabria, had a hardish time of it. Tom
Rance's brother whipped in for a season there,

---

and clothed   Their hardships make them more anxious to keep their children
from following their footsteps, and hence all the young men and women, without exception, strive to become farm-servants, and all who are of age have
striven successfully, except three girls who are still at home   At present there
are 13 families numbering 61, of which 21 are children, and of these 18 attend
school.   The gipsy school, which is so great a boon to the village of Kirk-
Yetholm, continues to be well attended, and the system of giving each child a
certain quantity (half-a-stone) of meal weekly in summer to encourage attendance has succeeded admirably.   A subscription in behalf of the gipsies
would be thankfully received by the Rev A Davidson, Yetholm Manse, Kelso "
    His late Majesty Charles I was hardly every inch a king, and looked
very wretched, though a noble lady for many years eked out the royal table
with 3 or 4 lbs of mutton and a loaf of bread weekly.   He was one of the
electors as well as chairman of the assembly when he was chosen king, and
made a speech narrating his many personal virtues.   The present Queen is his
daughter, and she purchased the Palace for £20 when it was sold by the parish
a few months since   She has no salary or emolument of any kind, and did not
attend her own election.   A more truthful or honourable man never lived than
the first king " Will Faa," and he kept a publichouse for years.   The farmers
and proprietors all tacitly gave him a ticket of leave to fish when and where he
liked.   He was a grand football player, and gained several matches, and was
quite a terror with his fists to the Northumberland tinkers   .The hardest fight
he ever had was, during a journey for gin, with two excisemen, one on foot and
the other on horseback and armed with a sword; while Will had only a willow
wand.   The exciseman worked round him in a circle, clipping a bit off the
willow wand at every sword-stroke, and at last, as Will would not give in, he
reached his hand, and left it dangling by the flexor muscles   The wound was
dressed at Alnwick, but the hand was useless ever after.   His Majesty was upwards of 84 when he died, and suffered much from dropsy at last.   For further
information as to gipsy habits we must refer our readers to the third volume of
Mr Alexander Jeffrey's very learned and elaborate work on " The History and
Antiquities of Roxburghshire "

but unfortunately died of a broken leg and typhus fever combined. Unweaned from the Chase by Philip's and Gondolier's Turf success, his lordship took to the Berwickshire and Northumberland country in 1843, when Mr. Robertson gave it up, and Talisman's blood did best for him out of the eighteen couple of that old Lambton pack, which he decided on keeping. This gave him seventy couple, and he hunted six days a week with three packs. He now hunts five days up to February, and four after that time. The country is not picked up for the dog and bitch pack, but the latter go to the outlying meets simply because they are lighter in the van.

Channing came to his lordship in '39. His father hunted Mr. Yeatman's, and he himself had ten seasons with the Blackmore Vale, under Mr. Hall, afterwards of the Heythrop, Lord Portman, and Mr. Drax, before he moved North. He then served for twelve seasons under Joe Hogg, and the last was his fourteenth as kennel huntsman.

The Amisfield kennels, near Haddington, where the horses and hounds go for the summer, were built originally for the Duke of Buccleuch. The move is made to Coldstream the first week in October, and they leave again on April 3rd or 7th. During that time they go for a fortnight to Belford. They enter from 14 to 17 couple, and walk 40 at least every year in Peebleshire, Perthshire, East Lothian, and the country. Sutton's Albert and Trueman, Burton Contest,

Rufford Playmate, and Drake's Duster, all died at Amisfield; for as Channing says, "If we get good blood, we never let it away again;" and he points out with pride that Trueman, Drake's Tarquin and Duster, and Osbaldeston Furrier blood are all combined in the Fencer and Heroine entry of last season. Albert was a very close hunter, with a rare nose and stout, and Trueman had grand ribs with capital second thighs. Contest was full of drive, and was used for three seasons, and 5½ couple are still left by him. Foljambe's Hazard and Herald were both here, and the latter won the scarlet cloth in the private sweepstakes. Beaufort Primate got some good hounds, and the stern placed far into the back makes the sort good to know. Pilot came from the Oakley, and Hermit and Harbinger, two of the leading stud hounds, are from one of his daughters.

Among the bitches we noted Rumina, a puppy prize-taker with Rhoderick, and the hare-pied Rarity, bred by Captain Percy Williams, and once condemned for her love of hare. Old Relish from Rally by Highflyer stands beside her, with her grey head and short and straight legs; and old Ruin, a capital one-eyed, sixth-season bitch, still challenges time, and runs at the top of them in difficulties. Blue heads may not be popular in a Leicester shape, but Blowzy and Buxom were two good ones, as they took off from Mr. Grey of Millfield's, and ran their fox ten miles in couples to Thrunton Crags, and so came ready entered. Welcome throws back to the

2 · M

Contest light tan, which mixes with her Albert and Trueman blood, and is still the top of the '63 entry; and she and her sister Dainty led alternately in the two runs, on one of the last days they were out on the Lammermoors. Heroine, the old black and white, was grouped for us with her fine Fencer litter, of which Heedless, Hebe, and Harmony were the foremost; and there was old Costly, a grand-daughter of Drake's Chaplet, one of the Earl's especials in her time.

The 24½-inch Galliard, "one of the finest big dogs I ever saw," according to Lord Henry Bentinck, came out first of the dog hounds, and his sire, the old smutty-faced Frederick, "who brings the fine skins," stood beside him with his sister Gaudy; but Goldfinch was not there. Frederick came from Sir Watkin's, and has not quite the style of his stock; but, as Channing says, "he never did anything wrong to my knowledge." Against Galliard he has only to urge that his fine deep kennel note never rises beyond a falsetto squeak in cover. Hazard was a glorious dog, and those who saw him on the flags for the Cleveland Cup could never forget him more. There, too, were Ringwood, "Drake's Duster about the quarters;" Rhoderick, "one of the best sires we have;" Banker and Rubicon, part of the Cup three couple, but the former minus an eye since that pleasant Guisboro' day. There, too, were grouped Hotspur, a grandson of the Belvoir Rallywood; Hector, who is quite "the Furrier of the kennel;" Trimbush,

a clean little Irish dog; and Royal, "old Contest
all over, but a little darker in the coat," and better in
his thighs as well as 31 inches round the heart and
7⅞ round the arm. Right well does he carry out
Mr. Campbell of Saddell's aphorism, that "hounds
are never illnamed, be they Mischief or Madcap, or
anything else."

The country extends from the Mill Knowe under
the Lammermoor Hills to Thrunton Crags. Mr.
Gray takes it up there with a scratch pack, and then
the Morpeth come in by Rothbury and the river
Coquet. They have but little cubbing, and the hounds
are generally blooded in Twizel and Kyloe woods
near Belford, or in Polwarth woods, and the great
chain of plantations from Greenlaw to Dunse. His
lordship does not go with them to Dunse, but only
meets them by train, and he mostly goes to the
hotel at Belford (half-way between Berwick and
Alnwick) for the fortnight. There are some good
gorses both in Berwickshire and Northumberland,
those in the former chiefly ranging from ten to
twenty acres, and with a belt of trees round them.
In character the countries differ essentially, Northumberland having more grass and single fences,
and being more open, while Berwickshire is stiffer
and more confined. November and December are
much the best months for the latter, as after February it is all under plough, and the dust flies in
clouds. The great drawback to Northumberland is
the difficulty of stopping, and from Ford to Twizel,

and so on to Alnwick, it may be said to be "all under ground." There are also some very craggy streams, and many a gallant couple have died at the Blue Braes on the banks of the White Adder. Artificial manures and sheep smears, whose patentee, whoever he is, may take notice that they can be "smelt a mile off," are answerable for many a check.

The stud is very grand, and owes much to Sunbeam and Turnus, the former of which was only just dead. Bob Carlyle, his lordship's head groom, and one of the best known men among horses in Scotland, bought him, in one of his voyages of discovery, at the Lucan steeple-chases, and his lordship rode him for eight or nine seasons, and never knew him tire. He was a dark chesnut of fifteen-two, and got all his stock great natural jumpers, bigger than himself, and generally chesnuts. Bob liked the sort so much that he picked up his own brother another year, but he died early. The Turnus blood is very strongly represented, thanks to Bob's constant pilgrimages to Knockhill; and the premier, a six-year-old chesnut of immense substance, very fast and great at his fences, bears that name. There, too, are his bay brother, and Hoddom, a very sweet one, Tom of Linne (half-brother to Lord of Linne), and The Friar, quite "the boy for the hills."

Old Dumfries, on which his lordship is painted, bears in his drooping back the mark of nine seasons; Wellesbrook is a long and smart brown Irishman of about half as many; and the Glasgow horse by The Rasher has fine style and stride. Of his half-sister Governess, Channing avers that he never saw her off her feet—a fact which he cannot exactly allege of Glasgow, as in a fast thing from Cranshaw's *" he fell ten yards, and I fell ten further."* Garibaldi is a horse of great power, and The Roan is of four seasons' standing, with a wonderful arm and substance, and like the Marotto mare, a clipper in a close country. For five seasons Channing rode The Pig, but of late he has been more on The Bird, a rare hill horse, as he proved in a day from Copeland gorse over the Cheviots; and Banker by Chanticleer, who won the East-Lothian steeple-chase, possesses the same faculty. Marden is a very knowing old-fashioned horse by Little Known, and goes back to Rocket and Little Thomas, " the last of the Mohicans;" at least so said Lord John Scott, who knew and loved the sort.

Jemmy Twitcher, who won seven steeple-chases, has gone, and so has the beautiful grey Pallinsburn,* who was more at home in a stiff country than on the hill, and one of his lordship's best for five seasons.

Bob Carlyle, who never broke arm or leg till last season, has been with the Earl for thirty-eight years, and is not only photographed beside his lordship and the grey, but appears in Mr. Gourlay Steell's presentation hunt picture on Wellesbrook. He can go back to Prince Le Boo, Cannonball, Rob Gibb, and

---

* The portrait of this horse appears in the group entitled " A Glimpse of Knockhill, 1864."

Little Phœnix of his lordship's hard-riding Leicestershire days, as well as the grey half-brothers Reformer and Canteen. Once he whipped in with Joe Hogg, and portraits of Waverley and Ringwood, the hounds of his fancy, form part of his collection at Amisfield. He was also playing in the same character from '29 to '34, when the Earl kept harriers at Kelso to fill up the two days that the Duke's did not hunt, and when, with Lord John aiding and abetting, they would " go like the mischief" with a fox over Cessford Moor. Bob's picture gallery of man, horse, and hound is a pretty extensive one; and Mr. Hay of Leatham Grange and Mr. Hunt' of Thornington are not forgotten, as men from whom the Earl has bought many a good horse. The stuffed fox's head has also a peculiar reminiscence. " *We killed it*," says Bob, " *thirty-five miles from this park, the very last day that I was a bachelor.*"

CHAPTER VI.

COLDSTREAM TO HAWICK.

"Forth from his den the otter drew;
Grayling and trout their tyrant knew,
As between reed and sedge he peers
With fierce round snout and sharpened ears;
Or prowling by the mountain cool,
Watches the stream or swims the pool."

SCOTT.

The Hawick "Lads"—Messrs. Oliver's Auction Sales—The Hawick Ram Sale—Dr. Grant's Otter Hounds—His Dandie Dinmonts—Robin's Education—Sandy and Billy—Mornings with the Doctor on the Teviot, Ale, and Jed.

HAWICK is not the prettiest; but there is a sturdy, industrial independence about it which gives it a high rank among Border towns. It remonstrated in good set terms with Manchester for rejecting Milner Gibson and John Bright; it plumes itself on being peopled by the descendants of heroes who fell at Flodden; and one of its poets has packed its greatness into this couplet—

"Spite of lawless fraud and pillage,
Hawick rose by trade and tillage."

The last trace of their martial ardour is to be found in the selection of a "cornet" annually. Garlick Jock, Black Wat, and "Adam Hart (carter)" are all on the roll, and two of them flourished when the "town clerk headed the horsemen armed with swords, and pedestrians with clubs," to race on the Muir the first day, and to ride the ancient marches, beginning at the Commonhaugh, on the second.

It doesn't take much to wake up the "lads" now. An otter, or even a foulmart, will do it most effectually, let alone a meet of the Duke's at Grundiston or Chapel Hill, so that summer or winter they are pretty well "up to their cruppers" in sport. We found fully five hundred of them waiting at the station to meet a local hero, "The Gover," who had been trained near Bradford for a mile race. One grim cynic growled out, when we asked for information, "*They're only a set of daft bodies—it's just this foot-racing*"; but, daft or not, if "The Gover" and his trainer had been the Premier and Mr. Gladstone they could not have been received more reverentially.

At present, however, we have to pluck up the ancient landmarks, and look upon Hawick as the great sheep and cattle centre of Upper Teviotdale, extending from Denholm on the East to Mosspaull on the west. There is a half-yearly market for cattle and hiring of servants, but the cattle department has of late years been entirely superseded by the weekly auctions of the Messrs. Oliver. This firm, which was the first to establish such auctions in Scotland, began some twenty-five years ago with a monthly one. Gradually this mode of selling came into favour with the farmers, and now a weekly one is held, at which the greater part of the fat and other stock reared in the neighbourhood is sold.

The store sales in spring and autumn are in a measure a transfer of yearlings from the hill to the arable farmers; but the hill breeding is not on an extensive scale, and the supplies are principally from England and Ireland, and from Red Water and the West Country between Jed and Liddesdale. Kelso and the Rood Day Fair at Jedburgh both help to fill the yards with two and three-year-olds, principally short-horns, in September, which are gradually sold off from December to May, either privately or at local sales to dealers, who take them to Leeds, Manchester, Newcastle, and the South. The turnip crop has increased twenty-fold in as many years in Roxburgh-shire, and the number of cattle fed in a very large proportion, whereas it once sent its stores to the south. Finger-and-toe bears heavy on the mangels, and East Lothian is relied on for potatoes.

The late Mr. Andrew Oliver also began the public wool sales before 1840. They were the earliest in Scotland, but not exactly on the Girdwood system. Catalogues of clips were published, and buyers went round and examined them, and then met at Hawick or Jedburgh and bid. Now the wool is warehoused, and there are three or four sales a year. The stock sales, which began about this time, were at first a mere name; and now Mr. Oliver sells as many sheep and cattle weekly as he did monthly, even when the neighbourhood warmed to the scheme. Inde-

pendently of the regular Monday ones, three or four
special sales are held for half-bred lambs in August
and September, and two principally for draft Cheviot ewes in October, and occasionally extra ones
for cattle. Mr. Oliver's new sale-yard will hold ten
thousand sheep and lambs; and after the last Melrose
fair it was full, and a contingent of a thousand were
billeted in the adjoining space. Liddesdale, Teviotdale, and Ewesdale all send Cheviot and half-bred
lambs; Fifeshire, Perthshire, and Forfarshire come
for the latter to feed off, and the English dealers
principally for Cheviot and half-bred ewes. Mr.
Penny has similar sales at Kelso, they also thrive
under Mr. Oliver at Galashiels, and Mr. Davison
at Melrose. There are plenty of other outlets for
sellers, and flock-masters on the Jed and the borders
of the Cheviot hills take their lambs to Pennymuir,
on the old drove road to Newcastle, in July, and their
cast ewes in October. Those in Gala Water, the
lower parts of Roxburghshire, and the upper part of
Berwickshire, who have a half-bred stock, sell their
three-parts-bred lambs at St. Boswell's and Melrose,
and buy half-bred ewes to keep up their flock of
breeding ewes on the improved land or parks. The
Cheviot lamb buyers from the Highlands generally
come after the wedder tops, and the ewe lambs (of
which flockmasters will only sell the seconds) are
dispersed round the district, while the cast Cheviot
ewes are invariably Cumberland and Yorkshire
bound.

The Hawick ram sale is of old date, and at one time fat sheep, tied by the legs, were shown along with them in the street. The Highland flockmasters very seldom come now, but do nearly all their business through commission agents, like Murray, the Swans, and Kennedy, &c., of Edinburgh, who have quite superseded the dealers. Once all the business was done by private sale, till Mr. Riddell of Hindalea sold the " Calroust Rams " by auction in Hawick Market a wholesome innovation on the private system, which must have dated back to the Union. Hawick and Moffatt are now the Cheviot capitals, to which Ettrick, Yarrow, all the Dumfriesshire districts, and the dales journey once a year for interchange of stock and good Border fellowship. At Hawick alone, from 1,500 to 2,000 rams are sold, at all prices from £21 to £2 10s. In exceptional cases they will range as high as £50, and Linhope, Hindhope, Hopesrigg, Georgefield, and East Middle have generally carried the day. The sale of Leicester rams has also much increased, and the principal Hawick district supplies come from East Middle and Spittal.

To pass through Hawick without having an introduction to Dr. Grant and his Dandie Dinmonts was not to be thought of. We first met him in the outskirts journeying professionally towards Teviotdale, with three of them in his dog-cart. Greyhounds, terriers, otters, and a good practice form his quadruple tie to the district, and he has almost ceased to think of his native Highlands. His house is a faithful reflex of himself. There is an infant badger stuffed on the staircase, and an otter of 25lbs. on the landing. The spotted skins of some sixteen puppies by the otter hound Pibroch, from Dowager, of the Duke's breeding, constitute a colony of mats. You wipe your feet at the bottom of the stairs on all that is now mortal of the black-and-tan Merryman, who made merry with water-rats when there was sterner work to do, and was put down as a trifler not worthy of his salt. Billy and Bobby are the only dogs which enjoy bed and board in the house. They dress each other's wounds most devotedly, after a hard morning's work, and share the doctor's bed. Their presence is his only soporific. He takes his rest with these martial retainers at his back and legs, and dreams of the glories of the Jed and Teviot, and the covered drains on the Ale. During the past winter he has used up most of his spare minutes after nightfall in designing and building a drag, which is drawn by Robin and a thorough-bred. The iron part is a blacksmith's handiwork, but the wood and the painting—claret picked out with red—are strictly his own. It is on four wheels, and built for twelve couple. The driving-box is placed on two tiers, one for hounds, and another for terriers, and there is plenty of scope for hounds beneath the seats of the car behind.

The Doctor's best affections have always been, not so much with the clan Grant, as with his Dandie Dinmonts, and his back-yard is quite a Charlieshope.

Nettle and Pepper, from Paul Scott, of Jedburgh, were the first arrivals, and Sir George Douglas's keeper gave him Shamrock, who had recently devoted himself to worrying collies. "Shammy" is of the Birsieslees branch of the Dandie Dinmont family referred to by "Stonehenge on the Dog." He was bred by Mr. James Scott, of Newstead, from Vixen by *brown* Pepper, or Pepper or "Pepper the Second." In short, the Doctor believes in no other blood than that which is derived from James Davidson, of Hindley and almost primæval Pepper and Mustard renown. He had bought many things in Dandie shape before he cast in his lot with this breed, but his trials were too high for them. They were entered with rats, and mounted the scale to cats, as age and performance might warrant. Too many of the puppies stopped there, or did not get any further than a muzzled fox; and then if age gave them solid confidence, they took their B.A. degree with the badger. This species of culture tends upwards to the otter, in which Tom and Teddy (the sons of Shamrock and Nettle) have become quite Regius Professors. Teddy gains in pluck what he loses in style. He goes quietly up to the "fish-slicer," and gets almost bitten to death on the head without a murmur, while he surely does the deed; but Tom dashes in with all the *élan* of a Zouave, and has it by the neck before it can get home with its "clinches." "A retreat for purely strategic purposes" is a thing they wot not of.

For the first two seasons that the Doctor was
Master of the Teviotdale, he and Shammy and William Broadwith (a very plucky little fellow, with,
alas ! an iron hook for a hand), who hunted Sir
George Douglas's for many years, were "almost the
only otter hounds." The Doctor might, in fact, have
never become an M.O.H at all, if he had not yearned
for even a higher "trial horse" than his badger, and
set out in quest of one on the banks of the Ale. The
hard-bitten trio were not long in finding an "aged river
poacher" (as the *Hawick Advertiser* puts it), and
bolted him into a sack. He was borne home tenderly by the Doctor; but he did not relish a mena-
gerie future, and in less than twenty-four hours he
had climbed up a wall eight feet high, worked a hole
through the slates, and given his new medical attendant leg-bail for his pains. Nothing more was seen
of him that season; but one of 25lbs., by four-feet-
two, and very like him, was found in the Denholm
Pool the next summer, and the chase was so long and
the dog punishment so heavy that the Doctor and
Teddy were the only ones up. The waters of the
Teviot never witnessed a more bloody fray than when
the former tailed him, and the latter held him by the
throat, and the three rolled over and over in the
death grip together. Walter was a rare adjutant
on these occasions. He was with the Doctor at
thirteen, and then became a herd laddie; but he
"returned to nobler pursuits," and held this staff
appointment for some years. His master's great

anxiety was to see him well bitten, and he quite grudged him all his narrow escapes. Indeed, the principal clause in the Grant articles of war ran thus: " If the otter breaks your arm, Walter, you are not to let him go."

It has not been our fate, as yet, to see the Doctor engaged in one of these great water wrestles; but we have a keen recollection of him in a stirring tableau on a certain February night, holding up his badger by the tail, and casting the gleams of the lantern on its aldermanic paunch, to show the happy results of a three years' captivity. Its condition and knowledge of " the noble art of self-defence" are undoubted; but still the doctor considers it, intellectually speaking, quite a dull-witted brute. He has tried hard to touch, one by one, the finer chords in its nature; but it won't have him at any price. Perhaps it has learned to suspect him and his honeyed words, and knows his mission far too well, as he goes bending almost double into its cell. Hence it burrows day after day in the straw-tub, eats enormous rations of bread, meat, and milk, and sternly refuses to reciprocate on any terms whatever.

The voice of the charmer has never failed before. He attributes this remarkable cynicism to his badger's advanced age when it was dug out, and he secured one of tenderer years. They are the first creatures he ever failed to educate. As for his ferrets, he taught them nothing but affection; but his " performing rats" got quite a step beyond that, and would sit on their hind legs and beg like a dog. He has tried his hand on eleven foxes (one of which bred three cubs); but except a brace of vixens, which did a little in the acrobat way, and an old fox, which had the freedom of the borough, and would occasionally return thirty miles an hour down the High-street and its area bolt-hole, pursued by "the allied armies" of Roxburgh and Selkirkshire collies on a sheep-market day, their mental culture was not high. "Foxie" had been trained from cubhood till he became a perfect Robert Macaire. He would sit up for half-an-hour at a stretch, with the Doctor's spectacles on his eyes, a pencil-case balanced on his nose, and a gold watch hanging by his canine teeth. For a change of performance, he would wink with one eye, and then roll over, and, shutting them both, pretend to be dead. Teddy and he had been fast friends in youth; but a coolness sprang up between them about some porridge, and those fearful jaws sealed his death-warrant.

Dowager, from the Duke of Buccleuch's kennel, a couple from the Cumberland, with Tom Johnston's assurance that "they would tackle aught," Malak-hoff and Fairplay from the Dumfriesshire were, of course, all "slape-haired ones"; and Pibroch, from Mr. Keir, of Whithaugh, in Liddesdale, with Royal and Ringwood, composed the rough interest when the Teviotdale otter pack was first formed. This season it was at its full strength with three foxhounds, eight otter hounds, nine terriers, and the redoubt-

able " Sanderson's Billy" to take the general superintendence. " Ringwood was the biggest blackguard
of the lot." He cost 30s., and arrived late one
night. Before breakfast next morning, he had bitten
a friend of the Doctor's, the Doctor, and the
Doctor's servant-girl, and it " wasn't homœopathic
biting either." The Doctor was bitten again after
breakfast, and at intervals during the first week on
every conceivable part of his person; and if he had
not kept the dog tied up in his bed-room, nothing
short of a charwoman in chain-armour could have
ventured within his doors. At length, being wearied
out of this fierce ivory bondage, he dragged the rebel
down-stairs, and fought a most bloody Ahwal,
Moodkee, and Ferozeshah with him on three successive afternoons in a loose box, which ended in a
Ringwood treaty for peace, and the entire devotion
of his young life to otters. It must be in token of
this vow of submission that the Doctor has had him
photographed for us at his feet, with the handle of
the hunting-whip across his neck, and in the illustrious fellowship of Billy, " Shammy," and Royal.
He is the sire of Bugle, from one of Sir Harry Vane's
sort, which inherits his grand qualities, and took to
the drag at thirteen months. There is still some of
the old leaven in him, and he was the only one that
refused to come out of his prescriptive corner when
the kennel huntsman was sent into the Van Amburgh
sort of cage where they reside. The suggestive
tones of the Doctor (who never uses a whip to any of

them) were enough, and he rendered a surly
obedience at last.

A lot of black-and-white puppies by him, from
Rally, were in the compartment below, where Ruler,
" about the last living drop of old John Peel's blood,"
lay curled up. He was just alive, and that was about
all ; but he recovered after some months of the most
tender nursing ; and he will leave behind him a rare
character as a dragger, fighter, and marker. He
still requires a good deal of care ; and he, Royal,
Collier, and Malakhoff are all fed by the Doctor's own
hand. Collier has also seen a good deal of fun, as well
as trouble, in his time. He once returned from a
trip with what proved under the microscope to be
mange in three forms—disease at the root of the hair
bulb, the vegetable parasite, and the scab animal-
cule ; but the Doctor fell back promptly on his professional resources, and the enemy was smitten hip
and thigh.

The descent of the pack from the cage, one by one,
down a narrow gangway, with Ringwood growling
like a ratepayer in the rear of all, was the scene of
the evening ; and the white Malakhoff made us rub
our eyes to be quite sure that it was not Mr. Morrell's old Trumpeter come back from the gorse of
shadows. Like him he is nearly perfect at everything, and with quite as deep a tongue. He and
Ringwood both went down in '63 with special retainers to Carlisle, and distinguished themselves highly
before Mr. Justice Carr by their eloquence on Bre-

con Flatts, and their method of dealing with knotty points in the rocks near Kitty Straits. Fairplay, a "quiet, sensible dog," but "unfortunately with a smooth skin," and deep in seal or sprint mysteries, scuffled down from "the cage," with Royal, who is quite a water "philosopher and friend," to the Doctor, and gifted with a remarkable Southern skull, and a bell-like tongue, which has discoursed rich music in many a drag. There is a strange psychological sympathy between them, as neither of them can touch a bite of anything on a hunting morning. Bellman, who came with Billy, and began dragging the very first morning with the old dogs at Ancrum Crags, is not easily overlooked, from his gay style; and little Randy was there, too, "the last bitch of the Bowscale blood," yellow with a white ring round her neck, and quite "a devil to worry." Thunder, her daughter by the Carlisle Thunder (a great hound in his day), is like her, but bigger; and Pibroch's "cage" substitute is Fanny by Lochinvar, which is neither more nor less than a greyhound bitch in sheets. She eventually broke her back at Borthwick Brae, on the very spot where, seven seasons before, she ran her first trial. Pibroch, who occasionally looks lost in thought, and does not care now to get too much in the otter's way, always sleeps by himself before the horses; and he and Sarah Sibbald by Canaradzo, and a Gordon setter, seem to have tickets of leave in the yard. The terriers cast in their lot with the pack, and are a "most brave and affectionate family." There is only one son of Bobby (from Teddy's dam) in the kennel, and a regular clinker for mischief, whose chief amusement out at quarters was to hang on to the pigs' ears. Hence he came back in disgrace; but they soon "desired him vehemently" when the rats increased and multiplied once more.

Of course we were introduced in due form to "Shammy by Sir George Douglas's Pepper III., by his Pepper II., by his Pepper I., by old Stoddart's Dandie II., by his Dandie I., who was, perhaps, the best dog of the breed that ever lived." He "has always been hard wrought;" but his sire did not die at Springwood Park till he was upwards of 16, and Shammy looks wonderful for one only three years younger. His sons Teddy of the wonderful jaw, and Tom, a regular Yellow Dwarf, can scuffle along ten miles in the hour, and have wind for a battle-royal at the end of it. Any one who dares to say that the Dandie is cross-bred, must gird up his loins then and there for a vigorous course of polemics. Not only has the Doctor looked into the whole thing in a most learned note, but he can quote several lines from the Greek poet Opianus, who flourished in the second century, to prove that the "crook-limbed and blackeyed" breed were natives of Britain at the time of the Roman invasion. As for his rapture when he looked on Landseer's otter and cub in the Bowhill gallery, and recalled "the bonny beast" in the flesh, and how he had "heard it whistling" to its mamma, it was truly touching. His spirit has communicated itself to the stable. The little thorough-bred black and Prince Augustus by Teddington certainly know nothing as yet of the sport, but the Birdcatcher chesnut Robin has been duly initiated. He waits for the Doctor on the bank; but once upon a time, animated by the same spirit which makes him pull so hard with the foxhounds, he became deeply interested, and walked up to his hocks in the middle of the Teviot. When there, he essayed to encourage his master with a playful dig in the back ribs, which nearly floored him just as the fight was at the hottest, and the injudicious bottle-holder was dismissed with the whip about his hips. This cured him of all active participation in worries for the future, except strictly as a spectator. On land he is in a far higher state of tuition than the rats: he kneels to be mounted; he kicks with both legs or one, as he is directed; he curtseys; he will spar at his master with the science of a Mace; carry his whip along the streets; or execute with him, in more festive moments, a species of Polonaise. And yet the groundwork of this training was simply " riding him blindfold for two months till I got into his favour."

Robin's antecedents are frightful to think of. Some one got him in exchange for a mare at Musselburgh races, and couldn't ride him home. In fact, his antics were so peculiar, that it is still an " historic doubt" whether he entered the army in early life, or cast in his lot with the foot-lamps and the sawdust. After

Musselburgh, he was through the hands of half the cadgers of Edinburgh, and landed at last in a great terrier-home at Birsieslees. The Doctor had a fearful character with him, and as, after buying him, he declined to pass a cart on any consideration, a few half-crowns would have parted them. Once in Hawick he declined to leave his stable for a fortnight, and, when he did consent to go a mile out of the town, he suddenly desired to return. The Doctor was glad to let him come, though he did go shopping all the way; and then an eye-shade or a pistol were the two last alternatives.

Ancrum Bridge, where the Doctor may be often seen sitting and waiting for the dawn and a sprinkling of the Border chivalry as well, and the Abbey Bridge, near Jedburgh, are the favourite meets. The Jeddites are especially keen of the fun, and somehow or other they always seem to have the office. Three hundred will often turn out to see the otter " die a natural death," and the Doctor finds no crowd so accommodating and manageable. The late Duke of Athole and Lord John Scott hunted a great deal in these streams, and the Leader as well; and therefore with such tutors, past and present, it is no wonder that many of " the lads" have the winds of Arabs both for running by day and recounting by night " the great worries in the water"; how Billy brought him out from under a root, and how Teddy, Tom, and Shammy are always getting drowned, and coming up again like a cork. Each hound hunts with a strap round his neck, so as to be taken up when the terriers have an "in-go" on their own account.

The Doctor's hunting costume consists of boots, Tweed breeches, and a thin pink Shetland shirt over a woollen one, and he is armed simply with a pole. He seldom speaks to his hounds except with his horn, and never by any chance uses anything but his fist to fight them off from the otter, or to correct them. Twice over he knocked Malakhoff nearly silly with it, in that terrible struggle near Sandiestones, which he kept up for fully twenty minutes, single-handed, against the whole of his pack. He wanted a live otter as a school of puppy instruction for the natural drag ; but their blood was up, and he was fairly beaten, and dragged out nearly exhausted, part of a dead and living chain—*Hawick Lads*, ∞ *The Doctor*, ∞ *the otter*, ∞ *Teddy*. As for Teddy, he had been "drowned three times, nearly worried under the water by Malakhoff (of course strictly under a misapprehension), and yet he still held on."

Billy and Bobby may hunt in dreams; but the Doctor's eyelids knew no rest the night before a meet, and it goes hard with him if he is not in his dog-cart and away soon after three in summer. The country people say that they have known him "tak a notion three days running when he's lying in bed," and of course execute it. Such instances are, however, rare, and he is seldom out more than twice a fortnight. He is generally back about ten; and

when every hound has been rubbed dry, he changes
his clothes, jumps into his gig, and away on his
rounds, and "sleeps at night without rocking." His
season extends from April to September, and perhaps on the average he may be out thirty times, kill
five brace, and let nearly as many off on the thirteen
rivers of which he has the liberty. The Jed, with its
"rugged rocks" and eternal tree-roots, and the Ale,
which Sir George Douglas fitted up with such a fine
eye to otters, may be said to be his woodland country; and it was on the latter that he had his "Billes-
don Coplow run" of fully ten miles. It joins the
Teviot, or rather reaches the open at Ancrum Bridge,
where they are generally pretty safe of a long burst
with a "traveller." The meet is at Kelso Bridge
when they hunt up the Teviot; but the pack is not
large enough to attempt the Tweed, and if they did,
the velveteen order of the Trappists have been there
pretty often before them.

"Sandy," or Willie Sanderson, a young butcher
from Carlisle, has been a tower of strength to the
Doctor since they met on the Annan in the May of
'63. He was entered under Willie Robinson, who was
then the huntsman of the Carlisle pack, and learnt all
his dodges. "The merrie city" has loved the sport
since Dr. Hildebrand's day. From Cliff Bridge up to
Wrack Bridge is their favourite hunting ground on the
Lyne. The Caldew is always drawn blank, but the
Eden hears the music of their twelve couple "from
Cargo right up till Armthwaite." Irthing Foot is a

DR. GRANT AND "SANDY"

(FROM A PHOTOGRAPH BY W. BEATTIE, OF HAWICK.)

sure find, and " varra smittle for lying," and a wakeful passenger by the north mail may catch a glimpse
of them at work between Southwaite and Carlton, in
the bosky glades of the Petterill. As it fell out, after
the Doctor's first interview with Sandy, the Teviotdale pack " rather lost heart, and wanted a dog for
creeping." In short, the post of " a good grounding
tutor" to the Grant terriers was vacant, and Sanderson's bull terrier Billy, and the very apple of his
eye, seemed (as his owner put it) "*just the dog to 'tice
them in.*" He was 22lbs. weight when in condition,
and about two years and four months old when he
was booked by the North British and entered on the
duties of his office.

Sandy thus sums up his varmint history with all
the terseness of a Cresswell : " Billy played with his
first foulmart; his second bit him at seven months,
so he killed it; he won't fight with a hound, or kill
a hare or rabbit, and he won't notice a rat without
orders." His early promotion was thus strictly the
result of high training and continual self-denial. He
was not long in being entered to the otter, and he
had accounted for one on the Lyne (near which
Mr. Scott, a joiner, bred him) when he was only
twelve months old. His second had decidedly four
or five pounds the pull of him in weight. It had
been driven out of the Lyne into the woods the day
before, and but for a bloodhound belonging to Mr.
Standish's keeper it would have beaten them all
again. However, they worked up to it when it was

crossing a turnpike-road near Bracken Hill, and Billy looked, after the "clinching" finish, just as if he had been shot with peas through the head.

Sanderson was so impressed with the master of the Teviotdale, after they had exchanged minds, that he at once presented him with Billy—as a touching tribute to his gameness. Still his separation from Billy is only nominal, as he sometimes goes over, and takes the horn when the Doctor has a Wednesday meet, or any urgent case on his hands. Cheered by his old master's presence and the Cumberland dialect, Billy soon got to work in his adopted country, and Ringwood recognised him at once as a most able and business-like adjutant on the first day they were out. The old dog, who has had about enough of the worrying business, marked the otter under a root, pricked his ears, and "stood back for battle." Billy tunnelled up to the otter in a jiffey, and pulled it out by the under-jaw; but it was only 19lbs., totally without a tail, and not unlike a stoat about the face. The Doctor flew to the cry, and fished frantically in muddy waters for the tail. He is not to be trifled with at such a crisis; and yet "Sandy" would keep telling him that it was "only a diving pig," and that he saw (which was true enough) by the air bells on the water that an otter had just slipped down stream. At last he fished it up bodily, and held it quite fondly in his arms; but although he invoked the crowd all round, there was no plaid at hand, and so it was dropped among the terriers once more, and they finished it. On another occasion, when he was not in full costume, an otter fairly pinned him by the heel, and he never even felt it had hold of him till it tore his trousers right up to the knee.

After meditating on it all the winter of '63-64, and being assured by his friends that he never could do it, he succeeded in taking an otter alive! It was bolted from under a tree root, on the banks of the Ale, with Teddy hanging to its throat. The Doctor took his resolve in an instant, and plunged the pair beneath water to hide the otter from the hounds, and drown Teddy off. Just as he took hold of the otter by its neck with the left hand, it caught hold of him, and pinned him like an English bull-dog for some minutes. The pain seemed nothing in that hour of victory. He shouted to Walter to strip off his coat. Walter was in the water and his shirt-sleeves in an instant, and after delivering his "one, two" in the regular Grant style, on the heads of three old hounds, he wrapped the coat round and round the otter in his master's arms, and the deed was done at last. It was a very pretty dog otter of 15lbs. weight, and offered battle for a time whenever they looked into the box. On the seventh day it took fish from the hand, but it died soon after, the victim of its appetite. The Doctor's fingers were rather numbed and powerless after the bone-mill process, and he was tremendously bitten in other parts; but what was that to such a long-coveted trophy, fairly won in the teeth of a whole pack of infuriated hounds?

In his code of hunting rules he is inflexibly merciful to the hunted. He will not have the dogs aided by any cudgel play, and the man who loosed a fresh dog in the middle of a general engagement on the Jed was pretty speedily " pronounced in contempt." On one occasion the field begged him in vain to let them see a kill in a mill sluice. Nothing would move him. He tied up the hounds, and chased out the otter over the bank with the terriers into the Teviot, and when it took to a stronghold there, he would not dig it out. Let the " dry-shodded ones" also beware how he offers them a back for the future. In short, as his Boswell observes of him : " He's sic a man. I can hardly tell you what he is : he's here, theer, and a' roads ; always moving—he's likest a dog through the water of aught ;" and then, throwing all his cumulative force into the simile, " He'd think nought, wad Doctor, of swimming across the Solway, clicking an otter's tail."*

* Impurity has been hinted at in the case of the Dandie Dinmont terrier bitch " Meadow," so I send you this genealogical note " Stonehenge" says Sir George H S Douglas's Pepper was the sire of Meadow, and Schann her dam I fear there is difficulty and error here Besides others of the same name, Sir George had *three* Peppers of *fame* in succession, at Birsieslees Which of them Stonehenge means I cannot say, but it matters little, as *neither* was the sire of Meadow Her sire was a " young dog" which Sir George Douglas got from Mr. Brisbane He afterwards gave him to a clergyman in Yorkshire His name, I think, was Mustard, certainly *not Pepper*. This dog was bred by a " mud student" in the Coldstream or Cornhill district, and had for his sire a dog Dandie, bred by Mr Fram of Trows The dam of Mustard (that is the *paternal* grandam of Meadow) belonged to the said " mud student," but *where he got her or how she was bred has never been satisfactorily determined,* and it is solely on this point that the *imputed* impurity of Meadow rests. I am satisfied that the bitch was pure I have a great-grand-daughter of Meadow's at this moment, and it is the greatest beauty of its age and species I have ever yet seen. My Shamrock was by Sir George's Pepper III. (from Vixen),

After this " evening with the Doctor," we longed
for the summer and the waterside, and July found us
at Hawick once more. Sandy, with his white flannels, his red cap, and his brass-tipped pole, had come
from Carlisle by the train, and was seated snugly on
one side of the fire-place, discussing the science and
swagger of his darling Malakhoff, and the courage
of " old John Peel." The little fellow quite warmed
up as he told how the old white was always " a rock
hunter on stones and likeliest places," and how of
all dogs he most fulfilled his wish to "see them
swagger and hunt with natur." Of course we ad-
journed to the kennel, to see what was drawn for the
morning. Bobby, the ex-pugilist bull-terrier, never
goes out, as, if another dog comes among the pack,
he cracks it up like a nut ; and then there's a row,
which the Doctor, who knows the full advantages of
conciliation, hates of all things.

So, like the grim but " liberal-hearted dog" that
he is, Bobby stops to keep house ; and if any of the
young dogs are to be entered at the badger (which

---

he by Sir George's Pepper II. (from his Schann, bred at Bowhill by the Duke
of Buccleuch's "old grey Pepper"), he by Sir George's Pepper I. (from Mr.
Lang's bitch), he by old Stoddart's Dandie II (from Schann, bred by Scott of
Hindley, successor to James Davidson), he by Stoddart's Dandie I., who was
the most renowned sire of his day, and perhaps *the best dog of the breed that ever
lived*. This dog was out of James Davidson of Hindley's Gyp (Gypsie), but
his sire is unknown Vixen, the dam of my Shamrock, was by Mr. James
Scott's Shamrock (from Spice), he by Mr. Brisbane's Dandy, which came
from Annisfield, and was bred by Lord Elcho, who got his terriers from the
late William Reid of Jedburgh, one of the greatest breeders of the race at an
early period Reid obtained his terriers from James Davidson of Hindley,
Mr Dun of Whitelee, the Bells of Hindalea Mill, and others Spice was by
Mr. Brisbane's Shem, which leads us back *(paternally)* to Mr Sumner's Shem,
Mr Todd's Charlie, and again to the renowned " *old* Dandie" of old Stoddart
of Selkirk.—J G

once got under the kitchen-floor, and gave the Doctor two hours of hard digging), he is always ready,
as resident professor, to instruct them in the art. A
little white bull-terrier, which thinks nothing of a
badger three times its weight, is equally troubled
with the bump of combativeness, so it stops at home.
Billy was of course ripe for duty; and even old
Shammy was to have a treat There must have been
four more Dandies, Teddy, Tom, and Piper—which
latter was Walter's peculiar charge—and a most remarkable fossil called The Dwarf, which never tired
in its life. Add to these a black-and-tan English
terrier—Nettle—which was there on a visit after its
rabbit coursing labours, and followed the Doctor in
the most implicit faith over stone and scaur, won-
dering what it could all be about. Billy never goes
with the hounds, but conducts them with a patronizing
" confide in me" air about a mile out of the town,
and then trots back to accompany his master. No
dog has a higher sense of his position in the Cabinet,
and it is a "moral" to see him come home with the
pack, swelling with self-importance if the otter is at
the doctor's saddle-bow, or if he is generally satisfied
with the sport. In the town he is most popular, and
considering the number of houses where he is on
visiting and luncheon terms, it is well he can hold
his condition as he does.

"*Only two hours and a-half, mind !*" said the Doctor, before we went to bed; and at two o'clock precisely he appeared, "stern as Ajax' spectre," in his

boots and Garibaldı shirt, and ordered us up forth-
with. It had been a busy night in Hawick. Members and followers of the Buccleuch Hunt had arrived,
some from a radius of thirty miles round. The supply of hacks was exhausted, and about a score of men
had been scouring the country for horses, and made
nothing out. Some had got horses, and failed to get
saddles, though they had spoken with many a night-
capped agriculturist at the lattice. One of the latter,
as the story went next morning, was " put up five
times," till he wished Malakhoff and all the concern far
enough. An unhappy man who did come out with
nothing but his handkerchief on a sharp back-bone,
and thereby laid the basis of erysipelas, rued the day
he was born. A certain lender was most magnani-
mous, as he sent his black pony specially for ourselves, and a pair of spurs with it. There was a
good watch kept on the Doctor by the Hawick
lads all night, to see that he did not steal away
before them; but the lights in the bed and break-
fast-room windows reassured their *védette.*

Even the police lent a hand, and kindly took their
station at the head of " Walter's Wynd," while the
Doctor quietly slipped the most noisy of his pack, one
by one down it, to Walter, at the river side, before
he brought out the body. And now, by twos and
threes, the hunters, horse and foot, came dropping
down the street, in the misty morning, through which
the illuminated clock struggled faintly to tell of
twenty to three; and still some would not believe

Sandy's assurances, as he issued forth with his pole, that the Doctor was "not forrard." He is such, an early bird that they are never quite sure of him. Catch him lingering among the blankets or near the coffee-pot at dawn ! A mile-and-a-half's walk, and we were on the Knoll at Haughhead, with nearly half-a-hundred horsemen round us; and up came the Doctor, on Robin, at last. It was all Walter could do to prevent his being greeted by a regular " As-sheton Smith" chorus, which would have sent the otter flying down-stream, if he had heard it. The moon was still up, and the mist-wreaths were curling far too heavily along the river to permit of action; but it " lifted" about half-past three, and the Doctor peeled, and, tying his coat, with the scarlet lining outside, behind his saddle, as a token, set out to look for " my old friend, which has beat me these three years."

At last we stood on the north bank of the Teviot, and the deep bell of Malakhoff, who was whiter than the mist, in which he was working, rung out the maiden note of the drag, when they were scarcely over the first stretch of shingle, near the Trow Mill. They were so busy and musical for a minute or two by a willow-bed close to the dam, that some thought he must be at home, or that the Doctor would again have to prefer his celebrated request to be allowed to crawl under a mill-wheel after an otter, because *" I'm smaller than a dog; and I dursn't let them go there."* That is even going beyond Admiral Ex-

mouth's principle, " Never tell a man to do what you
dare not do yourself." He did it once this season
after Royal, and very nearly got drowned.

Then came a regular rattling burst over a very
rocky part of the river, the non-mounted straggling
along as they could over scaur and shingle, through
deep copses or oat crops, which left the dew-point
from the waist downwards, over meadows and along
the turnpike, sometimes in the water and sometimes
out of it, tailing off farther and farther, and so up to
Midshiels. Sandy and his pole ran well into the
front rank of course; and Walter on his bay pony
Meg Merrilies, with a great bunch of couples behind
him, had been sent forward to the dreaded drain.
Poor Mr. Morrell delighted to tell how Jim Stracey
took his celebrated four-miler to the head of earths
at Wood Hill, on the Milton Hall day, and "just
beat the fox by thrice the length of his boots—not an
inch farther." Walter was not so lucky, as the old
one had "lapped up" his fishing for the night, and
scuttled down stream the two miles post-haste,
leaving his kind regards for Ringwood, in the shape
of his damp seal on the stones at the drain entrance.
As for taking up the drain in any part, and putting
in the terriers, it was hopeless. When Sir Wilfred
Lawson and Mr. Hilton Wybergh used to come from
West Cumberland to touch up these rivers with Tom
Johnstone, they were very fond of this fastness, and
opened it in the middle, to make a lying-up place for
otters out of the water level. "*It's miles long,*" said

the Doctor, "*we had best draw on,*" and on we went once more.

Mr. Edward Maxwell was with us now, from Teviot Bank, and in the full spirit of the thing, with two hunters out, a grey, and Flibberty Gibbet, the winner of a Berwickshire steeple-chase. The mounted field had swelled to seventy-six, and very disgusted Will Williamson was when we told him about it that afternoon, and how, of course, we all looked out for him to drop on us through the Minto Woods, on The Kaffir. He would not have known what to make of it, as the river was fearfully low, and the Doctor on his chesnut was hunting his hounds, or rather watching them hunt (for he had trained them to do it all themselves); while Walter waited down-stream, to see if the varmint slipped over the shallows. Some of the weavers got so anxious here that they tally-hoed a water-hen; but there was good hedging for the mistake, as a few minutes after, the Doctor was cheering "Old John Peel." "*That's the right stuff!*" said little Sandy, as the old dog spoke again; and then Ringwood, the Palmerston of the pack, came fairly to the front, took the water at Denholme Cauld, and swam the drag right down the pool. This was a very finished bit of hunting, and the foxhunters sat down in their saddles quite enraptured, as the old dog leant in his stroke from side to side, throwing his deep bass tongue as the air-bells, with the rich hot scent in them, floated down to him. Then a loud tally-ho was heard at the weir, and the wild

Indian dance of some foot people, who had gone terribly forward and got the hounds' heads up, told that the otter was away. "*He's over! Lift 'em—lift 'em!*" was the cry from the infantry. "*Lift them, indeed!*" said the Doctor, who had kept his patience wonderfully, and only made one address, and that in the quietest tones, from the centre of the stream— "*Leave my old dog when he's swimming the drag all by himself—not for fifty otters!*" "*You won't kill them when you can,*" was the excited retort; but the Doctor is far too fair by dog and otter to do such unsportsmanlike things, and the foxhunters were quite with him on the point.

It was lucky for his credit that he was so firm, as the sport would have been in another minute quite a burlesque on a fox-chase, and he would have fairly split up his otter in the open. The otter saw that he was headed, and short of water; and crawling out at that point, he went through a bolt-hole in the hedge, and away over the oats. In a few minutes, Hassenden Bank Haughs were all alive with the melody, Walter and the Doctor riding to points, and Sandy lobbing away close by the tail hounds, cheek-by-jole with old Shammy, who shambled along like a young'un in his glee. The ring was fully a mile, but the white crops and the glen were no protection to him, with three foxhounds running the drag. It was no use facing the open any more; so he worked back to the Teviot at Spittal Ford, swam another half-mile, and was out of it again, and cut off a corner across the fields once more, to get to the Rule. They marked him to a stronghold at Bedrule; but the gamekeeper told the Doctor that they might dig till Christmas, and be no nearer to him. Then we drew Wells, and there was music once more for a few minutes; but it was only the remnant of an over-night drag, and we were glad to take refuge from the heat under the canopy of the giant beeches. The world was now up and doing once more, and the turnip-women leant on their hoes, and looked in wonderment at the *posse comitatus* as it swept by. We were so hot and parched, that it seemed as if we had been at work for hours, but it was only six o'clock.

Then we sauntered back down the Rule, over trunks of trees and amongst boulders and through farmyards, till we were in the Teviot once more; but the fun of the day was over. The horsemen stuck on well, and there was a ceaseless splash, as at least forty of them followed the Doctor up-stream. There, too, was a lad on the bare-backed donkey, who had been in front all day; but we looked in vain for the brave trio who hunted in the gig, and were so great at Spittal Ford. The sun got up, and our spirits went down. Ringwood, Teddy, and Billy would have no-thing to do with it at Lanton Cauld or Manselaws Hutches, a perfect Mamelon of otters, when they are not away fishing at the lochs or getting into traps on the Tweed. At Spittal Bank they spoke to it but very feebly, and Billy's depressed manner, when he

had completed his observations, decided the Doctor
not to persevere, even after his second whip had gone
for a spade. And so there was a conclave in a meadow, and the word was given for home; and be-
guiling the way with a most welcome breakfast at
Teviot Bank, we left the Doctor to thirty miles of
practice, and like Sandy, who was fairly wearied out
with three otter hunts in four days, we turned into
bed. Sleep would have been all the sweeter if we
had killed an otter. They will not come, like spirits
from the vasty deep when you call them, and like
many other things they are often there when they
are not wanted. We remember Mr. Gallon having
a blank week, and on the Sunday, when he was
walking in a friend's grounds, one of them "like an
eagre rode in triumph o'er the tide," and surveyed
him patronisingly as it passed. Those who know
him may "phanzy his feelinks." Another of our
friends, who hadn't found one for some time, stumbled across what he thought was his leviathan black
cat, at the edge of a corn field near his house, in the
moonlight, and for some moments kept objurgating
" Simon" for his lack of friendliness, till he glided
into the stream.

The hounds were well looked to, and had six hours'
rest before they were sent on, and next morning we
followed them to hunt the Ale. They were waiting
for us on the bridge at Ashkirk, an hour after sunrise, and a right pleasant morning we had, watching
them quest at their own sweet will among its co-

vered drains and up its rocky sides, steady as a rock amongst hundreds of rabbits, without any crowd to press them. Half the village were out at Lilliesleaf —the baker who seemed the spokesman, and as learned on otters as quartern loaves; the shoemaker with his thumbs in his apron armpits of course; the carpenter, with his rule peeping out of his pocket— all members of the great council which sat on the whereabouts of the brace of otter cubs, which had been in the drain. Alas! it was all to no purpose; we opened the drain in the middle, but Teddy and Billy soon said "Not at home," and on we drew again, sending the horses for a short space round by road.

The old white house with the trellises looked out from the quiet, deep-wooded park, as we skirted Riddell, and anon we were over the palings, and among the roses and rhododendrons of Lint Hill, which Sir Frederick Graham once had for his hunting-box. We did not linger among these calm delights. On we went, and the hounds went up with a rush to try every place where there had been an otter before, but the streams were far too low, and the game were off to far happier fishing-grounds among the bul-rushes. Then Sandy—who has ridden for "four-mile saddles" at Kingmoor, besides winning several foot-matches—mounted behind the Doctor on Robin, and gave up his pole to "Young Druid," and Walter brought up the rear with Shammy on his pommel, and old Malakhoff came as he could, shambling behind everyone, and so we reached the Teviot once more in procession by a four-mile cut, down by the Minto covers. Walter longed to pluck a fox-glove for Sandy's cap in honour of that celebrated find; but Sandy was true to his Border love—"*Give me the blooming heather!*" Spittal Bank was blank again; but the drag of our first friend, who had evidently revisited the glimpses of the moon, and dwelt quite leisurely on some stones, to eat and digest his trout, was most satisfactory at eleven, and ten minutes of beautiful music closed the day, and atoned for hopes once more deferred and drains blanked on the Ale.

The Jed remained, and on a cold September evening we stole away fourteen miles with the Doctor among the hills to Mr. Scott's of Merving's Law, a most hospitable farmer, on its banks. Three miles to our right, and marching with Liddesdale, was Hindley, the "Charlieshope" of Sir Walter Scott, near which the Rule and the Jed have their rise, but there is not a terrier on the place now. At six next morning we were all up and breakfasting. A lassie, who had known Royal as a pup at walk, was one of the principal features of the meet, with a bit of bread in her pocket for him, and then she revealed a wealth of information about Newcastle and its otter hounds, which at once charmed and puzzled the Doctor. We did no good dragging up the river, and the loch to which we wandered a full mile in the Sheriff's grounds was vocal with no challenge. So we turned

down the Jed ; but the mill-dam, and the deep black
pools under rocks which are tenanted with countless
wood-pigeons, knew him not that morning, and the
horsemen who rode for points and met us, got fairly
wearied out. Seven miles were over, and Ringwood
began to fancy there that he " smelt a Lollard in the
wind" at last. Into the water he went to complete
his commentaries, and tried for a broken air-bell, but
in vain. The whole pack took the hint without a
word being said to them, and for half-a-mile they
were feeling for the drag by the river side. Malakhoff's great white stern went waving like a banner,
and yet he dare not speak.

> " There was silence deep as death,
> And the Doctor held his breath
> For a time."

It was quite agony not to cheer Bellman, as they
turned short, and the young dog went to the front,
led them to a gate in a clover field, but not one yard
beyond, and then back to the river, where one loud
burst of melody round a tree-root proclaimed the
marking to ground. Billy was of course field-marshal,
and a very grimy one with his exertions, while Malakhoff stood like a white statue on the root-top, with one
eye on Billy and the other down-stream. It was
pretty close quarters, as Old John "received on the
nose." In vain did the Doctor dash into the stream,
and call off his dogs by a feint; in vain did "*did
the darlings follow me just like a brood of young
ducks*"; in vain did Walter stamp on the earth,

while others watched the bolt-holes. As the school-boy said of x in his quadratic equation, we had "run him to ground under a root, and never could get him out again;" and Walter wore no otter cravat through Jedburgh streets that day.

CHAPTER VII.

HAWICK TO MOSS PAUL.

" And we will pu' the bell sae blue,
    And the gowan opening free,
    Wi' the red, red tinge aroun its fringe
    On the links o' Linhope lea."

SCOTT RIDDELL.

The Links of Linhope Lea—Moss Paul Inn—The Wisp Club and its
    Objects—Scott of Priesthaugh—Old Lymeclench—His Weighing
    Match—His Opinion of an Orator's Attitude—Sheep and Shepherd
    Losses—Mr. Aitchison on Mountain Hay—Sheep Management—
    Davie Kyle—Yeddie Jackson—Dandie Dinmont.

"Let's *awa' and see the tups,*" is the unvarying
watchword on "the wild green links" of
" The Dales," and we cheerfully obeyed it when
Malakhoff was once more only marking in dreams.
Our route was up Teviotdale, with The Doctor and
" The Dwarf" to beguile the way, past meadows blue
with wood-pigeons, and Borthaugh, dear to Will
Shore and "the Bold Buccleuch," 'neath the beeches
of Branksome Tower, where "The Gover" won
and his foeman fell a few yards from the post. At
Branxholm Bridge, there opened on us the wide, rich
meadows of the Teviot Valley, in which lies Johnny
Armstrong, the great Border Reiver, happily un-
conscious of the dairy herd and half-bred sheep all

round him. Once at Frostley Brook, " that uncommonly cold name," and we are among the Cheviots at last, and the somewhat variable pasture changes into the uniformly hard and sound lea of far-famed Teviotdale. It ascends with a slight gradient as far as Moss Paul Inn, whose post-boys were therefore said to follow the Teviot to Hawick and the Ewes to Langholm.

> "The braw braes of Linhope
> And lofty Moss Paul"

have long been linked in song. Mr. Aitchison's ewes crop the Linhope Lea, and nothing but a peaceful knoll of that name is left to remind the Borderers how " Jeannie Hall's tongue" was wont to wake the echoes, when she spied Jemmy Telfer on another of his raids. Like that watchful wife or spinster, the inn is a tale of the past. Peacocks scream in those ancient silences, and there is no relic of the old *régime* save Jemmy Ferguson, who has been ostler, man and boy, " eight-and-forty years come Martinmas." The very stables of his heart have been unroofed before his eyes, "forty-two stalls," as he says so mournfully, "for bye looseboxes, and sic grand hay-lofts." Gowanlock, the landlord, lived to see the last of the posting, ten miles to Langholm and twelve to Hawick, and to hear the last horn tune of the mails and the Locomotive, but he was gone before the Engineer took its final journey in the June of '62. Black-cocks still club on the heights behind the house, where the

cocks of the district were wont to meet and feast
each Martinmas tide.

The Wisp Club, as it was called, began in 1826,
but it was given up about the time of Gowanlock's
death, as Mr. Aitchison and one or two others had
outlived nearly every one of those jovial comrades,
who discussed punch after dinner, and settled, after
many an animated debate and division, the average
prices of cattle and sheep stock, white and "tarry 'oo."
In its earlier days, when newspaper information on
these heads was so ill marshalled, the list of prices,
which was regularly registered in the Club books,
had an especial value, and they were often referred
to both by landlords and tenants, when a lease was
to be renewed.   No paper reported its proceedings till the late James Steel, whose statue stands in
the Carlisle market-place, came over with two
friends, and took one of his terse and pithy reports
home for the *Journal.*

Gowanlock was the treasurer, and always returned
thanks at these Club festivals, as we read in a record
quite yellowed by time, "with his usual simplicity and
readiness of manner."   Scott of Priesthaugh was one
of its choicest characters.   If he wanted anything
down to a horse to ride to Stagshaw Bank Fair, it
was "only for a minute."   He was also a good man
with hounds, and the best jumper of the lot.   When
he was regularly put up, he had jumped twenty-four
feet at one bound on the haugh by the side of the
Moss Paul Burn.   One of the Club was so pleased

with the performance, that he vowed then and there
—" *If I could do it like Priesthaugh, I would not envy
the author of* 'Paradise Lost.'" Like the old school
of the Regency, Priesthaugh was not averse to the
Fancy. *Oliver* v. *Carter,* at Gretna Green, was
quite "a leading case" with him, and he could illustrate Tom Sayer's style most accurately, when he
had seen him put on the gloves at Carlisle.

Elliot of Lymecleuch was known far and wide as
a Cheviot breeder and dealer from Falkirk to Stagshaw Bank, and round by Settle and Rosley Hill.
A great spirit was old Lymecleuch, "very quaint, and
a famous plucked one" Free Trade never had a
sterner advocate, and it and " Sailors' Rights" com-
prised his political creed. Why he took up the latter
topic no one could ever tell, as he lived inland, and
hardly knew a jibboom from a shoulder-of-mutton sail.
Gowanlock surveyed him, as each club day blenched
his locks, and did not decrease his waist-band, with
increasing admiration and silent awe. At last he
could hold out no longer. "*If I had a stable full of
horses,*" he said, "*with that man's constitution, in
these days of opposition coaching, I'd run Croall and
the whole lot of them clean off the road.*"

Peter Brodie of Clarielaw, who drew 23 stone, once
upbraided "Lymey" with being a "toom hemlock."
At this Laidlaw of Falnash bristled up, and although
it did not just look like "a good thing," he backed him
then and there for an even sovereign against Peter
on the scales. It was not recorded in the club

minutes, but Lymecleuch got the turn of the beam, and won with a pound to spare. In his light-weight days, when "the herds" fought the "weaver bodies" of Hawick, and Dandie Dinmont was said to have been quite competent to lifting two of the enemy, smashing their heads together and then dropping them, Lymecleuch was a most able lieutenant. Sheep and cattle dealers at that time were all very handy with their fists, and the muttered menace was common enough between the dances in the ballroom, "*You and I'll square up that little bit of business some day,*" and they invariably did. Lymecleuch, when occasion served, was as sharp with his tongue as his fists. When Sir Robert Peel's portrait after Lawrence had appeared, one of the leading debaters rose to address the Club, with his left hand resting majestically like the great statesman's on his hip, and heard Lymey's hoarse whisper in the midst of his finest passages: "*Has that guff gat a sair hench?*"

William Aitchison of Linhope, Menzion—

> "Him with the nut-brown hair and hollow voice,
> My kindest, warmest-hearted friend the Borderer,"

as sang the Ettrick Shepherd—was one of the chief speakers, and is still the Sellars of the Lowlands, with about twelve thousand Cheviot and blackfaced sheep in the three counties of Selkirkshire, Roxburghshire, and Peebles, and hoggs on turnips in Cumberland as well. Sheep-farming, both in the Highlands and the Lowlands, has been a weary business at times.

In 1772 much more than half the sheep in Scotland died; in January, '94, there was hardly a farm without a dead shepherd, and twelve were laid one Sunday in Moffat churchyard, after the week of the "Goniel Blast." Beattie of Muckledon lost seventy score of sheep, and the mouth of the Solway was literally dammed up with carcases. The Ettrick Shepherd has told of those gloomy days, and so has the late Lord Napier of Thirlstane Castle. Black frost did the deed in 1816 and 1837, but '60 was a still more fearful year, and in Ewesdale one farmer alone had to spend £1,500 extra to keep his stock in life at all. The value of the sheep which did not die was fearfully deteriorated, and the mortality helped to prove that of late years a larger-boned but softer sheep has been introduced to the Cheviot sheep-walks. In spite of the corn, lentils, and hay, from a fourth to a sixth perished in the South of Scotland. A great deal of Dutch hay was used, but it was sadly deficient both in weight and quality.

It was generally found that in such adversity no flocks throve really well, except such as had stores of mountain hay to fall back upon; and in a paper which Mr. Aitchison read before the Farmers' Club at Hawick, after the disaster, he dwelt most earnestly on its value. "Sheep," he said, "make up nearly half the rental of Scotland, and yet landlords are sadly remiss, and very little is done for them. Sheep drains, sheep stells, and March fences have done much; but more is exhausted on forty acres of wet lowland as would put a sheep-walk into form." Hay-feeding was not practised before '99, but nothing can supply its place in a fierce winter. "Partial feeding is worse than no feeding, as the sheep listlessly wait on it, and no longer, in the absence of fresh weather, search after regular food. Giving it in handfuls may do for calm weather, but sheep hecks will alone prevent the wind pilfering, and save one-third of the hay. Corn, beans, and bran, with hay, may enable the flockmaster with a heavy purse and willing heart to tide through the dreary time till verdure begins again, and nature dethrones art on the hills;" but still, mountain hay must be his sheet-anchor. Mr. Aitchison's recommendation was that every hirsel of thirty score should have four enclosures of a few acres each (with sheep-houses and hecks), which should be properly limed and cut, two and two, in alternate years. "Go in for mountain hay," he concluded, "and the storms of winter may drift up the valley, and tempests whistle over the hills in vain."

Till after New-Year's Day the Roxburghshire flockmasters never dreaded storms, but between Candlemas and the middle of April the heavy pinch comes. Land that abounds in every variety of keep of course makes the heaviest fleece. Towards Sletrig Head it is very good, and so it is towards Jed Head and Rule Water Head. When you get to the range of the Cheviots there are very few mosses to be found, and the fine lea grass does not afford

nourishing pasture to sheep during the early spring
months. The consequence is that the sheep are reduced lower, and shed their fleece more freely, when
the abundant herbage of spring returns. The mosses
of the other part of Roxburghshire prevent the sheep
from being so reduced in condition, as they do not
grow so high up the hill, and are therefore available
in a severe spring. Sheep in Teviotdale are especially subject to foot-rot; but the louping ill or
trembling between the old and new grass is not
known on the Cheviot Hills, or near the source of
the Tweed and the Clyde.

Smearing the sheep with tar has been given up for
years, and fish oil is objected to as gilding the wool,
and hence Gallipoli or olive oil is most used, except
where poisonous dips have to be resorted to. The
gimmers are generally put to the tup, but many of
them do not nurse their own lambs, and the cast
ewes after four crops are for the most part passed
over to Cumberland or Yorkshire through dealers.
Teviotdale is rather higher than Ewesdale in its
sheep rent, and the Roxburghshire sheep-farms
generally vary from £200 to £1,500, at from 7s. to
10s. 6d. per sheep. In the North of Scotland it is
computed to take 2 to 2½ acres to keep a sheep,
whereas 1¼ to 1½ will suffice in Roxburghshire and
Selkirkshire.

The Lowlands are not a wedder country, and save
Elliot of Hindhope and Pringle of Hindley, nearly
everyone parts with his wedder lambs. The High-

landers once liked to buy their tups as shearlings, but now they have taken more to two-year-olds. They used also to pay higher prices for them, but of late years the supply has quite exceeded the demand. There was a reaction in favour of the black-faces when the winter of '60 sent the Cheviots to par; but still, there are very few in Roxburgh-shire, and the Cheviots have not yielded up their Selkirkshire heights. In the upper walks of Lanark-shire, Dumfriesshire, Selkirkshire, and Peeblesshire the half-breds are found as high as 600 feet above sea-level on partly cultivated and partly hill holdings. Higher up, taste rather than elevation decides the Cheviot or " curly-horn character of the flock," un-less land be very bleak indeed. Sometimes black-faces are surrounded by Cheviots, and even grazed at lower elevations on inferior lands.

Davie Kyle of Broad Lee, beloved of Lord John Scott, could not be called, like Scott of Singlee, " a singular grand divine among sheep," but he was quite a shepherd's friend in his line, and though he might be led at first in the hunt, no shepherd could live with him till the close of day. He would not keep a shepherd who could not hunt, and his brother Arthur was nearly as keen. Kyle once ran against Routledge, laird of *The Flatt* at Christenbury Creggs, near Newcastleton. He never met a better man, ac-cording to his own confession, but Routledge thought himself as good, "bar louping the hags." Davie had no great hound language, but he loved to have all

the dogs round him when he had a dram, and then
he was highly colloquial, both with them and his
friends. He lived at the head of Hermitage Water,
and as a stock-farmer he had one peculiarity—his
tups must all be horned. Liddesdale and Teviot
Head were the cream of his country, and from New-
Year's Day till the middle of April he would be
there with a dozen or fifteen shepherds at sunrise,
each provided with a pocket pistol and a lump of
bread and cheese.

Old Kyle was a good wrestler and fighter for his
inches. In early days he was entered to hare, but
he changed to fox after thirty, and killed nearly 800
brace in his fifty years. Cauldcleuch and North Tyne
furnished some of his best foxes, which were all of
the greyhound breed, and took a world of catching.
He always knew them again, or said he did, and
spoke of them confidentially as old acquaintances.
The drag was generally hit off from certain syke
heads, and when the foxes did go to ground they were
always " spaded" and never smoked. Bolting them
for "an afternoon fox" was not the custom of his hunt.
His terriers were of the Dandie Dinmont breed,
and latterly, as the neighbours said, he looked like a
terrier himself. They were high and leggy, with
wiry coats of a red-grey, and black points on their
ears, tail, and feet, and got well over the bogs. The
smaller ones with their out-turned toes did a deal of
business, lying flat and working like a share plough,
when they were tunnelling up to " Charley." Kyle's

hunting mantle fell on Ballantyne of The Shaws, and his old dog Ringwood, the sire of nearly all the good ones about, not only won a first prize at Bellingham Show, but was running still in the spring of '6 t as a ten-season hound. Kyle himself died in 1861, but he did not lack the *sacer vates*, as his memory has been sung in eloquent strains by the son of Christopher North.

Adam or Yeddie Jackson of Fairloan, at the head of Liddle, was also quite a king of the hunters, and had been, as Tom Potts, a brother shepherd, said, at a "vast o' banes breaking." His opinion about whisky was that he should like to be "a whaup and live by suction," and he did live into his ninety-eighth year. He was quite deaf at last, and wore spectacles, and when they drew Deadwater Fells he would hobble to the house end with his grand-daughter to take a look at them, and told her to nudge him whenever there was music.

Davidson of Hindley or "Dandie Dinmont" did not care for a pack of dogs, and with a shepherd or two to help him, two hounds and the terrier bitches Tug and Tar, he was about a match for any Liddesdale fox. Be it foulmart, cat, or even a collie dog, he had a turn at it. He always went over to Abbotsford, and met Hogg, Laidlaw, Captain Clutterbuck, &c., at the annual coursing meeting, when Sir Walter, with Maida at his feet, watched from a hill the doings of what the latter evidently considered an inferior race. It was a merry night at Selkirk, and

the Club mull went round with Sir Walter's own
inscription, "May the Foresters never want a friend
at a pinch." Tom Potts, than whom there was no
hunting shepherd of "stronger bone and firmer pith,"
always said that Dandie "never hunted with the same
glee after he brought the wife hame." Still, he kept
Nimrod, a cross between a greyhound and a foxhound, to the last; and he rose from a sick chamber,
mounted "Dimple," and, with Nimrod at his heels,
obeyed the summons to see a bagman from Deadwater Fell turned out for him at Burnmouth. This
was in the year '19, and on the first Sabbath of '20
he died.

CHAPTER VIII.

HAWICK TO ST. BOSWELL'S.

" Charley, rest! thy warfare's o'er,
   You died the death, and bore the breaking ;
Dream of chicken poults no more,
   Hunting-day, nor bugle waking !
In the gorse no more you'll lie,
   No more you'll roam the fields of barley ;
John Musters' horn and Ringwood's cry
   No more shall wake thee, gentle Charley !

Annesley, Oct., 1843.   THE LATE R. B. DAVIS.

Will Williamson's Early History—His Opinion of a few Old Sportsmen—
The Buccleuch Hounds—Opening-up the St. Mary's Loch Country—
The Buccleuch Country—Will's Best Horses—A Walk through the
Buccleuch Stables—Moultan, Wyndham, Paymaster, Marotto, and
Star—The Great Marlfield day—The Moor and his Stable Comrades
—The Brood Mares—Will Shore and the Hounds.

WILL WILLIAMSON had never joined " those
rare fellows" at the grey dawn, but he had
fraternized with them at other times, and the above
was his professional opinion. We found him at St.
Boswell's in his old spot by the kennels, and still
hearty at 82, and often riding fourteen miles to see a
good draw in the Kelso country. He gave up the
horn in 1862, when he had completed his sixtieth
season with hounds, and during all his huntsman life
he had only varied from nine-stone-seven to nine-

stone-ten. Eildon's Hills tower behind his home;
but he did not speculate with us on

"The words which cleft Eildon's hills in twain,
And bridled the Tweed with a curb of stone:"

and that "triple height" only brought out the story
of how wonderfully a first-whip's mare crossed them
one day, and how she surprised them all by throwing
twins at night. Will's mind has always been of
an essentially practical rather than a poetic turn.
He has never visited Abbotsford or Melrose Abbey,
but he has once or twice run his fox up and down the
Tweed banks, and into the ivied ruins of Dry-
burgh. With Sir Walter he communed very little,
except in the pages of "Old Mortality," and had
merely a passing word when the baronet came out on
the road to see the hounds passing to cover. Scraps
from the lonely tombstones of the Covenanters in
the covers about Dreghorn and Woodhouselees on the
Pentland Hills have been his favourite out-a-doors
reading; and at home, a Delmè Radcliffe and Beck-
ford, "with the Latin interlined," serve as his
hunting classics.

He was not born, but "bred up from a month old"
at Pencaithland, six miles from Haddington. His
father was groom to Colonel Hamilton, and his only
brother, a major-general in the Bengal army, died
five or six years since. The Colonel and Mr. Baird,
grandfather to the present Sir David Baird, had a
joint pack, and hunted East Lothian. They were
both good men with hounds; and when Mr. Baird

was on Bounty or the "Eclipse chesnut," and
Colonel Hamilton on Ben Yalder, very few, if any,
could go before them. When little Will, who took
messages on a pony for the Colonel, and then rose
to be pad groom, first knew that country, the
"great corn and potato garden" was only yellow
with gorse from Dunbar to Soutra Hills, and held
many a "traveller," who had stolen down from the
rock and heather of the Lammermoors to the low
country for meat. Dirleton and Gosford were
barren links bound down with sea-bent, and tenanted
by rabbits and sandpipers. Haddington Hill Park
and Amisfield were in the centre of a wild moor, with
whins high enough to hide Phantassie's horses when
his lad went to seek them. The country adjoined
Berwickshire on the Dunglass property in the east,
and touched Midlothian at the Elphinstone Tower
grounds. When the joint mastership was given up,
Henry Duke of Buccleuch united the East and
Midlothians, and hunted them three days a week.

Will's father, who was one of the whips,
then laid aside his scarlet, and became head
groom at Pencaithland. His son still rode after
the Colonel, but the chase lure was too much
for him when he was on duty one day near Haddington. The Colonel was speaking to a farmer
at the turn of a road, as the Duke's brought their
fox across it, carrying a great head to Saltoun Wood,
and when he looked round, after his colloquy,
lad, horse, and coat were gone, and were well

up at the finish when they ran to ground in Ormiston Wood. The Colonel told the boy's father not to be angry with him when he got home, and things went on as usual till a few months after, when Mr. Baird became commander of the East and West Lothian Fencible Cavalry, and in 1799 went " soldier·ing through England." Sudbury and then Newmarket were the head-quarters of the regiment when Hambletonian and Diamond were all the talk ; and in one of Will's rambles on The Heath he saw Sam Chifney and Will Edwards ride their maiden race as feather-weights* together. Old Chifney had passed his zenith; but between his son Will and the Scottish stranger there sprung up a fast friendship. The former sealed it at parting with a pair of braces, the buckles of which have done duty on generation after generation of straps to this hour; and the latter in later years, when the great days of Priam and Zinganee were in the dim distance, reciprocated with a suit of Scotch tweed.

Another two years brought these military wanderings to a close, and at twenty Will became second whip to the Duke, with John King as huntsman and Frank Collisson as first whip. His second and first whip probation lasted for fourteen seasons, and in 1816 he got the horn. The first fox he ever killed was from a meet at Armadill-toll-bar, and they

---

* Will Edwards won this race over the last three miles of the *B C*, on a two-year-old colt of the Hon C. Wyndham's, which was afterwards second for the Derby Will was fetched from school behind a boy on a pony, and was returned in the same fashion after the race

pulled him down after seven or eight miles before he could reach Callender Woods.   Mr. Baird managed the hounds for his Grace. They were still a subscription pack, with kennels at Dalkeith, East and Mid Lothians, and part of East Berwickshire as their country, and Pencaithland and Newbyth as outlying kennels. Mr. Bailey of Mellerstain, "as good a racing as he was a hunting man," hunted Roxburghshire and part of Berwickshire, as far as Foggo Moor in the Dunse country; and Will always speaks of him most reverently as "an old Roman, polite to all and bow to none."   Mr. Hay of Dunse Castle joined Mr. Bailey for a season; and ten years after he had the Dunse country for himself, and, joining it with the West Lothian, moved backwards and forwards.

There was a Hamilton pack, with Holy Town as its kennel, before Will became a Buccleuch "colt," and its Wild Irish huntsman, Merton Bourke, "rode over everything in Lanarkshire. Stars and ribbons were wont to cluster in those days of the Regency round the Newmarket cockpit, and there were mighty Scottish "Gillivers" as well. Occasionally a carriage full of cocks would come from Lanarkshire to the East Lothian, which paid return visits. A celebrated in-go took place at the "George" at Haddington, and it was long remembered how one of the cuckoo sort had knocked a black-breasted red clean out of the front window, and how the town fully expected to see a brace of bulldogs tumble out next.

The Duke of Hamilton was a tremendously hard
rider, and the groom's horse died following him on
his trotting chesnut from Edinburgh to Hamilton.
It was bought at Longtown, and Mat Milton
offered his Grace one thousand guineas in vain on
behalf of the Prince of Wales. "I can ride a
thousand-guinea horse as well as his Royal High-
ness" were the proud terms of the refusal. The Earl
of Lauderdale, then Lord Maitland, kept harriers at
Dunbar, and "understood horses and hunting well."
The late Lord Minto was also "a good rider, and
all the sons more or less met with my approba-
tion in the field." The Hon. John Elliot kept good
harriers near Hawick, and was the "best judge of
hunting of them a'." Will, in fact, often looks back
to "my three best heavy weights"—Elliot, Tweeddale, and Saddell. The first Lord Melville, says
this inexorable and impartial historian, "was always
knocking horses up." He was a heavy weight, and
Lord Advocate and Treasurer of the Navy, and an
earlier generation would speak with awe of the
waggon-loads of guineas which went to pay the
sailors. He got Will's brother the cadetship,
and Will retains his East Lothian silver hunt buttons
in memoriam to this day. Lord Elphinstone of Cum-
bernauld was also "a great authority"; and Major
Maclean of Ardgower, on his "very grand mare," and
Mr. Wallace of Kelly "had nothing to beat them."
The Major gave Will five shillings to buy his first
pair of spurs; and the other, an "awful Radical, but

first-rate sportsman," stood him his first tip of a
guinea.

Earl Moreton of Dalmahoy was also "a good
sportsman and rider;" and Lord Kennedy would
"follow all things, ride occasionally, and catch as
many grouse as another man shot, at least so they
said when they joked him. "   Mr. Campbell of
Saddell, "so full of his fun," was often one of
the field; and so was Mr. White Melville, "a first-
rate man from Fife."   Sir David Baird, who once
hunted Ayrshire and Renfrewshire, had many a day
with the Duke; and Mr. Hay mounted Will in the
only season that he ever accompanied Captain Baird
to Melton, and saw Tom Sebright and Dick Burton
at work.

About this time he caught a glimpse of "Gentleman Shaw."   His only comment on him is more
curt than scientific—that he "got well into his boots;"
but there is a world of hidden meaning in it.   Will
Crane of the Fife he considered "a devil to ride and
fall; he'd seen more of the world than all the huntsmen in it."   Lord Campbell he never saw but once,
when the hounds met at his place near Jedburgh. His
lordship came out on to the lawn to see them,
and the veterans of the English wool-sack and the
Scottish pig-skin shook hands.   Mr. Liston "nearly
as good a horseman as he was a surgeon," was also
seen as much on this side of Edinburgh as he was on
the other.   Will always says that much of his good
health "was owing to having him to look after me,"

and "there was always room for me at his house if I went to Edinburgh or London."

With the exception of Mr. Frain of Kelso, Will was never painted by any one except Mr. Frank Grant. Of him and his early studies in Edinburgh he retains one precious memento in Ruby and Blue Maid, which went in from Dalkeith to be drawn, and "had a narrow escape for their lives." "There were hounds," he observes, "in that studio, and all over the place—hounds from Fife and all places, till the mistress said she would have them hanged." These two, were only sketched in by the young artist, and Mr. Watson Gordon finished them. Darling's head is by Mr. Grant, and a present from the late Sir David Baird; and the silver fox's head testifies to Mr. Campbell of Saddell's recollection of the hunts, in which they had ridden side by side. With all these relics and reminiscences of the grand old school, we can hardly wonder at one great article of Will's belief: "The young'uns are a deal mair consequence in their ain opinion, and we don't ken if they're so much better. Faith! it's quite true."

As to hounds, Pleader began him from Mr. Bailey's kennel in 1816, and for this slice of Lonsdale Jester and Yarboro' Tidings he gave the huntsman £1. Saladin, the sire of Osbaldeston's Furrier, was very old when he came, and did no good, whereas Lonsdale's Javelin, a bigger dog and a capital hunter, did a great deal. Harewood Merlin came in a young draft, and had a wall-eye like a hawk, to which he owed his name. Lonsdale Harper brought in blindness, and as Will observed in italics, "*Mark that down as a beacon!*" Drake's Bajazet, Sykes's Trickster, "a capital finder," and Yarboro' Dashwood, the sire of Driver, all did well, and even Foljambe's Vaulter, "a great flat-sided soft brute," got rare stock. He was the only hound that Will ever left on the road home, as he tired to nothing in the Hirsel country, and had to stop at the schoolmaster's near Blinkbonny. Still, his Viner and Vesta (whose brother Victory was drowned in a conduit) he considers "the very best I ever saw." Rutland's Bertram he dismissed in his own quaint way : " He was not knocked on the head, but sent to me ;" Rutland's Fervent was "a wild flyaway beast—Will Goodall shot flying about him a bit ;" Rutland's Rocket was " well enough ," Rutland's General " was sent here as a good asylum, but his son General was a capital finder, and in look and disposition a thorough foxhound —that was my best hit from the Rutland kennel." Assheton Smith's Senator was used a great deal, and was "varra weel ;" York and Ainsty Tarquin, "a plain dog but a good stallion," was the sire of Trywell, " who would do her best to knock over her fox, and then would never join in breaking it up." Lunar— " that's a sort of astronomical theory—when Lord John Scott saw this name in the entry, he dropped heavily on to me about being among the stars. They chaffed me about everything, Lord John and all the rest of them. No one rode a fast run better than Lord John—quite a master at it."

The Fitzwilliam Feudal crossed well with the Marquis blood, and his daughter Helen was the dam of Hector. Monitor of this sort was a great hound, and Driver, his sire, a wonder. In the best run that Will ever had, and the only one he ever wrote an account of, they had very nearly lost their fox, owing to a very large sheep fair. Driver picked up the scent, and almost knocked Will's horse down by the crash with which he came through his forelegs, and at last pulled his fox from below a conduit near Carfrae Mill. The run was over a rough and wild country; and the rougher and wilder the country, and the more liberty for a wild fox, the better Will liked it. Finding on the Lammermoors or the Cheviots was his delight : "There were my best foxes; that's my taste—it's not a common one." Penicuick of course suited him, and he was quite in his element opening up the country by St. Mary's Loch, "an outlandish place," where none but Willie Tweedie, a few old hounds, and "all and sundries that could fire a gun" had ever been before. "Mercy! no one else would go near it. I got away from the Edinburgh rattle, deil a one would ride in it. One of them had such a tumble on the Pentlands; he put his hand to his face and felt the blood— *'Mercy on us, Williamson ! I'm spoilt for the parties'*— deil do I care about the country, so that the hounds and the fox have their liberty."

The hounds do not go higher now than Bowhill, where the Duke lives during the hunting season. His Grace's ardour for the sport speaks best through the fact that on the last day of the 1863-64 season he rode forty miles to cover, and as many back after hunting. Twelve miles is the average distance of the meets from the kennel, but at times they go more than twenty, and nearly up to Coldstream. The Kelso country is the biggest, with the hedges, banks, rails and doubles below, and stone walls higher up : wire fences have increased and multiplied on the hills; but there are plenty of hunting gates, with posts eight or ten feet high as beacons, at the Hunt's expense, so that the "iron age" here is no symptom of foxhunting decay. "Faldonside — one of the flyers of our hunt—you may put that down Mr. Druid" — twice over made himself independent of them, by hanging his coat over the wires, and then jumping them—"a fact for Scottish history," as Williamson observed when he heard of it. The Hawick, Chapel Hill, and Drinkstone side, and from Wolf Lee to Yetholm, are quite the "Turkey carpet country," "all grass and no fear of bogging." Most of the foxes lie in the heather at the bottom of young plantations, and the earth-stopping account is a pretty heavy one. There are some good ones at Mellerstain and Bow Hill, and Eller Bank Wood, and many others along the Tweed. Gala Law is a great gorse, and Chapel Hill, Wilton Bourne, and Grundiston, all made covers, with a belt

of trees round them to bring them within the arson
clauses. Cessford is, after all, the great cover of the
hunt. It is a grand wild moor in Roxburghshire, with
rare foxes, and nothing but grass hills on their inva·
riable line to Bludie Laws. The sport is generally
best in the spring, and February is a capital month.

On Monday they hunt the west side by Riddell
and Mount Teviot, on Tuesday the Jedburgh, on
Thursday the Kelso, and on Saturday the Leader
Water. Will always says that he never had a
greater treat than seeing his Grace ride Paymaster
over the walls in the Riddell country, and he adds,
" If the country was half up to his knees he would
go as well as ever, and still make good his fence."
In fact, he thinks the brown quite the best he ever
saw, and for ten seasons he never gave his Grace a
fall. The grey racer Richmond, Stuffie Major, and
Stuffie Minor were all Will's particulars, and so were
Sam Slick and Snip, which figure respectively in the
Grant and Frain pictures; but the roan mare Sofa
was his delight, and " lost neither pace nor pluck for
twelve seasons."

Mr. Hodge, the stud groom, succeeded Mr. Marshall
six years ago, and has just completed thirty years of
service in the Buccleuch family; and Charles Sharpe,
brother to Teddy Sharpe, the Newmarket jockey, is
the " Dick Christian" of the stables. The horses
move with the hounds between St. Boswell's and
Dalkeith, and generally leave the former place about
April 25th. The stables are beautifully kept, and

everything except the horses is out of sight. Every
new horse is measured for his Cuff saddle, unless
there is one in the collection to fit, and the names of
the wearers are all labelled above them, and in purple
morocco under the flap. "Moultan's" and "Wyndham's" labels still hang as escutcheons, and so does the
bridle which his Grace used when he was a fellow com-
moner at Trinity. Wyndham was bred in the Berwick
country, and served the Duke for eighteen seasons.
His Grace did not ride him so much latterly, and he
was such a perfect fifteen-three model, both in mouth
and temper, that he was more a sort of all-comers'
horse, carrying ladies or any visitors by winter, and
acting as Captain Bowman's charger at Dalkeith in
summer. Lord John rode him at times, and revelled
in him over the stone walls on the moors, and skim-
ming over the fine turf of Drinkstone and Chapel
Hill. His Grace rode Moultan once a week as his
first horse, and he broke down with him over a stone
wall near Alton in his fourteenth season. He was
brought home to be painted by M'Cleod, and then
he was shot, and buried with Paymaster, who was
also twenty-three. He was very handsome and
fast, and fencing no object, and as Mr. Hodges says
rather despairingly, "I may ride a dozen hacks to
death, and never find his equal again." He was by
Wintonian, from his Grace's celebrated Rosa Mar
by Springkell out of Helen Mar by Viscount. This
grand combination of Caledonian Hunt winner blood
was bought at Mr. Bailey of Mellerstain's sale, and

had seven foals at Dalkeith, six of which were ridden by his Grace. Marotto by Valparaiso was her half-brother, and did the Duke good service for seven or eight seasons. Still, he was never very canny with hounds, and Williamson was always "jealous of him" on this head. He was a short-legged, dark chesnut, of greater power than Moultan, and generally got his stock bay with short legs, and very good the Midlands thought them.

A big grey skin, which Mr. Hodge preserves along with the feet of Moultan, was all that we saw of Star. During eleven seasons he had shown no symptoms of failure, but in the March of '64 his Grace found the field riding away from him in a sharp forty minutes from Minto. The old horse seemed as willing as ever, but nature could do no more, and the second horse, Paddy from Cork, was called up. The grey was bought, "pedigree unknown," from Mr. Kench in the Dunchurch country, and stood nearly sixteen-two. Just three years before, his Grace had ridden him and hunted the hounds in one of their hardest days, with a second fox from the little whin at Marlfield by Marchcleugh across the old Roman road, without touching Bludie Laws, past Kinnearton and straight over Bearhope Hill, pointing to the Horse Shoe plantation. Here he was headed, and bent towards Gateshaws, where the hounds got to slow hunting, and were stopped near Moor Battle after $3\frac{1}{2}$ hours. Only four or five were up beside his Grace, young Hope of Luffness on another grey,

"The Indian," Elliot of Clifton, Swan on his chesnut, and David Henderson.

The hunters and hacks are all washed over with
tepid water when they come in. Four of them are
brought into the place together, and two grooms are
occupied about forty minutes over each. They are
clothed and left quiet for an hour and a half, and
then dressed over for the night. They also get linseed tea when they come in, a pail at twice, and have
their feet stuffed with linseed, fore and aft, twice a
week. The linseed is always bruised at the mill just
before the stones want setting, and then mixed with
water. It leaves a fine oily mixture in the hoof when
it is picked out next morning. But for this care the
feet would often be very much bruised, although
the blacksmith, who always accompanies the horses,
bevels out the inside of the fore shoe, to try and
prevent them from picking up flints.

There are fifteen servants' horses, and Will
Shore, who has just finished his third season,
has five. Rebecca by Isaac of York, a game light
mare, goes into the light-grass and moor country on
Tuesday, Ilston does the hilly work on Saturday, and
either Chesters, Titus Oates, or Tipperary is certain
to be told off for the stiff fencing on the Kelso side
each Thursday. Ilston is one of the best in the
stud, and was bought by Lord Walter in Essex, and
Williamson's comment on Chesters hits him off to
the life : *" There's a multum in parvo, quite a contradiction to the Paymasters—he's so short-legged. The*

Duke's Chamberlain bought him." "Old Terrona" has furnished a couple of Ravenhills, and they and Milsington by Russborough, who can stride away nearly as fast on the moors as his sire did when he stole up to Voltigeur at the St. Leger finish, are the cream of the whips' horses. The Duke's twelve are all thorough-bred, and Earl Dalkeith and Lord Walter have each six or seven. Young Paymaster is a little on leg like all his sort, and great in a light country; Barnton by Barnton is a little plain in the quarter, but not in the head, and strips deeper than he looks.

There is a nice, airy, and yet wear-and-tear style about the chesnut Baron by Bolingbroke, who is up to much more weight than Kate, a pretty-looking little Jericho mare. Birdcatcher claims Birdsnest, a fast daughter from the dam of Bridegroom, whom his Grace has ridden for six seasons past, principally among the heavy fencing on the Kelso side, for which Pale Ale, who was bred by the late Sir Tatton Sykes, has always had a standing retainer. Lord Stamford bought him from the old baronet, and he was sold for 160 guineas at the Quorn sale, and was, in fact, the only lot that Mr. Hodge bid for. There is an old-fashioned look about him, which would make him unsuitable for a flying Midland country. He seems well up to 15 st., and therefore his Grace rides with some $2\frac{1}{2}$ stone in hand. Paddy from Cork by Blight, and the only stallion in the stud, was just out of Sharpe's

hands; and Newton showed all the fine old fashion of
the Belzoni blood, with arms, shoulders, and hind legs
moulded for jumping, but he is a little gone in
his back, and is the only one of the lot that had a
bar sinister.   The Fawn was a light sherry bay, and
a little shy about the ears; and Dandy, a little quality
bay, and Undergraduate, an appropriately-named
Birdcatcher hack from Simmonds's of Oxford, stood
in the same stable with The Moor.   To our eye this
dark-brown, with the game, lean-fleshed head, was
the nicest and handiest horse in the stable, not up to
the same weight as some of them, but looking, as
Templeman said of Cossack, " as if you could place
him anywhere for the asking." Lord Walter's
" Mugger" was by Marotto, and so was Earl Dalkeith's Garotter, "a right stamp," as Williamson
said.

Canteen, Scarboro', Marotto, Wintonian, Oakley,
and Valparaiso have all furnished their contingents
at one time or another to the Buccleuch stable, and
the present young stock are principally by Leaming-
ton, Kingfisher, and Sir John Barleycorn.   There
are four mares and their produce at Dalkeith; and
" the old old blood" is handed down in Flirt, a nice
short-legged daughter of Rosa Mar.   Pearlin Jean
is there as a remembrance of Cawston paddocks, and
Songstress by Birdcatcher, which would have been
an annuity to many a Yorkshire shower.   In carriage horses his Grace is steady to bays, as the
Earl of Wemyss is to blacks.

We saw the hounds again in the morning, as Shore on Laaykirk and the whole pack accompanied us along the hard frozen road for the first five of our one hundred miles straight across Scotland. Among our party of "Guides" was the old slate-coloured Marquis, rather down in his toes, but still a standard hound with his Grace, and handing down his Assheton Smith Senator blood through some very useful stock. Shore summed him up best as "good when he's there, but he can't always get to it." The nice topped Trimmer by Hector is of the same season as Marquis, but a harder runner, and there is no need to look beyond old Trywell to see whence he and his neat sister Tempest derive their spigot noses. Barring this little defect Tempest's head and neck are very neat. There are no harder and honester workers than Comus and Chanticleer by the Grove Duster from Belvoir Comfort; and under rather a shabby black guise we have old Gulliver, "the lowest-scented of the lot." Harriet was one of the good Yarborough Dashwood sort that Williamson is so sweet on for their own and Driver's sake, and he has always been puzzled to think why she should be his "lady with the pig-mouth." Victor cannot be said to be pig-mouthed or mouthy, as he never has a word to say in cover or out, but in a road difficulty there is no better counsellor. Selim, whose stern seems never at rest, and Splendour are good ones of the Harlequin sort; Old Susan is another rare bitch at a road, and she and Tempest one day

held the line and helped each other for a mile and a
half, near The Bellion in the Jedburgh country,
when nothing else could speak to it. But we had
gradually got round the side of the Eildons past the
three small ridges of gorses which so often hold a
fox, and wishing Will as satisfactory a season as his
first, we bent away to the right for Faldonside.

CHAPTER IX.

FALDONSIDE TO DALGIG.

"Was it absolute truth, or a dreaming
Which the wakeful day disowns,
That I heard something more in the stream as it ran
Than water breaking on stones—
Now the hoofs of a flying moss-trooper,
Now a bloodhound's bay half-caught,
The distant blast of a hunting-horn,
The burn of Walter Scott?"

ALEXANDER SMITH

A Peep at Faldonside—The Landseer Gallery at Bowhill—Over Minchmoor—The Ettrick Shepherd—Sheep in Ettrick Forest—Points of Blackfaces—Crossing with Cheviots—Lanarkshire Breeders and Fairs—The Clad Score—Curling Enthusiasm—A visit to Dalgig—Scotland Yet and Canaradzo

"IT's a regular Noah's Ark," said Will Williamson, when we told him that we were bound for "Faldonside." Mr. Nicol Milne lives in this snug eyrie on the banks of the Tweed, just above the Abbotsford ferry. Wood and valley backed up by "a Cheviot hill" compose a pleasant landscape from the front door, and the swans and wild-ducks besporting themselves on the lake gave proof of the incisive character of Will's simile. There is a considerable extent of grass land, on which pure shorthorns have been settled for fully thirty years. Mr. Milne has always sworn by the St. Albans blood, and his two tribes, The Prendwick Princess by Bachelor (1366) and The Rosebud by Emperor

(1784), have both got it in their veins. The former came from Crisp of Doddington, and Mr. Milne went to pluck the Rosebud from Holywell when Crofton was in his zenith, and winning everything with his Gainford heifers. He used Tretter's Dusty Miller (9055) and Raines's Lord Stanley (18277); and in Ettrick (14518) by Tam Glen (10780) by Ethelred (5990) he combined a treble Gainford dash. The Princesses and Rosebuds are closely crossed in; but their short legs, fine hair and general robust stamp show that when you have made a really good foundation, you need not heed the popular cry against in-breeding. Mr. Milne has now adopted the Towneley plan of prefixing the bull's name, and thus "Wolviston Rosebud" and "Napier Rosebud" were both among his herd-book dames.

The Cheviot ewes on his hill hirsel are kept up each year by lambs from the Menzion flock, and he takes three crops of half-bred lambs from them. His flock of half-bred ewes are kept below the hill, and the lambs of both by a Border-Leicester go annually to St. Boswell's fair. The three-parts-bred lambs made 32s. 6d. last year for Fife, and the cast half-bred ewes 42s. for Mid-Lothian This system of breeding prevails between Galashiels and Edinburgh, where there is a great deal of artificial grass. Three-parts bred ewes are very rare, and only one farmer in the district h asadopted half-bred tups.

The pigs have been pretty nearly as long about

the place as the shorthorns, and came originally from
Mr. Nutt, a solicitor in York, who fled in his moments of leisure from calfskin in the smooth to pigskin
in the rough.   It was to Yorkshire that "Faldonside" also looked for a cross, and found it in one of a
prize pen of Lord Wenlock's.

A bull with a fine deep forehand, and of course
with a dash of St. Albans, thrust his head over the
rails for a word, as we passed to the stables.   There
we found George Goodfellow, who would remind us
of a celebrated ex-jockey grown a little older, as
cicerone to three hunters, and a grey pony " *as good
as she's bonny.*"   There was Empress by Marotto,
the heroine of the wire-fence feat once on the Cheviots and again in the Vale, but George was not
surprised at it, as she " *always goes as straight as an
arrow.*"   The Falstaff mare has not been tried as yet
in this high art jumping, but she seemed to have
quality and cleverness enough for anything, as you
stand behind her and look at those hocks and
quarters, and the pleasant white reach head with
which she was always saluting the terrier " Dunny"
below the manger.

Pepper and Jock are two more of the Dandie breed,
and in direct descent from the "Charlieshope" terriers.
Greyhounds live only in stone on each side of the
door ; but John Jardine, an old class-mate at Galashiels, and the sharer of many a holiday with the
gun and bag, fell back on his Faldonside recollections for a name for one of his Judge-Ladylike litter,

and took care that the bearer of it should be a good one. Still, if there are now no long-tails, "The Ark" is rich in liver-and-white pointers, with beautiful heads, and a "Gordon setter" shared the yard with a blue-mottled "Culley," or a "Belton Blue." Tame wild-ducks are tenants in common of the pond with Aylesburys and Rouens; Lauderdale and speckled Dorkings seemed to start from every laurel bush at their master's tread, but the pheasant sort had nearly died out from the lack of a suitable cross, which Mr. Milne cannot find. As for the Russian dog with a three years' clip on him, we shunned, and with good reason, him and his hole in the wall, and then set the mare's head westward by Peebles, Biggar, and Douglas for Ayr.

There was no help for us by rail, even if we had desired it, as the line only runs to Selkirk. In one respect it is unique as far as it goes. A woman was waving the safety-flag at Galashiels, and at Abbotsford a woman was station-mistress, and, as a passenger observed, "ringing her bell like anything."

We halted for an hour at "Sweet Bowhill," which was now under the influence of a nipping frost, to see Mr. Grant's picture of Williamson on Sam Slick, with Hannibal, Falstaff, Dainty and Destiny round him. A beautiful likeness it is of a loyal, old family servant, who is painted, by his special desire, raising his cap for a covert-side salute to his master. He also figures on a grey in a fast thing, from the same hand, in which Sir David Baird, Mr. Campbell of Saddell,

and other crack Scottish "green collars," dead and
gone, are all stealing away, and on which the Duke
of Buccleuch and Earl Wemyss can look and renew
their youth. The billiard room is quite a Landseer
gallery. Its prints are " artist's proofs" in the very
highest sense of the phrase, as Sir Edwin had been
over them with his chalks. It was delightful to trace
his sense of what points the engraver's art had been
unable to reach ; how vigorously he dashed his broad
touches into "A Distinguished Member of the
Humane Society," the reaper lass's kerchief, and *one*
of the interiors with the baby and the keery ; how he
stayed his hand from the hound and terrier troop in
the " Otter Spearing ," and just played with the
ripples and the waterfall in the Otters' Fishing ;
how reverently he touched the pall in the " Shepherd's Mourner," and how he just glazed the eye of
the dead standard-bearer and his horse in " War,"
and faintly heightened the smouldering of the
shell.

We had no time to go round by Yarrow, and we
cared less to see it in its wintry garb. Williamson
had told us that he " knew nae mair" about the
country we were going through than he did of Nova
Zembla. We did well enough as long as we held
on past Newark's Tower, over whose ruined gables
a hawk was hovering ; but when we gave up all
thoughts of Yarrow and " still St. Mary's Loch,"
and struck to the right up a bridle road, among
deeply-frozen ruts over Minchmoor to Peebles, it was

worse than a weary way. Large floes of ice stretched
across the path, and, mare in hand, we had to climb
the hill to get round the syke head, and more than
once we were all on our sides together. After this
rough experience of sheep-walk solitudes, it was like
enchantment to look down into a rich vale once more
among woollen manufactories, half-breds, and holly
standards, macadamized roads like iron, and rusty
iron gates, inscribed with 1745, leading up an avenue
to the ancestral grange of the Earls of Traquair, that
breathed of old family portraits and English quarter
sessions. "The shallow brawling Tweed" was ice-
bound, and there were hundreds of torch-light
skaters upon it as we cantered past, and fairly groped
our way to Biggar among such shady ways by Stobo
Castle, that the very darkness, as at Belvoir, might
be felt. It lingered, in one sense, at Biggar, as the
landlady, after going into committee with her husband and the waitress on the point, sent up the
latter as a deputation to inquire if the muffins we
had asked for were "a kind of pickle."

We own to a little twinge at having been so near
Ettrick without seeing it; but the mare had done
her two-and-forty miles as it was, and not even a
winter's tale was to be got out of the spot now that
the "Shepherd" was gone. His old associates speak
of him as a good runner at weddings till he was well
on to middle life, and he certainly acted up to the
spirit of the lines,

> "Nae wooer like the laddie
> Who rows me in his plaidie,"

as he would go thirty miles over the hills when he
was courting. One who knew him well says that
"some called him a sloven, and some called him
dressy; but, at all events, he shaved every day." In
his manner he was very familiar with every rank,
and social, though not a drunkard. "'Twixt the
gloamin and the mirkin, when the kye come
hame," was a great song of his, and he gave it with
remarkable spirit about the Gordon Arms and at
Selkirk festive meetings. At thirty Sir Walter
Scott noticed him, and then Professor Wilson, and
"he was lionized in London, and never did any
good as shepherd or sheep farmer after." A present of £100 from Sir Robert Peel, and £50 a
year for giving up his farm of Mount Benger, kept
him from want, and then he lived near the Gordon
Arms, and "just whistled and sang his life away."
Sir John Malcolm presided at the public dinner to
him in London, and he only lived till the next summer. He was buried in Ettrick churchyard, and
Professor Wilson was at the funeral with two
of his sons, and let down one shoulder into the
grave.

Ettrick Forest, and its old glories when it was a
hunting station of the kings of Scotland, are a theme
to which his enthusiasm has given an edge. To
Henry Duke of Buccleuch he accorded all the
honour of improving the Forest; but still, he never
could forgive him for being a catcher of moles, "those
innocent and blessed little pioneers who enrich our

pastures annually with the best top-dressing dug with great pains and labour from the fattest soil beneath."*

---

* The *Banffshire Journal* furnishes the following pleasant sketch of " Old Moley of Nethermuir" :—

"Deceased was the first professional molecatcher that ever practised his trade north of Aberdeen. Born in Westmoreland, he was apprenticed to a regular molecatcher, who, in the course of his calling, traversed the southern counties of Scotland, and then penetrated as far north as Forfar. Here William Irving (for that was Moley's name), impelled by his love of adventure, and a prying disposition, deserted his master, and determined to start on his own account. Journeying north, when near Stonehaven, he got into conversation with, as he supposed, a superior farmer. After a few miles' walk, this person invited him to his house. He proved to be the celebrated Captain Barclay, then rising into fame. He stopped at Ury a week, and many a story did he afterwards tell of that memorable visit.

"William afterwards turned up at Old Deer, causing a considerable sensation. His fame reached the ears of the late Mr. Crombie of Phesdo, who sent for him and appointed him molecatcher to the Earl of Aberdeen, which office he held for forty years. The Earl never passed him when in the grounds of Haddo House without saying a few words, but they seldom went beyond ' Well, I see you are there.' Moley had the highest admiration for this good and distinguished nobleman.

"Having been employed by the Earl, William was soon sought for by the lairds of the district, far and wide. His abilities in his trade were great, and although molecatchers are now numerous, it is questionable if an equally expert one could now be found. Few moles could ' trick' him; but he had other qualifications, which rendered him not only agreeable, but almost necessary to them. He was a great antiquarian, and came to acquire an intimate knowledge of the families of the proprietors. He was a botanist, and had an excellent knowledge of the culture of trees. He was a first-rate marker of game, and in slipping a greyhound had not a rival. At the Turriff Coursing Club Meetings he was in his glory. Several of the lairds in the district nearly fought for the possession of Moley on the 12th of August. His herculean strength enabled him to carry fabulous bags of game any distance. It was no uncommon thing in those days for the sportsman to walk ten miles to the moor and the same back, with Moley carrying twenty brace of grouse and half-a-dozen hares on his back. It is true he swallowed as much whisky as he could get to assist him on the road.

"William went to Nethermuir in the year 1802, and, as the place suited him, he remained there ever since. This was his head-quarters, but he was often months absent, plying his trade far and wide ; but Haddo House, Brucklay, Aberdour House, Pitfour, and Troup, with a rare excursion to Duff House and Gordon Castle, were his principal haunts. Everywhere he was a welcome visitor to the lairds ; but not so to the servants, who sometimes rebelled *en masse* against his admission, as he was accustomed to find many flaws in the establishment, which he was sure to communicate to the astonished master. Moley was very fond of Gebbie of Troup, the last professional fool in the north, and retailed many of his wise sayings.

"Moley is supposed at his death to have been 85 years of age. He retained

The Duke secured royal rights over the Forest, and stocked it with 20,000 blackfaces, which some will have it came from Fife. It was not until 1785 that Cheviots crept in. The old shepherds raved against them in their death-throes, and called them "white-faced shilpit things," which had been attended to like "fine leddies," and, as the Shepherd adds, "the blackfaces sought the heights in disdain." They had to stay there like moody Jupiters till '60; but that fearful time, added to the barren spring of '64, produced a reaction in the higher sheep-walks, and Lead Hills, the birth-place of Allan Ramsay and the highest inhabited village in Scotland, had "its ain again."

In Lanark market, blackfaced ewe hoggs, which could be had once at from £1 to 25s., have lately ranged from 28s. to 35s.; and in the upper parts of Peebleshire and Lanarkshire the Cheviots have had to retire. Still, with the exception of Mr. Aitchison's, there are hardly any Cheviot wedders in these two counties. Mr. Denholm, who has a large flock, both of blackfaces and Cheviots, in the upper ward of Lanarkshire, has quite given up the idea which many

---

his vigorous faculties of mind to the last gasp of life. For the last twenty years he had been a pensioner of Mr. Gordon of Nethermuir, to whom he bequeathed his album, composed of two large thick volumes of extracts of newspapers, containing accounts of the Aberdeen races, murders, executions, Turriff coursing meetings, comings of age, and other remarkable events in the northern counties since the commencement of this century. It is a most unique, instructive, and amusing album, though not well adapted for the drawing-room table, as its leather covers and soiled pages are nearly black from tobacco-smoke and peat reek, the combined odour of which not all the perfumes of Arabia could overwhelm."

flockmasters cling to—that the Cheviots are as hardy
when they are well turniped as hoggs. With him the
winter of '60 did comparatively little damage to the
blackfaces. They can fight their own battle, and do
even better than the hay-fed Cheviots. They work
up the hill and hunt the country fair for their food,
under difficulties; whereas the Cheviots (which are
straighter behind and not so free in the hock for hill
climbing) will lie at the foot and lose courage in the
snow. The " curly horns" have another advantage,
that they will thrive on high mossy land, whereas the
Cheviots require much lower quarters. If the two are
kept on coarse wild land, four Cheviots eat as much
meat as five blackfaces; but if the land is superior, as
in Roxburghshire, you cannot increase them to the
same extent. Others, on the contrary, think that,
instead of keeping a score more blackfaces for every
five score of Cheviots, you should read for every fifteen score. They will also eat coarse stuff which the
daintier Cheviots won't touch, but the price of wool
and their slower maturity will be always against
them.

A three-year-old Cheviot wedder will make 36s. or
37s. by his carcase, and 9s. by his wool; whereas 27s. to
30s., and 4s. 6d. for wool, is all that can be set down
for a blackface. The difference is strikingly seen in
this, that a Cheviot shepherd can get £48 for the
wool and lambs of his 46 ewes on a hirsel of 38 score,
whereas a blackface shepherd can only get £33.
Again we have the comparison, 23s. for the 24lb. stone

of blackfaced wool unwashed, and 40s. for Cheviot washed. Comparing well-fed wedders at three, the average of blackfaced will be from 15 to 17lbs., and of Cheviots from 17 to 21lbs. The blackfaces " grow like mischief" the first year on pasture, and after that they slacken, but still they are the daintiest morsel to set before a club, with currant jelly in aid.

The larger-boned ones are always better growers, and hardier, and flockmasters like them with a long neck and a short face, if they can get it. The head should be broad between the eyes, and free from wool; the nose full and Roman, the jaw broad and strong, and the eyes not too near the root of the horns, which should be flat and well apart, not too large, and coming away free from the head. Rams whose horns grow upwards from the same root invariably get their lambs with those lumps on the crown, which are so fatal at lambing time. The horn grows stronger in deep boggy land, and as, unlike the hart, they cannot

"Hang their old head on the pale,"

and leave it there each April, some of the heavy-headed ones grow sadly weary, rest it listlessly on a stone or dyke bank, and are careless about the ewes. Many have their horns sawn off at the first bend, or cut close and fired at the end of the flint, to prevent them bleeding to death. The roundness at the root of a horn will often indicate in a tup lamb that he will get them with soft bloody horns, which will grow into the head. These bloody horns suffer very much in cold weather, as they get frosted to the flint (or bone in the centre of the horn), and the sheep sink in condition.

Upon the colour of the faces there has been much diversity of opinion among the learned. Some of the flockmasters, and the Watsons of Culterallers among them, liked them very light, under the idea that it indicated faster feeding and more wool. This point was so steadily kept in view in choosing rams that the sprittle-faced began to lose their clear white and black markings, but now the dark sprittles have taken the lead again, and seem generally allowed to be hardier. Dark legs are an essential point, and no one seems to dispute that; but how to get the faces light and the legs dark is as hard as the solution of the riddle which the late Archbishop Whateley propounded and would never divulge :

> "When from the ark's capacious round
> The world came forth in pairs,
> Who was the first to hear the sound
> Of boots upon the stairs?"

The great Cheviot farms are above Ewan foot Station, and now there are nothing but Cheviots to Muirkirk, where twenty-five years ago they were all blackfaces. The Gillespies of Douglas Water began the Cheviots, and they go on to Glenbuck. Seven miles from Douglas, the blackfaces take it up again, and spread over the hills round Carnock, Sanquhar, and Kirkconnel. In Ayrshire they are chiefly black-faces, but in the North the Cheviot is creeping in fast. From Abington Station the black-face district bends away by Carnwath to the Pentlands, and towards the head of Tweed. They still hold the Dalmelzies and Stanhope hills, but they are gradually being put out of Nithsdale at the back of the Luther Hills. About the head of Clyde, at the summit of the hill from Beattock, the Cheviots have been crossed in with the blackface for the sake of stamina, till at the third cross the lambs look full Cheviot, and are sold as such. The last farm that did it was Crooked Stane, ten miles above Beattock, and nearly the highest land in Scotland. It kept to the blackfaced as long as it could, and then it silently followed in the wake of the fashion. The first cross has as little horn as the second, and a third or fourth brings the colour right; but still, the grey legs are obstinate, and the kemp will sometimes linger obstinately in the wool for years, and "fly away on the machinery when they try to work it." A great many mules are bred in Lanarkshire. Dealers bring the rough Leicester rams direct from Yorkshire, and take back ewe hogg shots to put to the Leicester there. The mules bred in the district are sold at four months for 15s. to 18s., and generally go South.

Coultar parish, and ten miles round it, is the great centre of the Lanarkshire blackfaces, and Lanark is their market. The Watsons of Coultar, Murray of Pentland Hills, Fryer of Knowhead, on the Campsie Hills, Sandy Denholm of Baitlaws, Dryfe from the Sanquhar Hills which range between Ayrshire and Dumfriesshire, Blacklock of Minny Gap,

and Craig from the heights of Black Craig in Ayrshire
are all there, vying with each other for sweetness and
strength of face, and weight of carcase and wool.
The Cheviots are all sold "bare" south of Falkirk;
whereas the clad score is always adhered to in the
case of the blackface, which are supposed to be "the
inferior clergy." The breeders made a stand about
twenty years ago, but the buyers checkmated them,
by sending the drum round Lanark to say that none
would be bought except they were double clad, and
the breeders had to put up with the double injustice
that year. Tups are never sold by the clad score,
and on Lanark Muir they seldom get as high as
£20 nett.

The show of tups is in June, and the Highlanders are the best customers, but do not care for
shearlings. They range from £3 upwards, but for
the leading sellers £4 to £5 is about the average.
The Watsons of Culterallers and Watson* of Nesbitt
are the heads of the profession, and sell some six or
seven score between them. Once they were great
exhibitors, but they have given it up, and Dryfe took
it on, but won principally with tups not bred by himself. There are three markets in Lanark annually.

The rough blackfaced ewe hoggs (of which breeders
sell fully half their store) are brought out on June
3rd in their wool, and are bought up by dealers for
crossing in England. At the next market in the

* This name was omitted by mistake from the list of the Highland Society
winners in p. 89.

beginning of August nothing comes out but the wedder lambs, sometimes 10,000 strong. They are dropped in April, and generally average about £10 the clad score, and go into Forfarshire, Perthshire, and Argyleshire to be wintered, and sold to the hill farmers in the spring. They are kept to three years old, and then come out as "hill sheep" at Callow or Falkirk, at all prices from 24s. to 24s. At the end of August, the ewe lambs and the mid (shot) wedder lambs come out to the number of eight to ten thousand each. The Northumberland and Cumberland men buy them up, and many go down to Askrigg, from which Yorkshire supplies itself. Part of the shot lambs go north, but they are generally wintered in the neighbourhood. The ewe lambs are all wanted for mule dams, and some of the lots will fetch 17s. 6d. There are a few double flocks in Lanarkshire, and Mr. Denholm has one of the largest—sixty score of blackface and fifty score of Cheviots. The most extensive blackface proprietor is Mr. Lindsay of Stanhope, Peeblesshire, who has 3,000 ewes and ewe hoggs, and Mr. Paterson of Birthwood, in Lanarkshire is not far behind him.

From Biggar we passed on our way through Lamington, where the hand of the proprietor, Mr. Baillie Cochrane, M.P., may be seen in its neat cottages, and a small English church and lich-gate, which Pugin would not have disdained. The Ayrshires began to come thick when we had crossed the Caledonian line, and "Ayr forty miles" met our eye,

near those Douglas sheep-walks for whose cup days
Sunbeam, Sea Gull, Patent, and Rebe were not
pupped in vain. It was an exhilarating ride through
the windings of the hills, with ice ponds in deep ravines,
made vocal by the curlers, and then through the iron
country among an infinity of dark sprites wearing
lamps upon their foreheads—in fact, "the roaring
rink" by day, and the roaring furnace by night.

People who talk about the Scotch as phlegmatic
would alter their note if they saw them at curling
time. We have no conception of the mysteries of
"chap and lie" and "outwick," and all that sort of
thing, but it was grand to see the enthusiasm of the
players of every degree. Corpulent farmers, whom
we couldn't have believed capable of it, crooked their
lusty knees; and the lads swept the ice frantically
as the smooth grey stone came gliding on towards its
fellows. Inn stables near the favourite ponds were
so full that it was a mercy we could get a stall for our
mare at all. If we passed a cart about 10 a.m., we
generally found it full of the paraphernalia of the
game instead of ordinary farm produce, and stalwart
men and boys strode gaily along every turnpike and
bye-lane with whin brooms of a delicious green under
their arms. At night we heard desperate discussions
on the events of the day, and orations fully ten
minutes long on the glories of some particular rink.
It once seemed strange to see a Yorkshire and a
Lincolnshire breeder of blood stock draw their chairs
close one evening, put their hands on one another's

knees, and fight out inch by inch the stud merits of
Stockwell and Orlando; but the Old Cumnockites
went beyond that. They disregarded their ale and
their toddy, they stood up and held each other by the
coats, and cross-pumped into each other's sys-
tems their curling observations and criticisms. Almost from daybreak telegrams were flying about as
to the state of the ice, and the very farm lads looked
as if they contemplated suicide when the thaw came
softly stealing from the south.

A six-mile ride over the hills from Old Cumnock
brought us to Dalgig, which Ivie Campbell and his
Canaradzo have made so famous both in Scottish and
English leash annals, and our first notions of the
place were gathered from a distant view of Mr.
Campbell and his renowned white, surveying a rink
of curlers. The group on the bank was completed by
a slashing (May 3) son of Canaradzo and Snowdrop
(who died after pupping), a red bitch by him out of
Butterfly by Judge, and a very small white by Daring
from Canopy. They may not, perhaps, like Milton's
lubbar fiend, have "earned their cream-bowl duly
set;" but still the life of saplings at an Ayrshire
dairy farm is a right royal one; and we found them
invariably curled together, basking in all "their
hairy strength" on a rug by the kitchen fire, and
complacently surveying and levying a capital per-
centage on whatever kail and porridge were flying
about. We remember a lady once telling us that
she never could get her servants to treat the foxhound

puppy with due consideration, till the huntsman
called one day, and asked, in severely important
tones, "*Do you give that puppy his exercise regularly?*" and that ever after it became the subject of
the deepest respect and solicitude. The bump of
reverence is equally developed among the domestics
at Dalgig.

None of the above three had received a name. There
were many deep searchings of heart, countless brown
studies, and endless dislocation and collocation of
syllables in connexion with the standard initial letter
C, in prospect, before Mr. Campbell would get that
point settled. We have a floating notion that we
found many learned exercises of this nature not
only on the fly-leaves of his books, but on stray enve-
lopes and the margin of old *Ayrshire Advertisers*.
In fact, his evenings are one series of strenuous phi-
lological wrestles. His coursing friends have often
a joke with him about his taste for nomenclature,
and one of them had the temerity to infringe the
patent, and call his dog "Dalgigaradzo." Some
of them will have it that he keeps a lucky-bag of syllables at Dalgig, and draws them out at haphazard; but
luckily there is that telling title, "Canaradzo," to confute such impious cavillers. One energetic and speculative stranger at the Waterloo had rummaged every
dictionary and gazetteer that he could lay hands on,
and, failing in his search, reverently approached Mr.
Campbell on the ground, and, with a preface
to the effect that "it sounds well," begged to be

informed where it came from, and what it meant.

"*Excuse me addressing you, sir, but Johnson's Diction-ary does not hint at such word.*" "*Doesn't it?*" replied the proud author of its existence; "*if the dog wins the Cup to-day, you'll find it in the next edition!*" And with that the querist subsided into himself. Still Mr. Campbell seems to think "Coodareena" and "Carabradzo" quite as happy inspirations; and he has been dreadfully bothered by the way in which the outer world persisted in pronouncing another pet name "Ci-ol-og-a," in strict contravention of the Dalgig canons. Twice over we were pulled up, and told that it was Chi-o-*lo*-ga; and yet such was the force of habit that we "went and did it again." Cups and photographs are a great point with Mr. Campbell. On the piano there stands the goblet which Coodareena won at Lytham, separated from her Brownlow cup by one which Canaradzo gained at Islington last year.

The chimney-piece can also boast of two similar Canaradzo trophies; one of them the first at Birmingham, and the other the second at Leeds—a decision, by-the-bye, which "no fellah can understand," and at which Mr. Randell, who bred the first-prize dog, and Mr. Nightingale* as well, raised their hands

---

* The latter thus speaks of him: "He has the particular point which settles all dispute, in my mind, as to a fast *v.* a slow greyhound, viz., the proper description of loin. A broad, thick, vulgar loin denotes to a dead certainty the slows, that worst of all complaints in a greyhound. What is wanted is a well-developed loin, not heavy, nor too long or weak, but growing finer and narrower from the middle to the couplings, just as you see it in him."

in dismay. There, too, is Mr. Borron's Ardrossan
Cup, which was brought to Dalgig by Highland
Home; and the Kyle Club Collar, with its wreath of
name-medals, was not long in its sideboard lair. It
is dated 1852, and bears, among other winning names,
those of Brighton, Picton, and Baron Garnock; and
Calabaroono and Cadazooro, brothers by Cardinal
York out of Canopy, were its joint holders on Mr.
Campbell's behalf. Their dam, and their grandam
Scotland Yet, hang on the walls; and Canaradzo
and Ciologa join partnership in the slips, with young
Mr. Campbell holding them. We have read in
Becher Ward of "the short, hot glitter of a rat's
eye," but it is nothing to a bench of sixteen terriers,
whose gaze and grouping the photographer has
managed with wonderful tact. The stuffer's art has
also been called into requisition for a black-cock and
a squirrel; and there, too, is the head of a small
Roman-nosed hare, the identical one which was the
humble instrument of deciding the Biggar St. Leger
of 82 dogs, when Hippograff ran up to Condolorado
by Bedlamite out of Swallow.

Dalgig derives its name from Dal-gig, or The vale
with the rise. It seems to be in the middle of a sort
of rough grass moor, which suits Ayrshires, as Mr.
Campbell has a perfect heap of medals to attest the
victories of his bulls Clarendon and Cardigan, and
has twice over beaten the whole county for the best
lot of milch cows. There are plenty of stone fences
and ditches about, and not many hares. The grouse

and blackcock lead the white division many a hard gallop; and the smaller trials are sometimes brought off on a big moss two miles away. Still, when—as John Wilson *alias* " Jock O'Dalgig" the trainer (and a very quaint little character) expresses it—"*We want to ken the Watterloo boys; we tak them eight miles doon the country, to the Duke's land at Kirk-connel or Dalmellington.*" The hounds have only once come that way, and John almost speaks under his breath to this day, when he tells how he had just time to couple up his charges before they threw up, scarcely three hundred yards from him, and his deep thankfulness that his kennel was not eaten up bodily that day. Not a man was within miles of them, and when they had discovered and discussed two dead calves which had been thrown into a pit, they con-centrated their attention on a cade lamb, which had been left in a shepherd's plaid, and it soon departed to the Happy Pastures. Cox, huntsman, had re-turned to Eglinton Castle without his pack, and a telegram next morning informed him of their where-abouts, and requested his immediate presence, as no one cared to go near such cannibals when they were once coaxed into a stable.

So much for the local traditions of Dalgig, where Mr. Campbell was born shortly before the present century. Strange to say, he cared no more for a greyhound than he did for an opposum until 1849, and he never attended a public meeting until what racing men still fondly call " Voltigeur's year." He then began at some private coursing days for half-crown stakes with Dido, and inflamed his ardour considerably by beating Wigan at Kirkconnel.

This future stud hero was bred at Bank House, near New Cumnock. Mr. Pagan had him as a present from Mr. Heslop, and not caring for the responsibility, and being deeply impressed by the Dido defeat, he arranged with Mr. Campbell to become his confederate. It was settled that they were to share the expenses and winnings, and that Jock (a Wigtownshire man who used to lead the prize-bulls to the ground, and helps still with the cows), aided by Mr. Ivie Campbell, junior, were to combine their forces, and train the brindled-and-white, who was then in his second season, and generally ran at 63 lbs. He was a sweet-tempered dog, but his two preceptors had rather a tough job getting him fit. When they did, he won the Douglas Cup twice in succession at Biggar. As time went on, Mr. Greenshield's Veto (by Marquis of Douglas's Dux out of Tileside lass) arrived to Wigan, and Mr. Campbell stipulated for two pups as the price of the wooing. They were suckled and sent in due course; the dog puppy turned out a complete idiot, and was handed over to a local Calcraft, and the bitch was neither more nor less than Scotland Yet, that kernel of all Mr. Campbell's fame. Wigan just won £80 a-piece for the confederates, and was sold some time after for "a pony," to a gentleman over the Border. He left another great Scottish pledge behind him in

King Lear, the winner of the first 64-dog Waterloo Cup.

Jock's principal comments on Scotland Yet seem to be confined to an entry on our notes, that "*she was varra fast and of a varra jumping sort; Ah! she was a grand bitch.*" In the slips she looked one network of veins, and all her litters have inherited her beautiful skin. She was beaten in her first course at Biggar, but she afterwards ran up in a 64-dog stake at the Caledonian meeting, to Mr. John Jardine's Baron, and won the Caledonian Cup; and she seemed to excite quite a *furore* among the Scottish division, when she did so well at the Waterloo of '54. We were not there the next year, when she ran up to Judge for the cup, but Mr. Campbell still declares that it was "Noe course avar," as the hare only weighed 4 lbs. Mr. Nightingale says of this course: "She killed her hare too soon. Judge went a tremendous pace, and went round and turned his hare to the bitch, who killed before she could get into good solid work, which was her great forte." Barring her colour, which was pure white, she was to Mr. Campbell's eye more like her daughter Coodareena than anything he has had in his kennel. Her light was nearly quenched before she became a brood bitch: as she was seized with dropsy or some such ailment, and became such a swollen object about the head more especially, that she was within an ace of being put away like her brother. However, Mr. Campbell tucked up his sleeves, and summoning the whole strength of the establishment, placed her three or four times a day in a warm bath, and swathed her in flannel so effectually, that he gradually brought her round. Ranter by Bedlamite was her first love; but the puppies, nearly all of which were black, came at a bad season of the year, and were wrong in their legs as well. In short, none of them ever gained any note of admiration or even an entry in "Stonehenge's" Coursing Calendar. She had another trial of the Bedlámite cross through Jacobite, but except Mr. Begbie's Blitz (who ran up to Canaradzo in a 32-dog stake at the Caledonian Meeting), they all died as puppies. The blue strain of Bugle was tried next; Mr. Marfleet's Beacon, who had just been purchased from Mr. Borron for 60 gs., was chosen as her consort; and Canaradzo, Crested Lochiel, Cazzarina, Canopy, and Harvest Home formed that memorable litter.

Canaradzo was always the best looking of the lot, but Crested Lochiel had the most bone. Respecting the merits of these two brothers, Jack spake thus: "Crested Lochiel was about a neck the faster of the twa, but Canaradzo always wrought the inside of him." The former was a very game dog, and a rare fencer, but unfortunately in his third course for the Caledonian St. Leger, he spiked himself striking at his hare, between the breast and the shoulder, and wrenching himself loose with a great effort, killed the hare after all, and lay down ruined for life. Canopy was very fast, but not so close in her work as some of the rest. She divided the Caledonian St. Leger with Mr. Ewing's Lucknow, an eight-dog stake at Biggar, with Cazzarina, and a stake at Southport with Mr. Jones's Jeopardy, but never won anything outright. She was also second at the Birmingham Show, and has had three litters of puppies. Cam-ye--by Athol was one of her first litter of young Jacobites, of which Mr. Campbell presented one to Lord Eglinton. Cadazooro and Calabaroono (which the papers would persist in calling Calabaroona) are the cracks of her second litter; the saplings are by her first cousin Daring, " a nice little dog," who is making his way at the stud, and she is about to visit Cardinal York again. We may note that Cam-ye-by-Athol was sold for £80 before he was ever slipped at a hare, to Mr. Johnstone, who changed his name, without applying to any privy council, into Jock of Dalgig. This compliment Jock felt deeply, but alas! his namesake died soon after winning the North Lancashire Stakes at the Ridgway Club—in a wire fence near Blackburn. Cazzarina was sold for £50 to Mr. Gibson, after winning a Caledonian and a Clifton Cup, besides running up for the latter to Sea Rock, and is the dam of Gunboat by Jacobite.

But we must hark back to Scotland Yet. Nothing came of her Condolorado litter of whites and blacks, which arrived on the New Year's morning of '59, and Mr. Campbell was in a mood to realize when the second Beacon litter were ready for action. Sea Pink, late " Coorareena," and Sea Foam, late " Co-

2 s

looxardo" (a very cherished combination of syllables
in Mr. Campbell's eyes), produced £100 and £120
respectively. Then there was Coorooran £50, and
Ciologa £85, or £355 for one litter, and one of them
with a broken leg! Coursers shrugged their shoulders
when Mr. Campbell stuck to it that he had a better
at Home than either Sea Pink or Sea Foam, which
he sold to Mr. Spinks after they had been defeated at
Biggar, and had divided two Puppy Stakes at Abergele. It was, however, a true bill, and unbelievers
began to think so when they saw Ciologa win the
Vernon Cup and gold watch, and her brother, Coorooran, the sole companion of her journey from Dalgig to Derbyshire, follow suit with the Sudbury
Stakes as well. Of course she was jealously kept for
the Waterloo Cup, and Mr. Spinks offered £200 in
vain. Three hundred would not have tempted "old
Dalgig" to forego what he considered an all but
Waterloo certainty, after seeing her beat Coorooran
in a trial. She was very smooth in her style, and
almost as great a favourite with Mr. Warwick as
Riot was with Mr. M'George.

The Beacon litter No. 3 included Dixie, who was
presented to Mr. Dunlop, and won the Biggar St.
Leger, and Great Gun (both of them brindles),
Caroola, Jessie the Flower of Dunblane, Coodareena,
and Carabradzo (another composition triumph). Caroola, a white with blue spots, had quite a tragical
end, as she broke her neck in her Waterloo trial
course over Kirkconnel, where she had shown herself

a trifle faster than Coodareena. It was a sad sight
for Jock and his master, as she lay with the hare
beside her, her eyeballs starting out of her head,
and her mouth full of grass. There were still a fourth
and a fifth litter by Beacon from the old bitch, who
never trusted her progeny to wet nurses. The first
was a very early one, and out of it nothing, save
Mr. Gibson's Ivy, and Jeannie's Bawbee (sold for
£15 at five months), were worth their keep ; and the
last pupping scene of all culminated in a heap of five
dead ones. The old matron was a perfect wreck,
and soon after that she was put away, and buried
honourably in the garden ; and a veterinary surgeon
in Kilmarnock, stimulated by the account of the
Eclipse and Elcho skeletons, begged Mr. Campbell
for her bones in vain.

Canaradzo had not seen a hare for two seasons
past ; but he was quite emancipated, to the immense
improvement of his temper, from kennel control, and
seemed " always watching to get ben," and specially
improving his opportunities at meal times. He is a
beautiful dog, especially in his ribs and the outline
of his back, and with his tail set on so well, A dinner, but more especially tea and toddy, derive an
additional zest, when you have a Waterloo Cup winner stretched on the hearth-rug, dreaming of Will
Warner and the hares. He went by the name of
"Rector" but not a soul in the house could tell "the
reason why." April 12th, 1858, was his birthday, and
his maiden essay was dividing the Biggar St. Leger

with Lord John Scott's Terrona; but after that, the hard ground at Abergele, where he was second to Tipsy Cake, gave him a dressing which he did not forget in a hurry. Then he won the Western (32-dog) Stakes at the Caledonian Club Meeting, and made his score up to £220 before he went for the Waterloo of '61. Mr. Campbell would have sold him for £150, after he won his two courses; but Mr. Randell would not give more than £100 at first. Still, but for some telegraphic bungle, they might not improbably have come to terms. He ran rather wild in his first Waterloo course with Gilbert, and had the first turn given against him; but Mr. Nightingale, who was on the ground, marked his style with Faldonside, and assured his friends pretty decisively that they must take no liberties with him. Faldonside, Bude Light (the most teasing opponent he had), Seventy Pounder, and Ingomar, all met him in turn, and he finally disposed of Sea Rock, and got through his six trials without one "No go." He was a patient dog in the slips, always carrying his tail up, and never straining till the game was fairly before him.

At home he was never led to his hare except by Ciologa; and although he had virtually retired, and some litters were becoming due, he was obliged to come out and do battle again, when she broke her leg a fortnight before the Waterloo on the sands at Southport. He beat Coorooran in an Altcar trial, and did the same for Sea Pink and Jetsam, both favourites, in his two first Waterloo courses. What with Sea Rock one year and Sea Pink the next, he was quite a thorn in Mr. Spinks's side; and Jock lays it down as undoubted law, that his defeat of Sea Pink, after his stud service, was the best thing he ever did. Kingwater led him in his last Waterloo course, and both stumbled on the plough; and Kingwater not recovering himself so quickly, Canaradzo jumped over him, and killed his hare. He had one more course at home, and that was with Colossal, who jumped against a peat hag and killed himself, and got confounded by the newspapers with Canaradzo in his death. Pace and smoothness, as well as great cleverness with his teeth, were all combined in him. He begot some puppies the season he won the Waterloo, as Camden Town was sent to him in pursuance of an off-hand promise; but the produce—Canopy's Niece, &c.—proved no great wonders. In his first regular season he began rather late, but he had fifteen winners, and so far he may be credited with forty to fifty winners and runners-up, with a winner and a runner-up for the Waterloo among them. During his running and stud career, he brought about £1,500 to his owner, and he became Mr. Knowles's this spring for another £100.

The Scottish National, the Coquetdale, the Ridgway Club, the Waterloo, and the Sudbury were Mr. Campbell's coursing grounds, so that Jock was on circuit nine times a year. He has only been twice to Ireland, but was in great force with Coodareena and

Calabaroono when he did go. Abergele is quite out of favour with both master and man, and the latter observed that "its stubble and grass are as hard as the frost is now." Since he won the two best stakes at the Scottish National with Canaradzo and Cazzarina, in their first season, Jock has had a leaning towards Biggar, but regrets its relentless hills. He likes Southport quite as well as "that level mossy kind of spot," Lytham, which is "too heavy ground for Cliardona." He thinks it has far better hares than Altcar, but against the sloping sides of its ditches he decidedly protests. As for Sudbury, "it is all grass —sort of meadow—well enough; but I don't like them big hedges, they're no fit to loup, and its hard to get through 'em."

Such were the preliminary commentaries of little "Jock o'Dalgig," as we sat with him and Mr. Campbell in the bothy, which is turned into a kennel. A splendid fire blazed there night and day; and if we looked in at the window when Jock was off with the key, we might occasionally see the whole clan of Scotland Yet sitting or lying gravely round it, and holding a far more peaceful communion than any common council, London or provincial. The biscuits were in a rack above their heads, the muzzles and brushes formed a bristling array, and the "canopy" idea was carried out by the graceful tresses of the sheets. The bitch of that ilk was at Mr. Campbell junior's house, about a mile distant at Craigman, with two other matrons, Miss Julia by

Judge, and Highland Home. Farther away across
the hills at Knock Dunder, were two saplings
one (of Jan. 25) by Canaradzo from Di Vernon
and another by Canaradzo from Annoyance, a bitch
which won a 32-dog stake at Bridekirk. This brought
the whole strength of the stud up to about seventeen.
Eight were on the benches in the bothy kennel; and
while the wind whistled shrill outside, Jock called
them up one by one in that cozy little shop, and
fought his battles over again, as he showed their
muscle.

"They are all good-tempered," he observes, "except to collies and terriers, and they can't abear the
sight of them; and what's better still, they're all
winners or runners-up." Two brothers who divided
the North Lancashire Stakes, at Lytham, lay on the
nearest bench, and had precedence in his call.
"Here, Tom!" he began, and down jumped Cadazooro, by Cardinal York, out of Canopy, a black and
white dog, with a grey face, and a slight family
resemblance to his uncle Picton. Then it was a case
of "Come on, Macduff!" and down came the black,
with white toes, Calabaroono, at that inspiring kennel
call. He is not such a worker, but has rather more
pace, and was drawn, after an injury in a severe bye,
for the great Scottish National St. Leger. Still, if
he only got third honours, Skedaddler, by Canaradzo,
was the right dog in the right place; and Mr. Campbell found much comfort accordingly. On the fourth
day of that meeting, 15 out of 91 were left in, and

7 of them were in Jock's lot, which was only 8 strong to begin with. The cry, *" Mirth, come Mirth !"* was promptly responded to by Coodarcena, and her owner ·embraced her on the spot. This "little blue girl" has great length from the stifle to the hock, and with plenty of pace and working power, and it was quite evident that Mr. Campbell thought of standing upon her again for the Waterloo, as he did this year, and won three courses. *" Bugle !"* brought down, as in duty bound, a blue in the shape of the flashy-looking, handsome Carabradzo, who divided the Douglas Cup with her and Gilderoy.

Like his sister, he has lots of drive *" always waving them forward,"* as Jock puts it. He runs at 70lbs., and is " far war to keep down than ony yen of the lot." A little black spot on the near cheek was the only mark on the white " Snow," or " Cararando," who headed the Canaradzo quartet. He is out of Young Camarine by Jardine's Baron, and depended more on working than pace for his victories at Coquetdale and the Scottish National. His own sister, called by Mr. Campbell, "Calmaroona," and "getting nought but ' Fly' from Jock," was a sweet-looking and fast, but rather unfortunate bitch, and got un-sighted in her first Waterloo course. " Venus," *alias* " Ciorardeena," out of Resolute, a daughter of Restless, and fourth at the Scottish National, had gone on improving. She was '· beaten early on by Tom, and yen we put away," and they thought her slow till she ran up with Silver Rays at Lytham, and

then they quite changed their minds. She was a nice
bitch, but there should have been a transfer of names
between her and "Veto," or "Cliardona," in order
to render them strict poetical justice. This daughter
of Avalanche, a Welsh bitch, was quite the beauty of
the kennel. She had never run badly yet, and she
got first turn from Silver Rays at Southport (where
she was third for the Bitch Puppy Stakes) and divided a stake at Sudbury, with Mr. Steel's Schweppe.

There have been great changes since then. Calabaroono won a Waterloo Purse and the Brownlow Cup,
and was sold to the late Lord Uffington for £200, who
won the Sundorne Cup with him, and had the morti-
fication of seeing him put out in his first tie for the
Waterloo. He was always a very beefy difficult dog
to train, and from this cause he had been beaten in
Mr. Campbell's hands for his first Cup course the
year before. Cadazooro has also gone, and in fact
only Coodareena and some puppies remain.

Mr. Campbell has other specialities besides greyhounds, and his herd are well known through
Ayrshire. Cardigan, his best bull, won about £100
in Highland Society and other prizes, and that sum
was refused from Sir James Ferguson, M.P., who
wished to take him to Paris. Many medals, one of
them a £10 gold one for the reclamation of waste
land, and a silver one twice over for the best stock
on the Marquis of Bute's estate, under Sir James
Stuart's guardianship, when nearly a hundred stocks
were shown, have also come to Dalgig. Cardigan

was bred by Mr. Parker of Broomlands who has
a very celebrated winning stock, and most of the
cows are by Clarendon, a half-brother of Cardigan on the sire's side, who was first at Glasgow.
But it is difficult to regard a man from two distinct
points of view, and we like best to think of "Dalgig"
as we are wont to see him on that glorious day

"When north of Tweed and south of Tweed
Join hands at Waterloo,"

with a quaint good-humoured repartee ever ready
for those friends who will crack a joke over him, and
leaning on his gnarled and polished black oak staff
the while, as he scans the style of his cherished
Canaradzoes.

CHAPTER X.

DALGIG TO AYR.

"Through Carnwath he bounded fast,
By Douglas Mill rode he,
But weary, weary was the steed
When he passed Ochiltree"

SCOTT.

Ayr—Cow Districts—Rearing, and Points of Ayrshire Cows—Colours—
Vessel—Beef—Milking—Show Dodges—Ayr Milking Prize—Bowers
Cheese-making—Dunlop and Cheddar—Mis Jane Dunlop—English
Purchasers of Ayrshires

A THAW had followed frost, to the dire confusion of the curling interest, and then a frost had set in again. There was nothing for it but to get up in the dark at 5 a.m., to encounter the blast furnaces once more, and skate pretty nearly all the way on horseback between Dalgig and Ayr. This cheese capitol of Scotland looks quite a pleasant city of the plain, with its steeples, cupolas, and towers. The Wallace Memorial "contrives a double debt to pay," and has a dram shop below, and in the hostel, where Tam O'Shanter met Souter Johnnie, the green-moulded thatch has not yielded to slate. Our further Burns' homage consisted not only in walking by the sea-side, and home by the monument, but took the more practical turn at night, of looking him through from end to end for mottoes, and feeling most thankful for " Ca' the yowes to the knowes."

The " Puir Mallies" have been silently encroaching on the county. South of Carrick, especially, the Galloways have had to yield to the sprittle-faces, and " Galloway for 'oo" becomes a truer saying than ever. On the subject of the best cow districts there is much diversity of thought; and some will have it that Cunningham, Cumnock, Dunlop, and Kilbirnie rank highest. " It's a Kilbirnie cow" is a passport at once; but still, many lean to the notion that the best are to be found between Kilmarnock and Paisley, Largs, and Kilmalcolm, and West down Clyde on the Mearns.

A calf sucking would spoil the county theory as to the shape of the " vessel," and hence all calves, however promising, are pail-fed. The great majority scarcely ever touch new milk after the first six weeks, and then get a very scanty allowance of skim milk or hay gruel for six weeks more. They are, in fact, " dragged up" rather than reared to queyhood, and are put on a rough damp bite at six months. This treatment keeps the horn fine and the paunch big, whereas sweet feeding would do precisely the opposite. At six months their value will be about £2, and at fourteen months they seldom fetch more than £3 10s. to £5, as no estimate can be formed of their future milking properties until they are two years old, and therefore a buyer would work in the dark. Some few are put to the bull at fifteen months,

to the infinite detriment of their size. From the
middle of June to the end of August, in their third
year, is the best time, and during the winter they
are gradually brought into the byre. Twins with
them are of rare occurrence, which their hard bringing
up may in some measure account for. Many of these
"tidy queys" in-calf are sold off grass in October or
November to English commissioners, for £7 to £12, at
Kilmaurs, near Kilmarnock, at the beginning of November. The cows are in "the right tid ye ken" a
fortnight before calving, or two weeks after; and the
bloom is fairly off them at the end of July, unless
they are fed very highly. They are on the grass
from May to November, but after they calve they
get bean-meal, and boiled chaff and light corn for a
time. Their most general winter diet is bran and
bean-meal, cabbages and early turnips, and steamed
swedes with chaff and cut hay.

They should be short in the head, wide and free in
the jowl, broad in the forehead, with a large full, gentle
eye, totally free from a Roman nose, and with a
tapering expressive muzzle. Many dislike the hair
to be shaded off with tan up to the nose, from a belief that it betokens a wild, roving disposition, which
will operate against the milk-pail in both ways; and
a yellow muzzle is all the fashion. If possible, the
head should be set on with a slight arch, the neck
should be light, and the ear large and fringed. The
horn should neither be heavy nor sappy, nor have the
sweep of the West Highlander (who is said to have

brought in the action and broad forehead, centuries back), but should come away from the head at first, and then go upwards with a gentle rise. If it is an enamelled white, it is liked much better than the waxy. Well-laid shoulders are always a very great point, and a cow should be thin through the heart, with a nice straight top line to keep her plates up. Light bone below the knee and hock is another great essential, and so is a good flank curtain to the vessel. A curl along the edge of the belly is a capital sign for milk, and the tail should be as " thin as a rat's," with a nice brush at the end of it. As a general thing, they have not enough hair, and those that carry it are quite the hardiest. Too fine feeding is always found to spoil the pile. Whites (of which Mr. Ivie Campbell had once some very good ones) are not generally popular, and the shorthorn love of roans has no place here. The breeders like best to see them dropped dark red, flecked with white, and dark brown, provided they have no tan muzzle, as they are then sure of a good sale.

Ayrshire is always "a colour market." The Hereford or brocky-faced ones aie the remains of an old Ayrshire breed (in Dunlop, Dalry, and Kilbirnie), and they are always mellow handlers and very good milkers, but generally with crummy horns. Blacks are rare, and at a premium when they can be got; and the blues and whites, which are rather liked in some parts, carry a peculiarly short tail as their crest. Mr. Craig of Polquaise was celebrated for them, and his herd dates from Jock the Laird. Mr. Greenshields of West Inn, near Douglas, goes a good deal for white with blue spots, and finds them very excellent milkers. The light fawns, with a pure-white nose and light about the eyes, are not such milkers; but, after all said and done about colours, it is the orange skin and the orange tint at the root of the tail which betoken butter and cream. An eminent dealer assures us that he has known "crummies" give 12 lbs. and 14 lbs. of butter per week of 16oz. to the pound, and that thirty-six cows near Maybole once produced £14 a head, not to the bower but to the owner, who sold the milk to go to Glasgow. There must have been no weed or blind pap there.

The teats, to satisfy the mathematical eye of fanciers, should be at distances of one third of the vessel on the side, and of half the vessel across. The vessel should be oblong, with plenty of loose skin hanging straight down, flat at the bottom, and extending well below, so as to draw sustenance from the very belly, and to keep its shape with age. The orthodox shape of the vessel and teats is propagated in the tribes, and in one respect the Ayrshire men may be said to "milk the bull," as they look most jealously to his false teats that they be small and round and well apart before they use him. Both bull and cow, to ensure a milking tribe, should have large veins along the belly; but there is no milking creed of thirty-three articles like the Guernsey, extending to the direction which the feather should take on the twist and vessel. To constitute a first-class vessel, the teats should also be no bigger than a good large thimble. Still, very often, perfectly-formed vessels are by no means the best for milk, and many a cow who would have won on every point would have failed if the actual pail test had been applied. Still, the fashion is as rigorous as ever in public, though nearly every one jeers at it in private.

The English buyers never care for an orthodox vessel, but like a bad one with large teats, to prevent the dairymaids or milkers from grumbling, and to ensure more careful stripping. An Ayrshire lassie would think it treason to murmur, and gradually she gets into the habit of squeezing it with her fingers, and merely working from the elbow. In England, it is drawing with hand and shoulder, up and down, like a peal of marriage bells. There is a good deal of music in the more quiet Scottish elbow mode, and we were amazingly amused once, when a narrator—who seemed quite to agree with the lines that

> "Lads on lasses love to call,
> And lasses whiles are kirning" —

broke out over his toddy : *"When I was a young man, I've seen me dance to it like playing the piano, if I fancied the dairymaid."* Later in the evening he warmed to his subject, and said : *" I could have married her for nothing else than her milking."* Of course, we felt bound to put more milk into our whisky (we never could take it with water, hot or cold), and to assure him that it was a most laudable sentiment. The cows also repay a gentle dairymaid with their love, as they sometimes answer to their names, and we have seen them follow and fawn upon her, just like dogs, in a field.

In warm weather there is more cheese from the milk, but the cream does not come up so well. One cow will generally make about 10 stone of 24lbs.; but if forced with 2 or 3 lbs. of bean-meal, even on grass she will go as high as 13 stone. About Kilmarnock they give this stimulant all the season, after milking in a little whey. In very rare instances, when she has been "milkit to the bone" on bran and bean-meal, a cow has gone as high as thirty quarts a day, three weeks after calving. A heifer can be got as high as eight to twelve quarts with her first calf; still she is not in the swing of her milk till she has had a third or, fourth calf, and all good managers contrive to have her at least six weeks or two months dry.

If the vessel slips away, the system is evidently failing, and the milk becomes poorer. They will last up till eight or nine, and we have known them to go on to fifteen and upwards, if they do not take a weed in one of their quarters (of which cold shivering is one of the first indications), as very few people will work a cow with three teats. Mr. Harvey of Glasgow generally buys cows at six years old and upwards, as they stand the byre confinement better.* The im-

* The following details of this leviathan dairy have recently appeared in the *Agricultural Gazette* :—"There are several Glasgow distilleries, Mr. Harvey's among the number, and the spent malt (draff) and spent liquor

pression at a distance is that they will not feed; but the prettiest sight that ever loomed on us on a Scottish road, was a barren heifer of the breed, fed as level as a pea-pod, and beef to the very cheek. We were almost sorry afterwards that we had seen her, as it made it so very difficult to shake off a notion of beef points in Ayrshire, and stick to the purely milk ones. But it is nearly the same with all Englishmen, until you get a Colly Hill and an Airblaes well into your eye, and then you will not often find their marrow in Ayrshires. In fact, you do not see many crack things among the Ayrshire breeders, as the fancy buyers always know what is going on in the

---

of the stills (pot-ale) are good cow food. There has thus gradually grown up in this locality under Mr. Harvey's energetic management, one of the largest dairies in the kingdom—probably in the world. Cow byres some 56 yards long, and from 12 to 24 feet wide, according as one or two rows of cows are to be accommodated, stand closely packed, the whole surface of the ground being thus covered by a roof, and from 900 to 1,000 cows are pretty constantly in milk. They are fed during winter partly on steamed turnips, seven tons being steamed in order to give one meal daily to 900 cows, also on coarse hay, of which, as of straw, they get between 20 and 30lbs. a day apiece; also on draff, of which they receive half a bushel daily each; also on Indian Corn-meal, of which they have 3lbs. daily each, also on pot-ale, of which they receive three times a day nearly as much as they will take, from about 6 to 10 gallons daily. During the summer they are let out, a byreful at a time, for half a day to grass, and come in to receive their spent malt and still liquor, and hay in addition. They are managed, cleaned, and fed by two men to a byre holding about a hundred cows; the milking is done three times a day, by women who take charge of 13 cows in full milk, or double that number in half-milk, apiece. Between four and five o'clock (taking the winter management) the byres are cleaned out, and the cows receive a "big shovelful" of draff a-piece, and half their steamed turnips and meal, and a "half-stoupful," probably 2 gallons, of pot-ale. They are also milked thus early. At 7 they receive their fodder straw or hay. At 10 they get a "full stoupful" (probably 3 or 4 gallons) of pot-ale. They are milked at noon. At 2 p.m., or thereabouts, they are foddered again, and at 4 p.m. receive the same food as at the morning meal. They are again milked at 5 to 6, cleaned out and left till morning. The average produce is stated to be 2 gallons a day over the whole herd."

herds, and swoop down like vultures, with cheques from 50 to 120 gs., or more, if a crack is heard of. It is a very great thing to have this fancy demand, as there is always a sufficiency of good blood left, and it serves to stimulate private energy, and keeps the breed well up before the world.

If a bullock has been forced well on with bean-meal and bran or cake, it will fetch as much as £15 at two years old, and about two-thirds of that sum if only off grass. Aberdeen feeds Ayr, as the county roasting pieces are not large enough, and the Ayr-shire bullocks and heifers go to Edinburgh, where their beef is popular at the first-class tables. Bullocks rising five have been sold there as high as £30. A heifer is easiest to feed off after her first calf, and 28 stone of 24lbs. is very good for a dairy cow. Some dealers make a trade of buying up these "furrow cows," keeping them for four or five months, and selling them by roup at the end of the time. The bull-calves from common cows are killed soon after their birth, and when the rennet has been taken out for cheese, the carcase is stuffed with straw and packed off to Glasgow and Edinburgh for 7s. or 8s., to some of the beef-pie men. A well-fed bull-calf should get his four quarts of new milk morning and evening for three months. They are scarcely ever used as yearlings.

The show dodges of the Ayrshire men are inex-haustible, and not unattended with danger, as one man in his last twenty-four hours of a "strong prepara-

tion" fairly burst his bull. A great deal depends upon
the jockeying during that time. A cow is generally
kept sharp set till four or five hours before the show.
If she had been on too fine food, her paunch would
be drawn up, and the vessel would lean forward, and
the teats not in position; whereas if the paunch is
gradually filled in these few last hours, first by giving
her common food, and then by coaxing her into
quantity by bettering it at every supply, she is filled
to repletion, and the vessel hangs taut and square.
She often gets her pound of salt at night, and between the two agencies she should be turned out
quite the thing in the morning. Cows are also kept
well up to "tid" during the show season with gruel
made of linseed-meal, oat-meal, and flour, diluted
with their own milk, and sometimes as much as 3lbs.
of treacle in it. The shape of the vessel is also as
carefully looked to and adjusted as the Spanish cock's
comb, which was, while the fashion set that way,
kept up in pasteboard splints, till just before going
into Bingley Hall. A board is put below the vessel
with holes for the teats, and tied with strings round
the cow's back, so as to keep it in position, and the
vessel is laved with cold water all night, to make it flat
and contracted and give it consistency.

They are also washed over with butter-milk, and
the finer lights put in with soap and gum. Sometimes
the cow barbers use butter-milk for the legs, and take
to hair-oil, and the horns are rubbed with charcoal or
hawthorn ashes, in accordance with an old supersti-

tion. In short, the day and night before the show
are in many instances quite as important as an artist's
glazing-day at the Royal Academy. The judges are
all well up to "the little game," which extends to
scraping rams' horns almost to the quick, and then
japanning them, and is on all-fours with that artistic
clipping to hide weak points, against which old Val*
Barford, *K.C.B.* (Knight of the Clipping Board)
struggled so long, till the Royal English Society
issued its ukase.

Ayr begins the show season on the last Friday of
April, and brings many bull buyers from Dumfries
and some Lancashire and London men to look up
queys. Then follow Irvine on the first Tuesday in
May, and Kilmarnock, Mauchline, and Maryhill, all
in May. There is another Maryhill in November,
and with June come Tarbolton, at which there is a
good display of bulls and late-calving cows, and also
East Kilbride, near Glasgow, with its great trio of
prizes for the best Ayrshire cow in-milk, aged bull,
and farm mare. In 1860-61 the late Duke of Athole
gave a cow-in-milk prize at Ayr, and photography
has preserved the scene. The average result of the
milkings was as follows:

Mr Wallace's Glengall, 26lb 5½oz	Agnes Wyllie	1
Mr Reed's Cherry, 24lb 7oz	Janet M'Munter	2
Mr J Hendrie's Bell, 22lb 10oz	Kate M'Kail	3
Mr A. Hendrie's Ochiltree, 22lb 1oz	Charlotte Hunter	4
Mr A Hendrie's Lily, 22lb	Eliza M'Craith	5

The dresses were a sudden thought of the Duke's

---

* Called "Bob" by mistake at p. 112.

the night before, and were all made under Mrs.
Andrew Hendrie's superintendence, and each of the
five lassies, when they were called in to don them,
received half-a-sovereign from his Grace. Brown
stockings, white crazy (*Anglicè*, sun-bonnet), light-
grey drugget petticoat, grey-striped apron, dark and
light alternately, and blue-and-white-striped short
gown, were the pretty combination. Messrs. Dren-
nan, Telfer, and Smith were the milking judges. To
look at, Glengall was the coarsest cow of the lot, and
although the above was her average at 10lbs. to the
gallon for ten milkings, she was not nearly up to
what she achieved in the Duke's hands at Athole.*
His Grace gave £26 for her that day, and he also
bought Ochiltree and Lily, at £1 for each pound of
milk.

Not more than a fourth of the Ayrshire farmers
have bowers, whereas in Dumfriesshire and Galloway
the management is fully half and half. The bowers
pay from £6 or 10 st. of cheese and upwards, according to pasture, climate, and soil, which is considered
best on a freestone bottom. Many ploughmen look
upon it as their highest promotion to marry dairymaids and be off to a bowing. They generally find the
milkers and herdsmen, and the owner the food. If a
farmer finds bean-meal and green-cut corn for his
bower, he expects more cheese, and, in fact, the quantity of cheese always depends upon the style of
feeding. There is sharp watching for fodder on the

* See part "North," page 290.

one side and for cheese and accurate information as
to the whole crop on the other, and it often hap-
pens that a referee has to be called in. The original engagement is for twelve months, but some
bowers have gone on for 17 years, and there is a re-
newal of the lease every year, varying according as a
better or worse field comes into the rotation. Many
farmers get as high as 15 stone of 24lbs. for a cow,
and it has been known to reach 20 stone; and generally 2 stone discount is allowed for bringing up a
quey calf. The bower's profits are eked out by feeding a few pigs on sweet milk, whey, and bran, and
making skim cheese; and if a cow calves a few weeks
before the cheese season begins, he gets the advantage of the butter. Of course an owner has to look
out pretty sharp that the cheese is not starved during
the year, so as to embroil him with the cheese factor,
and therefore bowers, who do not keep their places
and are perpetually working up to a leaving, soon
get a bad name.

The Ayrshire Agricultural Association was the
permanent result of the Highland Society's visit to
Ayr in 1835 (a period of scum cheese and salt butter),
which it has never cared to repeat. The new
local Society moved about till 1851, and since then
its meetings have been regularly held in Ayr. The
introduction of the Cheddar mode of cheese-making,
and its extension throughout the south west of Scotland, have been its chief triumph. The Dunlop or "full
milk cheese" system (so called because made from

the milk of one day) began near Dunlop, eight miles from Kilmarnock; and Kilbirnie, Beith, Lochwinnoch, and Stewarton were also its strongholds. Still, there was no general mode followed, and most of it would not have been saleable in England. From time to time the Highland Society offered prizes for the best imitations of Cheshire and Gloucester; but it was not, we believe, until Mr. Robert Macadam, and his brothers James and Alexander, turned their attention to the improvement of Dunlop cheese in Wigtownshire that there was any marked advance. Mr. Caird, who was then at Baldoon, took up the thing with his wonted spirit, and sent his dairyman to England to learn; and afterwards Mr. Robert McAdam came to Baldoon as bower, and introduced the Cheshire mode. Mr. Caird had at this time a hundred cows, and his account of his success induced the directors of the Ayrshire Association to send two special commissioners to the English cheese districts. They reported in favour of the Cheddar system, on account of the lightness of labour, ease and simplicity of management, and high price of produce, and the result was that beginnings were at once made in 1854 on several Ayrshire farms, and at last Stewarton has adopted it.

The Association did not leave the farmers to grope among mere printed rules, but engaged Mr. and Mrs. Joseph Harding from Somersetshire as public instructors. They set up their apparatus in barns at five or six places in turn, and bowers and dairymaids flocked to them from Galloway and elsewhere. Mr. Robert McAdam (who is now, we believe, near Newcastle-under-Lyme) was one of their most strenuous pupils, and turning from Cheshire he introduced the Cheddar practice so successfully into Galloway that they were making their 73s. per cwt. when Ayrshire was only equal to 60s., and they have never been quite caught yet. Their strong, old land and cleverer keeping give them an advantage over the Ayrshire cold clays. The farms are generally larger and the milk and cream richer; in fact, the wilder the country the richer the milk, like an egg laid in the muirlands. Still even these natural advantages and strength of feeding, when not aided by science in the making, produced a very strong and bad flavoured cheese.

The first Ayrshire Association Cheese Show was held at Kilmarnock in 1856, and Kirkcudbrightshire, Wigtownshire, and Argyllshire have all figured in the lists. Draining, green-cropping, careful stock selection, and better house feeding have largely swelled the cheese produce of Ayrshire; and although thirty may be called the average both in it and Galloway, there are dairies with eighty to a hundred cows, and one farmer will occasionally have two or three sets.

The cheese season begins in May, and lasts till the end of September. Cheese made late, between harvest-home and Martinmas (Nov. 22), is seldom good, and the great bulk of bowers give up with September, and make fresh butter and skim-milk cheese all the winter. Very little of the latter is sold, except in the crannies of the Highlands, Oban and Tobermory, and perhaps in the dram-shops of Glasgow. Temperature is the very key-stone both of making and keeping. In summer the heat is kept up from 66 to 70 degrees, and at the end of September hot water and stoves come in. In Ayrshire many of the Marquis of Bute's tenants have capital making places, and cheese-houses heated with pipes; and in Galloway a few farmers make all winter. It is pretty good, but stiff and of a peculiar flavour, and does not pay for keeping. Cheese of six weeks old will sell in Glasgow, which has, in con-tradistinction to Edinburgh, "stomach for anything." It is in proper condition for using three months after making, and of course it ripens sooner if it has been kept warm by artificial heat. Eleven years ago the Dunlop system was universal, but the progress of Cheddar has been so rapid that in '63 it had quite got the lead, and now half Ayrshire and Dumfries-shire adopt it. A Cheddar cheese is sometimes made as big as 96lbs., and it averages 6s. to 10s. per cwt. more than Dunlop. The curds of a Cheddar are plot-ted with warm whey, and it is made up a little dryer, and is a little sooner ripe. It also takes rather longer making, and is steeped colder, and the milk is not so warm when the rennet is put in. Cheddar is more carefully worked out, whereas Dunlop is more hit-or-miss or rule-of-thumb. By the Cheddar mode more curd is got to work with, and the whole strength of it goes into the cheese. Hence the whey is far poorer than the Dunlop, which not only fattens pigs well, but even yields cream and butter at a pinch. Fine Cheddar quite holds the London and South Wales markets, and the demand makes the farmer pretty stiff with the factor, through whom the shippers generally purchase. Still, Glasgow regulates the cheese prices of Scotland, and its bazaar on Wednesday during the season is a great sight. Some people have a prejudice in favour of Dunlop, and therefore Cheddar is generally made on the Dunlop chessels, and keeps the old shape, instead of starting one of its own. Dunlops range from six to nine inches in depth and 20 to 56lbs. in weight. Even small Cheddars measure from a foot to sixteen inches, and beginning where the Dunlops leave off, reach as high as 90lbs., but they are still 60lbs. short of some of the "factory made" Americans. To obviate the retail difficulties in slicing them, the grocers cut Cheddar horizontally through the middle. It is naturally whiter, on account of the warm whey, and therefore annatto is very freely used. The Glasgow people do not care for colour, but the Edinburgh factors always stipulate for it.

Cheese factors always go round with their piercer in September, and begin getting in at the end of September and throughout October. English factors have different prices for the first lift, and the second, (which is generally softer), and the Scottish ones are gradually beginning to insist on it. Some of the largest dealers will have at times as much as 15,000 stone (of 24lbs.) in stock, and be under engagements for more, which the farmers send in by turn, although they all like if possible to clear their cheese-houses in October. All the lots are paid for in ready money, as the farmers could very ill afford to give credit. Once there was 1lb. given in every 24lbs. of cheese, and a fleece to every 12 stone of wool—"a pun to the stane and a fleece to the pack" —but the factors are "kind of beat out of it now," and of these hoary customs only the clad score is left, and that in a very mutilated shape.

A newly-made cheese should be turned once a day for six weeks, and then once a week for the rest of the twelve months, in order to prevent the rot of the skin. Messrs. Richardson of Edinburgh and a few others adopt the English system of putting elm boards between the rows so as to keep the skins apart. A factor who chooses to keep for a twelvemonth, and observes all these precautions, can sell occasionally as high as 16s. per stone, but that is the highest point Cheddar has ever reached. Cheddar, which is finer and sweeter in flavour, keeps better than Dunlop, and the latter generally becomes too strong in flavour after nine months. For very first-rate keeping, a fire is preferable to a stove, as the heat is too severe at times. A stone of cheese kept with the greatest tact will waste ten per cent. in a year.

Mr. Campbell, of New Cumnock, attempted to make
an Old Parr of one, but at the end of nine years it
had turned quite dark, and was so completely exhausted that it was hardly eatable.

Jane Dunlop of Stewarton is the largest dealer in
Ayrshire cows, and may be seen in the Glasgow market every Wednesday. She will bring as many as
170 to a leading fair, and they are to be found in a
great field at Strathbungo, near Glasgow, or behind
the Black Bull. The May and June fairs of Rutherglen are also great places with her. As a judge there
are few to equal her, and she does her own business,
driving up and down the country in her gig. The
business is now conducted principally by her son
Gabriel, and is still as extensive as ever. The
trade in Ayrshires is immense, and a dealer once
passed 2,073 through his hands in one year, and not
a few of them for France, Australia, Austria, and
Belgium. The dealers begin the first week of February, and go round to all the markets, Ayr, Glasgow,
Biggar, Kilmarnock, Renfrew, Rutherglen, Stirling,
Dumfries, Carluke (the largest of all on May 21),
and buy them as threes and fours. Before the days
of railways, they paid five visits in the season, but
now they are seldom away.

The English, who are not fond of black-noses but
of large flecks, give all prices from £8 to £18.
Some leading English dealers will advertise the
colours before hand, and then make a point of getting
cows to correspond. Many farmers breed on pur-

pose for the market, and in November the dealers will buy up late-calving heifers, and disperse them over different farms, and 2s. 6d. in the pound is taken off if they do not prove in-calf.

The styles of the six men who hold the English trade are so well known that the experienced breeder can tell, if he goes into the market, pretty nearly what each will take. Cotterill of Worcester goes in for little short-legged beauties, fawns and flecked reds or "leopards," with spots like half-crowns all over them. Broad backs and coats "that can't be too smooth" and up-horns are also great requirements in the "*Here's one for Cotterill.*" In fact, he must have neatness and no self-colour like red or black, but the shape of the vessel is no consideration.

If they're only big enough, they'll do for Bennett from Cheshire, who likes large papped ones, with a view to his dairy customers. Much of the importance of the Dumfries market has depended upon him for many years. Jackson of Lancaster buys the best young heifers chiefly rough in the coat and good growers. Hodgson and Parkinson from Staffordshire also like them strong and useful, and the latter especially buys the oldest and roughest for the Potteries. Rough rumps, bad backs, and thick horns are all the same to him, as there is no respect of age, quality, or colour with the miners, as long as they have a four-legged milk machine. These dealers will sometimes take two to three hundred from

Dumfries market each week southward. Burrell of Essex has often taken eight score in a lot, and would always rather give £20 for a good than £7 for a bad one. And so ends our "milky way."

CHAPTER XI.

AYR TO ARDROSSAN.

" Will Shakespeare, I wist, could never resist
The glance of a pet ' long-tail' ;
He'd down with his book, and up with his crook,
To find him a hare on Cotsale
Queen Bess and her court, in their love of the sport,
To A. Graham himself didn't yield ,
And she bade no churl, but proud Norfolk's Earl,
Draw up coursing laws for the field."

SPORTING MAGAZINE

Eglinton Castle—The Races at Bogside—Scene of the Tournament—
The Foxhounds—Bowls, Rackets, and Curling in the late Lord's time
—The Ardrossan Coursing Club—Waterloo—A Peep at Picton and
Cardinal York—A Visit to Mr. Borron's Kennel.

THE vane at Eglinton Castle faced south at last, and
the curlers had been duly notified that they need
not come to the garden ponds, unless they wished to
play up to their ankles in water. Eighteen hunters
were still walking round and round the straw
ride, in those dark-green plaid sheets which England knew so well; and the colour of the dark-
brown Rocket, who was last in the string, seemed to
bring back all those grand old days of Fobert and
Charles Marlow—The Dutchman and Van Tromp.
The Chase is the present Earl's delight, and for three
seasons his untiring enthusiasm has kept together
that Ayrshire country which has made other good
masters droop and turn aside to more hopeful hunting

grounds. Both his lordship and Cox are light-weights, and the stud is in keeping, and principally made up of horses which Mr. Napier, the stud groom, purchased in Ireland. Warlock was there, and he and Cox had been out thirty times already that season. Conqueror was the first that the Earl ever rode to hounds when he came back from sea and the nice-topped Bloxham, The Witch, the sweet-headed Mutiny, and Shamrock, who is second horse twice a week, were among his lordship's especials; while Deceiver, Lyons by Yellow Jack, Red Hart, and the grey Chicken by Bantam, all take their turn with Cox and the whips.

No race-horses have been trained here since Mat Dawson had Dr. Caius and The Potentate in charge. It was here, too, that he bred and broke Aristides, whom he sent to his brother Tom, when he had Blue Bonnet and the other horses at Middleham, with an assurance that he could "do what he liked *if* he liked." Dr. Caius was a very perfect little fellow, and there was never a finer finish up Snaker's Hill, the "Choak Jade" of Irvine, than when he beat St. Lawrence a head for the Eglinton Park Cup. Mr. William Hope Johnstone also won a great stake here with his rare weight-carrier William Le Gros, as he took all the money he could get about the Irvine Cup and the Stewards' Cup, and landed the double event. There was some rare gentleman-riding at this Bibury of the North, and the neat and yet vigorous finishes of Sir Frederick Johnstone, and the

fine patience of Captain Pettat—both long since gone
to their rest—won them many a race out of the fire.
The steeple-chase course went out from the bottom
towards Kilwinning, as far as the river Garnock, and
included several banks, a brook, and a wide ditch, as
well as a stone wall in front of the stand.   Sir David
Baird, on his clever little Pioneer or his cocky little
Dr. Syntax, was alike dangerous over it, and the
Marquis of Waterford fairly " skinned the lamb" by
winning thrice in succession in one afternoon on his
great, raking Blueskin.   Lord Eglinton did not care
much for the flag-line; but when the Marquis
thought that Multum in Parvo (13st. 7lbs.) was not
so good as his Saladin (13st. 12lbs.), his lordship took
him for 500 gs. ostensibly, but it was said for 1,000 gs.
a side, and, thanks to his own steady riding and John
Napier's training, beat the great Irish pair in a
canter.

There have been no races since '52; but a stick
cover has been made for the foxes in the park, and
thus one sporting interest rose when the other waned.
Major, Waterloo, and the beautiful Blackbird, "whose
eyes seemed starting from her head with life," are
all gone, and their monuments with them, but there
are a few greyhounds still at the Castle, and the
Earl won the Waterloo Plate with Rainbow in '64,
when both the Purse and the Plate winners were
Ayrshire-bred, and King Death by an Ayrshire dog.
There is no special trace of the tournament ground
among the oaks, elms, and beeches at the back of the

Castle, where six-and-twenty years ago the present Emperor of the French looked on through the three wet days, and the Duchess of Somerset was the Queen of Beauty.

Thither came among the rest Sir Francis Hopkins, the Knight of the Burning Tower, on a bay; the lord of the tournament, with his golden armour, on a chesnut; Lord Waterford, in steel armour, with six esquires; Lord Ailsa, Knight of the Dolphin; Captain Fairlie, Knight of the Golden Lion; Mr. Campbell of Saddle, of whom Tom Ingoldsby would aver that he was

" Somehow knocked out of his family seat;"

and Lord Glenlyon, as Knight of the Gael, with seventy-two Highlanders, who guarded the tilting ground, and, with boundless beef and ale under their belts, still sighed for their wonted porridge.

The foxhounds are made up of purchases from the Southampton, Mr. Drake's, and the North Warwickshire packs, and drafts from the South Warwickshire, the Doneraile, and the Yarborough. There are 58 couple for three or four days a week, and they always run them mixed. We noticed the smutty-faced Frantic; the short-legged Heroine; Tempest, with a head telling of Drake's Duster; Cheerful, with all the Belvoir quality; a nice Dainty; Duchess, sister to Dashaway; and Dauntless, with some of the Baker blood about her, and a great taste for roe deer. Doneraile's Transit was another of the Drake's

Duster sort, which huntsmen set such store by;
and there, too, were the deep-bodied Wary, Careful, a very nice mover, and a neat little couple
Chantress and Carnage.   North Warwickshire Prat-
tle wears well, and Drake's old Milliner sits apart
with Skilful.

The dog pack are principally of the Doneraile,
Southampton, and Drake blood. Four couple of them,
with Tapster, Trouncer, old grey Seaman, and the
stout-boned Oppidan, compose the Drake lot, while
seven couple have the Southampton and twelve,
with Challenger amongst them, the Doneraile brand.
North Warwickshire Damper earned his benison
from Cox as "full of head;" and Squires's pet
Launcelot is full of action. Old Chieftain is also from
the North Warwickshire, and Young Seaman, the
only one they have had from old Milliner, sits near
him, as if gathering thoughts of wisdom.

It is a great open country for the foxes, with deep
gills and a bad cold scent, which lies best by Dunlop,
Caldwell, and Ardrossan. It is thirty miles from
north to south, and the plough country on the Ayr
side is the heaviest and coldest part. Tarbert Gorse
is a great find, with a rare scent over the grass; and
Caldwell is also a crack meet, with a fine country,
up to Kilbirnie.   There were a few roe deer at Dal-
rymple Wood, but it has been cleared out with two
couple of draft hounds, who made some fine melody
over the job. The bottoms of the cover are all sedge,
which is down after November. There are eighteen

or nineteen litters in the country every year, and his lordship has put down several brace as well; but still, despite all his exertions, there has been a "fox famine," and they have once or twice left off before their time. Many of the gorses have only been planted within the last three seasons, and there is very little good lying; and if the foxes are driven out of the country, there is no outlying pack on the hills to bring them back. Sourlie Wood, near the kennels, is generally a sure find, and so is the stick cover of three acres, which they draw with the terriers. The trains suit them well enough, and the hounds are also vanned for the long distances, and, in fact, never did master struggle harder to deserve success.

The late Earl seldom hunted here even in Sir David Baird's day, and for the grouse shooting he went to Cleuchearn, beyond Eaglesham. Curling, bowls, golf, and rackets were his delight; and his racket player, Patrick Divitt, and the Hon. Mr. Montgomerie were making the tennis-court rattle again when we looked in. The late earl did not begin rackets till he was 35 or 36, and then Sir H. H. Campbell and all the county gentry came and had great matches at Christmas. In summer, his example set all the Ayrshire farmers off bowling. He would come down in the beginning of July, and play matches every week till nearly the middle of October. Hugh Conn, John Napier, and Walter Smith, V.S., played in his bowling, and

Robert Brown, one of his farmers, took Smith's place in the curling rink. He gave a 120-guinea Cup to be bowled for annually between the Ayr and the Glasgow men, and a ten-guinea medal for every club on his estate. On the bowling days when the great "jug" was played for, an immense table was laid out, and all the ladies bowled with their kirtles up to their knees.

When he challenged the clubs for twenty miles round at bowling or curling, the stakes were always a boll of meal for the poor. One year no less than £40 worth was distributed this way through the Minister of Kilwinning. He also made three artificial curling ponds with wooden bottoms or asphalte and polished ashlar. Two of them were fifty yards by thirty-six, and the other sixty by sixty, and he would have twenty rinks going at one time. Napier played the 50lb. stone, Brown the 46lb., Conn the 44lb., and his lordship himself directed the rink, and played last with the 40lb. one. No one was cooler in action and understood better all the subtle generalship of chap and lie, and outers, and yet he was always learning. He would be at the ice to a minute on a dark winter's morning, and keep himself warm by sweeping till it was light enough to begin, and then he would curl all day. If one curling rink was better than another, he would never rest till he played it, and Sir James Boswell's was one of the defeated.

He and his leading players had each three or four

pairs of curling stones, and none of them better than Sir Thomas Moncrieff's, which were very quick and polished. They were made of granite called "burnoch," which was got near Sir James Boswell's estates, and spotted white and black like a starling's breast. His lordship did not neglect golf, which he first learnt on the links near Stevenson. Some of the best men from St. Andrew's and Musselburgh came to Prestwick, near Ayr, to play with him; and he died on a return visit to St. Andrew's, when he was very little past his prime. No man was better known or more loved throughout the three kingdoms.

The "view house" still stands at Bogside, and one's sense of the desolation is not dissipated by that dreary spot, Kilwinning. In a vault beneath its kirk, which is a curious appendix to the ruined tower of the old abbey, his lordship lies with his two wives. He was erst the very life of the spot, when the archers of Kilwinning met once a year to shoot at the green papingo with the golden heart, on the summit of that tower. He who winged it got a broad ribbon for his prize, and the ribbon-men drew after dinner for the honour of the first shot for the Captaincy, which is conferred on him who first knocks it off its perch, and was twice won by the Earl.

Mr. Ewing's greyhounds, or rather a pack of fifteen or sixteen couple, passed us in the town. He has had far more, and when his Leven Water ran second to Neville for the Malleny St. Leger, he had fourteen among the 100 in the stake, and eleven of them were left in on the first day. "Leven Water," says Mr. Nightingale, "was not unlike British Lion in his work, a plucky good laster, of great strength and symmetry; he always ran well, but he never came to England." Many of the Ewing kennel were of Dr. Brown's blood, a well-known Ayrshire character. His dogs were kept by farmers, who got half their winnings, and some of them were very fast. The Doctor was a big man, with a perpetual scarf round his white hat, and an umbrella under his arm, and so nervous that he never looked at a course while his own dog was running. There were few faster than his Chance in Scotland; and Spot was one of six left in out of 178, when Read's Sultan won the great stake at Southport. He had also Whistler, and a good bitch Cantrip, and place them out where he might, they came in well and fit to run on their trial days near Stewarton.

Ardrossan lies some seven miles coastwards from Kilwinning. Its beautiful slopes which skirt the coast, where Arran holds its silent watch among the breakers, are dear to all Scottish coursers. The old Club livery was silver-grey with silver buttons, black-velvet waistcoat, dark-blue silk handkerchief, white cords, and Napoleon boots; and Mr. Borron and a few more are still faithful to these dress traditions of more than forty years' standing. The meetings are far more for sport than pelf. Every farm on the

Eglinton estate sent dogs, and members lent dogs to the farmers who bred them. As many as a hundred dogs would be entered, and sixty courses would be run off in a day. As Mr. Nightingale (who judged thirty-three times) says, " It was just like going from Lytham when you left the town end —rare quarters, and a happy, pleasant time of it." Lord Eglinton was always there, a leader in reality, never aspiring to be one, but always with delicate courtesy supporting those in authority, and ready to help in taking up a dog or in any other way. His seat on horse back was peculiarly stiff and upright, and he was never pale and anxious except when Waterloo ran. His Blackbird was small and strong, and won the Caledonian Cup, and a more beautiful puppy was never brought up at Eaglesham. Frolic by Waterloo was a great delight of the first Lady Eglinton's, and well she might be, as she was a very resolute, low runner, and won the Great Wiltshire Puppy Stakes at fourteen months.

It was at Ardrossan that her sire first ran. Old Baird Kirk, the keeper, would maintain that his brother Fingall was better, and they had one spin, and Waterloo beat him. The latter was by Dusty Miller from Exotic, for whom Lord Eglinton gave £50 to a South Lancashire breeder. "His head was always held high like Black Cloud's; he never pulled a yard from the slips, and was never in a hurry. In the first 100 yards he was not fast, and then he went harder and harder. His shoulders were beautiful, his forelegs nice and short, his tail long and curiously curled, his thighs very long, his ribs remarkably good, his hocks turned in a little, and he was made like Cerito about the loins.   He was not only very great on plough, but a wonder to climb a hill, which helped him not a little when he beat Gracchus at Ashdown.   Killing was his weak point; he would get possession of his hare, and put in some beautiful wrenches, but beyond that he was not clever with his teeth.   Cacciattore once just beat him in a trapping course, and he was thrown out at Waterloo by a very bad little hare, which came short back when he reached it half a dozen lengths first, instead of jumping the ditch, and met the other dog in the face.   He was in form then, as he won the £100." Such is Mr. Nightingale's " winter tale" of him.

Before calling at Mr. Borron's we walked four miles by the shore almost to Tarbert Gorse, in search of Picton and Cardinal York.   Mr. Richmond was pursuing his daily labour, and six or seven of his charges were playing in the meadow near the mill. Duchess, by Ptarmigan from Di Vernon, was good to know from the burn on her blue skin, and had made up for her Waterloo defeat by winning the Douglas Cup.   Marshal Forward and Silver Rays were there; and " York! York!" brought the yellow-and-white sire of Calabaroono out of a mysterious straw hut behind a door, and soon three white-and-yellow daughters were grouped round him.   He and Picton, Di Vernon, and Trip the Daisy made up the

Jacobite and Forest Queen litter, so well known in Walsh's Calendar. The Cardinal was " a fine steady-working dog, a sticker, and with a great share of pace." There was very little affinity in look between him and Picton, who has less length, and ran a few pounds lighter. They had a very strong trial once, when The Cardinal stayed the longest, but did not show such speed. Jacobite their sire was " a little shabby sort of a dog, who commanded and met his hares at the turn. He had great pace for his size, and, like his sire Bedlamite, he was rather impetuous. He was the best puppy in England ; and then he began to rush and run as wild as a deer." On his dam's side he inherited the rough-tailed Violence blood, which goes back to Mr. Fox's Fairy. The sort were very fast, and therefore just suited the Duke of Gordon.

Two white greyhounds in stone guard Mr. Borron's avenue. He is of an old Lancashire family, and the blue greyhound on his shield, quartered with the lamb and banner, is inherited from General Braddock, who fell on the British side in the War of Independence. Coursing has been with him a life-long passion ; at nineteen his name was in the Altcar and Ridgway lists, and more than thirty years ago he brought down greyhounds to Scotland, starting at 4 o'clock a.m. on the mail. His first good stake was won at the Lanarkshire and Renfrewshire Club, then held at Pollok. At Lytham and Altcar he has often carried off a leading stake ; but in the Waterloo Cup, even if he has had a first favourite, he has never got through more than two courses. He won the Purse with Black Cloud, but his nomination has been more generally among the sixteen Plate unfortunates, who "take nothing by their motion." However, this has been the fate of many; and David, for instance, went head over heels into the first ditch.

Scotland and England have cross obligations in the shape of sheets and slips. The Hon. Hamilton Dundas first brought the former from Newmarket to Scotland; and Mr. Borron, who had been struck with the swivel slips of Marsh, a Paisley gunsmith, took back the idea to Lancashire, which had previously only followed the Newmarket fashion of two ends of a strap coupled or parted with a wedge, or like the Oldfield Lane Doctor on Chat Moss, " started the whole fleet" for a St. Leger. Still, greyhounds do not monopolize Mr. Borron's hours of idleness in his new sea-home, as a grey mare and a chesnut were in his stable, waiting for their turn with the Eglinton at Tarbert Hill or Southennan. He has always adopted the plan of gilt electro-plating his bits, and considers that when horses have carious teeth it does not make them so fretful, or engender so much saliva. His horses are not bedded on straw, but on pine shavings, which he finds very efficacious in keeping off the plague of fleas. He has also taken a good deal of trouble to ascertain the right temperature of greyhound kennels, and first tried corrugated iron ones, lined with felt and wood, but they were too cold in winter and too hot in summer.

Three black pensioners, Black Flag, his sister Black Belle, and Bold Enterprise, were in the first one. Old grey-faced Black Flag won the Puppy Stakes at Lytham, and was great on every ground. He was a cotemporary of Black Cloud, Skyrocket, and Beacon, and is by Blue Light out of Wicked Eye, and one of the only litter of hers that ever did any good. Four of them died of distemper, and only Black Flag and Black Belle were left. Bold Enterprise by Beacon out of Judy (sister to Judge) is a lofty sort of dog, and carries his head well up. He was very good for the flats of Lancashire, but, like The Judge blood, failed at a hill. Mr. Borron bought Judy on purpose to put to Beacon, as there was a great deal of the Streamer blood in Judge, and he wanted to unite it again with the Bugle. Bold Enterprise shows his teeth, and is as savage as a tiger. In his running days they dare not keep him with the other dogs, as he was a complete lunatic; and the grave of Ivy, near the flower border, proclaims his latest victim. His victories have been varied; he once beat Canaradzo at Southport, and he killed a terrier, although he was muzzled. His sister Bit of Lace was away at Glasgow, and so was Billet Doux, both of them fast, and known at Altcar in their day. Mr. Borron is crossing the blood carefully, and has some saplings by Bloody Heart (brother to Bold Enterprise) out of Black Belle. Thus Black Belle is put to Bloody

Heart, and Black Flag to Bit of Lace. Brighton went seven times to Altcar, and won six prizes and ran up for the seventh. Archibald Cook, Mr. Spinks's present man, trained him, and Mr. Nightingale said of him: "He was a wonderful dog; he ran the truest of any dog I ever saw—true as a puppy to the last." Curler, his sire, was a grand dog, a great worker, and of rare bottom, and, being by Jason out of Rosebud, he combined Lord Stradbroke's blood with the old Ayrshire. Brighton was bought from a doctor at Kilbirnie, near Dalgig. The doctor was leading him, and Mr. Borron had Brightness in hand, when they went down to the slips to meet in the run up for the Dalry St. Leger, and it was arranged that the doctor should have first and second money (£70), and that Mr. Borron should take Brighton. He was sold at London for 50 gs., and went to Mr. Rendall of Brigmerston, near Amesbury; but he was no good at the stud, as he got his puppies far too fine, and he became a parlour dog at last.

The most wonderful hit that Mr. Borron ever made was buying Blue Light for thirty-five pounds, and old Lancashire reminiscences. He came in the middle of the season, when he had run twice and won twice at Altcar, and was then sold by Beale, the late Lord Sefton's trainer, who received him as a present, on account of his being worsted in his trial by Senate. In his looks he was rather insignificant, and weighed, like Brighton, 56lbs. He was got by Monsoon out of Stave, full sister to Bugle; and like

Bugle, he was blue with black hairs, and especially bare on the quarters. The blood has always been more calculated for the flat than the hill. He won 25 out of 26 courses, and was only beaten by Craigieburn, whom he paid off; and then he cut his back sinews on a bit of glass, and broke down. Beacon and Black Cloud were the results of his cross with Frolic; his Black Flag was from Wicked Eye, Bright Steel from Scotia, Blackness from Nettle (a sister to Steel's Japhet), and Skyrocket from Syncope of the Streamer blood, which was generally red with a little white. Skyrocket was given to Lord Sefton by Mr. Borron, and thus the Bugle blood came back to the Sefton Kennel with another cross of Streamer in it.

Frolic, the dam of Beacon and Black Cloud (who ran at 68lbs. and 70lbs. respectively), was by Waterloo out of Dr. Brown's bitch of Ayrshire and Biggar blood; and Bright Idea and Bonfire were of the same litter. The old bitch died, and they were brought up by bull-bitches, or "lady bulls," as Frank Buckle would have called them. In Black Cloud and Beacon the Streamer and Bugle strains are united with the old Douglas or Greenshields blood, and through Exotic with the Newmarket. Black Cloud beat Beacon in his trial the first season, and two years after Beacon had the best of it. Beacon was a good average dog, a regular runner and not brilliant, but so hardy that he won the Caledonian, Altcar, and Irish Challenge Cups within a month. He was sold for

60 gs., and came back at $6\frac{1}{2}$ gs. five years after, very fresh for a dog of ten seasons.

Black Cloud drove his hare, and kept her to himself like his daughter Belle of the Village, but he, too, went into a ditch in his second Waterloo course. His greatest performance was beating Mr. Randell's Ranter in an Altcar Produce Stake. He was a rare turner, and Judge's pace was never shown to greater advantage than when he just outpaced him down the hill near Carstairs; but his sister Bright Idea avenged him on the Cumberland red, after two undecided courses. This was in 1855, and Judge had won the Waterloo Cup a month before. Mr. Borron always thought Bright Idea better than either brother, and she was never beaten in public. She only ran twice as a puppy, and was drawn for the fifth course of the Biggar St. Leger of sixty-four in the spring. In her first course the next season she broke her leg over the rocks, and it gangrened, and her sister, Bonfire, died in a wire fence near Biggar.

CHAPTER XII.

AYR TO DUMFRIES.

"They spied a soldier with a Scotch kirn on his head Some of them had been purveying abroad, and had found a vessel filled with Scotch cream· bringing the reversion of it to their tents, some got dishfuls and some hatfuls ; and the cream being now low in the vessel one fellow would have a modest drink, and so lifts the kirn to his mouth, but another canting it up it falls over his head, and the man is lost in it, all the cream trickles down his apparel, and his head fast in the tub This was a merriment to the officers, as Oliver loved an innocent jest."

CARLYLE

Ayr Race-course—Kilkerran—The Dairies of Galloway—Captain Kennedy—Stranraer—Galloway Points—A Day at Meikleculloch—Ride to Southwick—Mr Stewart's Shorthorns—The Dumfries Pork Trade.

WE saw Ayr in its sunniest guise one morning, as we sat on the race-course stile, and combined our "silk" recollections of Lanercost, Philip, and the other heroes of the Gold Cup, with the "scarlet," as Lord Eglinton's men on a bay, grey, and chesnut, trotted past to the meet. Some Ayrshires grouped on the banks of the mill-stream, as if for a "sun picture," pulled us back to curds and cream, and the thoughts of how on earth we were to grapple with such a subject as cheese. We might wander off in the spirit for a time to the days when wolves preyed on the red deer of the Grampians; when "The Returning Hugh" established the first barley mill north of the Forth, and died in his bed and his yellow wig at the age of 112; when the old carrier drove his white ponies with

2 x

packs on their backs and bells on their heads over
the rough muirland road; when Madge Wildfire with
her crook and her plaid wandered through Ayrshire;
and when old "Keely Bags" supplied all Galloway
with sheep ruddle; but still, cheese, wool, and bacon
were ghosts that would not be laid, and fairly em-
bittered our life.

Of the route to Maybole we knew little enough,
as we rode it by night, striking, as it would seem,
inland, as there was no sea roar for company. Next
morning the scene opened on the Girvan Valley, with
Kilkerran House to the left. The hills are covered
with fern and heather, and go by the name of
"The Burning." They are so called from a seam
of coal, which once took fire on the Kilkerran property. It has been extinguished for many years,
but one at Dalquharran is still burning. On
the opposite side of the valley, the open freestone
subsoil of Kilkerran is admirable for silver firs,
spruces, and beeches. Mr. Fleming rents it at present, and as for animals it was quite a Noah's Ark
No. 2. His residence in India gave him a taste for
Arabs. A bay and a black mare were at exercise in
the park, and a grey horse, a much better specimen
than either of them, and an H.C. at the Islington
Horse Show, was leading gallops for Brewtey's string
at Newmarket. One of the Clydesdale mares was
the prize mare Rosie, a purchase from Merryton, and
had a fine partner at rather a lower figure from Dumfriesshire. Of sporting dogs there was also quite an

array, black and tan Gordon setters, three or four of them prize winners, and liver-and-white pointers for the Kilkerran muirs, which stretch miles away behind from Barr to Straiton. The late Duke of Athole's herd of West Highlanders, which were displaced at Blair Athole by the Breadalbanes, wandered in dun, red, and cream array among the meadows on one side of the river Girvan, and as many Ayrshires on the other. Among the latter is Arabell, one of the first-prize takers at Battersea, and bought for 57 gs. at the first Merryton sale, along with the red-and-white Beauty. The dairymaid was uncommonly sweet on her, and drove up the more Hereford-coloured Blossom, to show what a neat pair they made. The first-prize bull at Maybole, and the first prize one at Kelso, also stood side by side in the byre, while a group of Bretonnes outside lent their tiny aid to the dairy.

Between Kilkerran and Girvan we rode through rich bean and wheat land, in the midst of which is " the garden farm," as it is called, of Girvan Mains, which owes not a little to sea-wrack manure. As we pass the ruined church of Old Dailly, and the wayside stone which tells where John Aikin died, we may well revert to Old Mortality or Edie Ochiltree laying aside his staff and wallet, and calmly yielding up his spirit. After this it was quite a rocky sea-coast route past the gates of Ardmillan with the hooded eagles, where Lord Ardmillan passes his learned leisure. Half-bred lambs and Ayrshires

were in the Vale, and sprittle-faces on the heights;
and as the Highlands of the south-west began to
flank the coast, we saw Galloways or rough crosses
from them browsing on their sides. Forty years ago
there was not an Ayrshire in Ballantrae, and nothing
but these stunted blacks as far as Whithorn in
Wigtownshire; but Ayrshire dairies have gradually
overspread the Stewartry of Kirkcudbrightshire, and
away to the Mull of Galloway and Burrow Head.
The wild hard pasture gives it its pre-eminence as a
dairy country; but it was long before this faculty
was properly brought out, and twenty years
ago an Ayrshire would have been almost a raree-
show.

The farmers hated their neighbours' spotted kine,
, and would not allow their hinds or "bondagers" to
keep them for fear of the colour effect on the blacks.
Mr. M'Clue of Din Vin is one of the earliest Cheddar men, and keeps as many as 140 cows; and Col.
M'Dowall has a beautiful dairy at Logan House.
Ayrshire men found the price of land cheaper, and
crowded into Galloway, and so the idea has spread
on. In one respect the dairy management differs from
Ayrshire, as there are fewer bowers, and every year
lessens the number.

There are not many sheep till you reach the east
of the county. Half-bred lambs are on the holme
land near the river, and all the mountain district is
stocked with sprittle or brocky faced sheep, more
especially in the south-west, on the Minnigaff hills.

Once sheep were preferred much blacker in the face; but thirty years since the farmers thought that the lighter-faced wedders had most "tops" among them, and were quieter to boot, and held to rams of that shade. New Galloway is a great stronghold of the breed, and about Kells, where it is flanked by the Minnigaff and the Carsphairn hills, it is as wild as Westmoreland, all rocks and cairns, and with blacker heath.

Many blackfaced wedders and half-bred lambs are turniped in Galloway. There is nice and kindly dry land by the rivers Dee, Urr, and Ken (which divides Balmaclellan from Kells), and half-bred hoggs are not sent to Penrith now in such numbers, but kept on during a part of the summer. In fact, some of them are put on turnips a second winter. The breeding of half-bred lambs and grazing them as hoggs on arable ground is a practice of only recent growth. Many Clydesdales are bred and sold at three, after a year in the harrows. It does not pay to breed any other kind of horse, and for a roadster farmers fall back on Rosley Hill.

We struck rather more inland from Ballantrae to reach Finnart, through what seemed in the gloom to be a mountain glen, with natural oak, birch, and hazel on its sides. We can well give this Glenapp credit for all its summer beauty; but it was a time of rain and snow and mist, which half-shrouded the grand deep-sea anchorage of Loch Ryan, at the foot of the glen. Captain Kennedy, a distinguished grazier of sprittle-faces and Galloways, and a frequent judge at the Highland Society's shows, grazes a considerable portion of the hill and valley ground at Finnart. He does not breed Galloways; but his flock of sprittle-faced ewes number thirty score. Ayrshire Laddie of his breeding won a first prize in Mr. Dryfe's hands at Battersea; and the Captain has shown and won at Ayr, Glasgow, and Aberdeen sometimes with his rams, but more frequently with ewe hoggs. He generally buys his Galloway stores in September, and keeps them for one-and-a-half years. They are bought when they are nearly that age as " cuddaghs," in September, at Dumfries, and up and down the Stewartry. The sky and the hills of the glen are their only winter shelter; and however deep the snow may be they are kept out in the field, with oat straw, turnips, and hay. In Dumfriesshire yard-keeping is generally adopted; but the Captain's experience is to the effect that unsheltered bullocks come to hand quicker in the spring than if they have the shed option. Messrs. M'Combie and Heath, the great Aberdeen and Norfolk feeders, have been his leading customers. For many years Mr. M'Combie took forty at a time, and in his lot of 1859 he got the Smithfield and Birmingham prize-bullock, which was bred by Mr. Martin of Braco. Mr. Heath has dealt very largely with him of late.

Stranraer was of all towns the most dreary on a wet morning; and watching the oyster-boats in the

bay, reading most ancient newspapers, and looking
at Flying Childers, Eclipse, and King Herod—the
last testimony to its races, which have now been dead
and buried for more than forty years—on the walls
of a coffee-room, beguiled the weary hours, till we
could start once more to Dumfries by Newton
Stewart, and New Galloway, on that most sodden
and "most immemorial day."

> "The merchant rain, which carries on
> Rich commerce 'twixt the earth and sun,"

was never at rest from sunrise. We went past endless
muirs and moss hags full of dark-grey boulders and
small lochs, on which wild-ducks were sailing, as if
proud of the general suction. Still, after all, there was
certain grandeur about that damp desolation, and
when you thought of it in connexion with many a
dark episode, with the tales which linger still in the
western Lowlands, "of the black charger of Claver-
house, of the strange encounters with the Evil One,
of the cry of the plover and the peewit round the encampment on the hill-side," you might well allow
that it was "more instructive than many books."

Cumberland has done much for Galloway stock.
It is true that, before George Graham of Riggfoot
began to breed them forty years ago, there were good
bulls bred in Johnstone, Dumfriesshire, and equally
true that he began with a cow from Sproat of Renton,
and a bull from James Welch of Leaths; but still, he
was the "Black Booth" of Cumberland and the

Border counties, and none attended so systematically to the beef points. The late Sir James Graham had at one time a herd of thirty cows at Croft Head, which were purchased by Mr. Yule, his steward, and Mr. Wilkin, one of his tenants. They went to Galloway to choose them, and instead of medals or money, bull-calves were given as prizes to the Netherby tenants who showed the best lots of five yearlings and as many two-year-olds. Gibbons of Moss Band had once the best herd on the estate, and John Johnson of Pedder Hill was very close up with him. The showers of Galloway cattle at the Highland Society are comparatively small, and it is quite of late years that they have come up in sufficient force to bring the rule into play—that if there are more than three of the breed in a class, they are to be judged separately from the Angus.

In Wigtownshire they have no Highland Society men among them. The Earl of Galloway used to exhibit, and so did Mr. Stewart of Glasserton; and now James Gifford of Bladenoch, M'Whinnie of Milton, and Agnew of Balscalloch are generally foremost at the local shows. Kirkcudbrightshire gets most prizes at the Dumfries Union. The Earl of Selkirk had once a herd at Grange of Kirkcudbright, but it is now kept at Canee, and is not in its old form. The Sproat stock was once most celebrated, but he has not been steady to his early love, and crossed them with Anguses, and then with shorthorns. He was the breeder of Borness or Cumberland Willie, who was the first to make the fame of George Graham so fast and sure.

Graham of Meikleculloch has quite gone to the front with his females, and Semiramis, Harriet, and Hannah, all first-prize Highland Society cows, stood in his byre at one time. Wellwood Maxwell of Glenlee had the first yearling heifer at Kelso, and Clark of Culmain the best Galloway bull at the '62 Union Show. Shennan of Ballig keeps more cows than any man in Galloway, and owns the Nestor of black bulls, Bob Burns (235) by Geordie (234), whose failing back only just beat him out of the first place when he was shown at the Newcastle Royal in his tenth year. Biggar of King's Grange, Thompson of Blaiket (who bred the second prize yearling heifer Queen Mary at Battersea), and Cunningham of White Cairn, with his well-known Kate, all show either at the Royal or at the local show at Dalbeattie. Cunningham of Dunrod Mill only owns three or four, but Mr. Jardine won with his stock at Lockerbie, and he bred Sir William (222), who was the first two-year-old in Thompson of Blaiket's hands, when Bob Burns headed the aged-bull class at Edinburgh.

" Black and all black" extends into the Dumfriesshire dales, but not higher up Nithsdale than a few miles above Thornhill. Rae of Gaterslack, Stobbo of Halliday Hill, William Irving of Brandennoch, and David Martin of Braco, are all loyal to it. Graham of The Shaw shows good heifers at Lockerby, and the Kirkhill stock was in its prime when the late Walter Carruthers had ' Jock (66), own brother to The Squire (18), and when his Ranger was second to Wellington (22) at Carlisle.

Lockerby first introduced the Galloway bull sales on April 17th, 1851, and Castle Douglas followed its lead. Fifteen bulls and eleven queys were sold at the first Lockerby sale, and £16 was the highest figure. Twenty years ago as many guineas was thought very high for a black yearling bull, but prices have soared upwards since then, and now twice as much can be got from the Kirkcudbrightshire and Wigtownshire men when they "tak a notion," and an odd one goes at a good price to Cumberland. The bidders are not much guided by the prize positions, and this year the third fetched £11 5s. more than the first. The price of females has also gone up, and good queys will fetch £20 to £30 for Canada and Ireland, where they are crossed Aberdeen-fashion with a shorthorn bull.

The United Society of Dumfriesshire, Kirkcud. brightshire, and Wigtownshire, which must not be confounded with the Dumfries Union, meets once in five years at Dumfries. Shennan of Balig won well in '57, and '62, and so did Cunningham in the last-named year. There is a great annual sale at Castle Douglas in March, at which Kirkcudbrightshire generally fits itself with bulls for the year, and has gone as high as £60 rather than be foiled. Still, the best local show for Galloways is at Dalbeattie. Graham's Hannibal was twice first here, and that eminent breeder drew out his whole strength, with

Semiramis, Dinah, Matilda, Harriet, and Maud when he was first in the five-cow sweepstakes.

Galloways look best in October, as their brown-calf hair generally returns each spring. The head should be short and Roman, like a Cheviot sheep, with a full expressive eye (a point very difficult to get), a round bold forehead, and a good robust muzzle. The poll should be broad, and the ears large, with broad fringes inside, active in their movement and standing out at angles from the head, instead of lying back like the Angus. The sweetness of the head and bone, the finer skin, and the lighter hind quarters and thighs distinguish the Angus aristocrats from their Galloway brethren, and, in fact, the Angus may be called "Galloways with shorthorn treat-ment." Graham of Riggfoot laid great stress on short legs, and a good rough coat with wool amongst it, which sticks on till the new hair comes. It is said that Galloway men look too much to great length of hair without reference to softness, and that they are satisfied if the coats are as wavy as bears. *They* say, on the contrary, that they like long coats to throw off the water, but that there should be plenty of wool below, and that to be wavy from light-ness is an Angus vice. Once the Galloway tail was much too high, but that point has been amended, and the tops have become straighter and the loins less slack. A thin rat tail is looked upon with sus-picion, lest there should be a thin skin with it, which will not suit the climate. Bad thighs are nearly as rare as a horn or scur. Once they had white backs, and were brindled and horned as well, and some few were "belted," or white in the middle. For some years an advocate of this peculiar branch of "sparkiness" gave special prizes at South Tyne, and candidates came from up the Tyne by Gilsland, Stapleton, and Kingwater. Scarcely a belted or a brindled one is to be found now, but sometimes one with a white forehead. General Sharpe was fond of a sort which were "black with white facings," and were sometimes spotted under the eye or mottled on the face, exactly like a Hereford. The General was never without a bull of this sort, and a small herd of them was kept on his Tower of Repentance farm when he died. Many Ayrshires have been put to Galloway bulls, and the calves come with black smooth skins and narrow heads, which seem to grow narrower with age.

The best old grass in Galloway is supposed to be in the parishes of Kirkcudbright and Borgue; and Milton Parks in the former, cannot be excelled. The great majority of cattle in Kirkcudbrightshire get hay and straw, with a few turnips under sheds. In Wigtownshire the farmers feed higher, and use turnips and cake more freely, to push them on for the Liverpool market. The softer climate of Dumfriesshire suits the winterers best, but there has been very little loss from disease in Kirkcudbrightshire since the farming became higher. Poor land not broken up makes them very liable to red-water, and young cattle also suffer if they are brought in spring on to the granite. The queys are generally put to in their third spring. Galloway calves, which are dropped early with a view to the Highland Society, which dates from New-Year's Day, suck five or six months, as crack showers say it is "the cheapest thing, after all, to let them have their own rights." A great proportion of them are sadly sacrificed to the sale of milk and butter, if they are dropped near a town. After nursing a calf at the teat, £2 to £3 is often made in a black cow dairy. They are not remarkable milkers; but still, the faculty runs in some strains, and it seems pretty well settled by those who have kept both, and speak from no party spirit, that they give more butter for less milk than the Ayrshires. There is no better and finer mottled beef in the world than the Galloway and Angus, and so the Smithfield prices show, and perhaps the daintiest morsel is a three-year-old heifer that has never had a calf.

The Dumfries Wednesday is a great market for Galloways from May to November, and then it falls off before Martinmas. During this period yearlings and two-year-olds are dispersed all over the Stewartry, and then they are bought up again two years after for St. Faith's and Brough Hill. Woolpit in Suffolk is a great fair for them, and so are Penrith and Carlisle. The last Wednesday of September, which falls on the week before Brough Hill, is one of the largest Dumfries markets, and so is the October Wednes-

day which precedes St. Faith's, the chief Galloway
gathering in Norfolk.   Once the "St. Faith's cattle"
were bought up under that name all over the
Stewartry, but much fewer go there now, and they
are kept and fed off in the district, where every store-
keeper expects to get at least £7 a year for the two
years he keeps them.   Stewart's Auction Mart in
Dumfries does a great business at 3d. in the pound
for every sheep, and 4d. for cattle, and its proprietor
also gives prizes at Christmas for fat stock.

We stopped at Dalbeattie with a view to going
round by Southwick, and also specially to have
another view of our old Kelso friend Semiramis, in
her home at Meikleculloch.   Mr. Graham's farm is
about 2½ miles from Dalbeattie.. He came here in
1843 from Cubby Hill, and began to build up a herd
from eight cows.   A sort of Roman encampment behind his house, and fully 460 feet above the sea
level, was a tempting object for a climb, and, only paus-
ing to look at a young bay Wattie o'Harden, of that
old genuine Stitcher blood which has won in many
a Border ring, we soon planted our M'Combie hazel
staff on the summit.   Meadow, moss, and arable, all
struggle for the lead in the valley, which tapers away
towards the little V-shaped opening in the distant
hills, which tells of the road to Dumfries.   Ayrshires
and Galloways seem to have a divided empire. Half-
bred hoggs and blackfaced wedders were folded on
the turnips, and a powerful Dollond might have revealed in those woolly groups some Cheviot and

blackfaced ewe hoggs sent down from the neigh-
bouring hills. The Cheviots are principally on the
hill range towards Criffell, and beyond the Solway
Firth we catch the faint outline of Skiddaw, Saddle-
back, and the Cumberland hills—the first home
beacon in our journey. The engine sounds the knell
of Mosstrooper raids and feudal days, as it rushes up
the valley and calls at that dreadfully matter-of-fact
Dalbeattie, with its corn, its saw, its paper, its bone
and its bobbin mills. Its Craignair granite also
helped to build the Liverpool docks, and is now laid
under contribution for the Thames embankment.

The evening sun was just slanting over the distant
hills of Kirkennan, and tinging the quiet waters of
Edingham Loch. There, too, in the panorama were
Torr Katrine, Culmain, Blaiket, and Whitecairn,
which have always rallied under the black banner;
but not so Meikle and Little Firth Heads, where
they keep the Ayrshires, at which Mr. Graham's
Modesty by Guardsman gazed too fondly over the
hedge, and brought a red calf thrice in succession.
Bess, the dam of Freebooter and Modesty, was then
the queen-mother of the Meikleculloch herd. Her
lineage is undeniable, as she is by Fergy (19), who
was only shown once, and was then first at the Highland Society. He was by The Squire (16) by Cumberland Willie (1C0); and it was to The Squire,
bred by Graham of Riggfoot, that "Meikleculloch"
owes his show rank. Fergy's dam Riggfoot was
bought along with The Squire, who was not only

first at Edinburgh in '48, but was never beaten in his home circuit of Dumfries, Lockerby, and Moffat. Good hind quarters came in with him, and so did that nice docile eye (through Belle, the dam of Bess), which Galloway men so much prize if they "really ken a countenance." Three seasons were the limit of The Squire's stay at Meikleculloch, and then Walter Carruthers of Kirkhill and Graham of The Shaw used him. Two strains of Cumberland Willie united in Freebooter (203) through Bess, who was sent to Beattie's Mosstrooper, the bull which won so much both for him and Gibbons of Mossband, who purchased him as a yearling. He was of Riggfoot breeding, with rare thighs and ribs, and rather slack behind the shoulders, but, as the Battersea judges said, "a bull first-rate of his kind." Mr. Beattie bought Maggy from "Meikleculloch," and beat him with her at Carlisle, and then Hannah paid "Newbie" off at Glasgow. Harry and Wellington both came to Meikleculloch from Adam Corrie of Cairnie Hill. One went to the Emperor of Russia, leaving a capital daughter, Jess, behind, to die of pleura; and the other was not only a first Royal bull at Carlisle, and a first Highland Society one at Glasgow, but made £60 in prizes from first to last, and was sold for £80. His was not mere ring prowess, as he left Dinah, Harriet, and Agnes; and Harriet's prizes were within £12 10s. of his own.

Mr. Graham's love of showing has not been an unthrift one. The Squire won him the first prize he ever tried for at Dumfries; and since then the money total has been very considerable, plus two clocks, two salvers, a sugar-bason, goblet, and inkstand, and a medium gold medal for Hannah. This cow came "fra the fell side" in Cumberland, and was bred by James Thompson of Saughtree Gate. She gave twenty quarts a day when she was being "caked" for show, and went on nearly at that rate for seven or eight months, after calving. Her first calf, Dinah, was by Wellington (22), and her Semiramis and Hannibal (201) by George Bell of Minsca's Guardsman.

Semiramis and Lord Southesk's Quadroona were quite the black queens at Kelso, and Poet Close, the laureat to the sable King of Bonny might have been better employed singing their praises than making such delicate disclosures about Bonny's queen, as that she weighs 17st. with her parasol and crinoline, and that she liked the eating so well on board The Athenian as to make it necessary for the ship's crew to coax her out of the cabin, and then lower her by gentle violence over the ship's side into the long boat. As his rapture was lacking, we may say in sober prose that she is a long, low cow, with beautiful thighs and twist, and very snug in front, and nicely turned about the bosom; but still Mr. Graham has always a saving-clause for "Hannah at two years old." Cunningham's Kate beat both her and Harriet at Dumfries, but it was a case of table-turning when she met them separately—Semiramis at Kelso (with M'Combie as Chief Justice), and Harriet at Kirkcudbright and Dalbeattie. Semiramis also beat her at Newcastle and Kirkcudbright in '64.

Galloway cows are generally very safe breeders, and there was a singular proof of it at Meikleculloch, as twelve out of thirteen had live calves, and another was shortly due. Galloway twins are of rare occurrence, and, curiously enough, five-sixths of the Meikleculloch calves were heifers. They were all by Thompson's Sir Walter, a son of Bob Burns, a bull to whom Mr. Graham has always been faithful. We found his blood (through his son Sir James) in Second Hermione from Dinah, and Rose of Galloway from Semiramis; and there, too, just ready to depart to the Duke of Buccleuch's herd at Drumlanrig, after her Newcastle victory, was Harriet 2nd by Clansman, son of Harriet. The byre was full of other prize winners—Emma the first Battersea two-year-old, Matilda a second at the Highland Society, Semiramis, and old Bess, fourteen years old, and quite gone in her vessel.

It was a seven miles' ride from Dalbeattie to Southwick, first among peat bogs and then among the heather, and the granite boulders which Dr. Chalmers spoke of on his visit as " the riddlings of the earth." At last we got over the brow, and turned by Boreland side into the wooded vale of Southwick, with its warm farm steadings, and its silver firs and beeches, and so on to the home where Rose of Autumn spent the autumn of her life, and Pride of Southwick was

born. It is a fine early climate for cattle, sheltered
as it is from the cold North, and with two hundred
acres of good old pasture, enough to set some shorthorn breeders' teeth on edge. Mr. Stewart delights
in his garden; but we cared for none of those things
save the *Cryptomeria Japonica,* or Chinese cedar, and
the *Taxodium Semper Virens* from New Zealand.
They may be forest trees elect, but the price is at present prohibitive.

" Southwick's sunny vale" lies about a mile and a-
half from the Solway, just opposite Allonby. Grouse
bags can be made on the hills behind; the partridges
scurry away under the feet of the shorthorns; and
foxes wage their wonted war against the roe-deer
calves, among the weeping birches and the richly
tangled undergrowth of oaks. There are harriers
but no foxhounds in the Stewartry, and in vain do
the Commissioners of Supply propose a premium of
ten shillings on a fox's ears, and seven shillings for
a cub's, as " they are quite outbidden by the English countries." Trees grow down to the sea shore,
where the sheldrake with its chocolate breast and
broad ring hatches many a brood. The herons have
their fishing stations on the Solway, and build in
the silver fir near the ivy and holly-covered mill-
wheel, and patiently draw the burn for hirlings,
which come up from the sea in the second week of
July, and cause such doughty controversies among
the *savans* as to whether they are trout or salmon.

Two or three Alderneys were grouped under the

beechen shade.   The Five Sisters and the white
heifer from Hoddom did not disdain the company of
the "cream stainers," and formed our introduction
to the herd, which is, with the exception of a small
one at Kirkchrist, the only one in the Stewartry.   It
was commenced twenty-one years ago with Cherry
Blossom by Ronald, a daughter of Old Cherry by
Pirate.   This tribe crossed with Heir-at-law (13005)
has made more money than any, and it went steadily
on to Cherry Flower and Southwick Cherry.   Cherry
Blossom was bought from Colonel Cradock at Newcastle in '46, and it is a rare testimony to that sterling old breeder and his honest scorn of all bidding-
up tricks, that when he refused Mr. Stewart's private offer of 150 gs., and said that she would be
shown at Newcastle, and sold, win or lose, she went
for 80 guineas.   There were also several cows from
Watson of Walby, which, as well as Brilliant and
Victoria by Gainford, and bred by Crofton, nicked
well with the Baron of Ravensworth (7811).   Cru-
cifix came from General Sharpe, and Pride of Southwick goes back to her in straight descent through
Vanity, Hoddom, and Abbess of St. Mary.
Emily by Kossuth (11646), and a descendant of
Crofton's Emily, was bought by Mr. Unthank, and
went into Colonel Towneley's hands, where she bred
Emma.   Fennel, for which Mr. Atherton has always
stood up, and Polly Hopkins by Premier (2449),
also founded tribes; Rose of Autumn was bought at
the Athelstaneford sale; and her Rose of Promise by

Heir at Law made 283 gs. at the Southwick. As regards bulls, Jobson's Adam (2920), Whitaker's Fitzmaurice (3807) of the Fairfax sort, Lax's Baron of Ravensworth (7811), who gave good shoulders and bosoms, Colonel Towneley's light red-and-white Hudibras Heir at Law (13005 by Hopewell, who brought more money than any of them, and Ambler's M'Turk, a great useful bull with a dark horn, were all used in turn.

Mr. Stewart had many dealings with Mr. Douglas, and Brenda, Volga, Rose of Autumn, Rose of Cashmere, and the two whites, Clarionet and Venus de Medicis, both speculative bargains, were among his principal purchases. At the sale in 1860, seventy-eight cows and heifers and nineteen bulls were disposed of, and Rose of Autumn returned in her old age to Mr. Douglas, who had bought her daughter, Rose of Sharon, and at one time or another, Baroness Brenda, Heath Bell by Hudibras, Lord Raglan (13244), &c., all bred at Southwick. M'Turk (85 gs.) fell to Mr. Ambler, Heir of Killerby (157 gs.) to Mr. Stirling of Keir, and Pride of Southwick (70 gs.), then a yearling, to Lady Pigot. Hence, looking at the short and simple annals of those sixteen years, it would seem that there were plenty of plums. Lady Pigot had espied the merits of "The Pride" at a glance, as she grazed in the fifty-acre holme in front of the house. Her ladyship was then on her way to Mr. Douglas's, to conclude a purchase for the hapless First Queen of Athelstane, and decided to take her, because, much as she liked the Rose of Promise, she could not then pass over the darkness of her horn. First Fruits and British Flag from Warlaby and Red Bates were used in the next herd, which came to the hammer last autumn. Mr. Atherton was there for the Cherries, and Southwick Cherry Flower (100 gs.) and Southwick Cherry (61 gs.) went back with him to Speke. A heifer, Eliza (60 gs.) changed hands for Broadholm, and Clarionet and Rose of Cashmere went with good reason for merely butcher's price.

Joe Graham shall tell hereafter of the fun he had with the late Marquis of Queensberry among the Criffel foxes; and therefore we must merely wind round the foot of it past New Abbey and "The Durham Ox Inn"—a pretty plain proof that we are drawing near English soil—to the heart of that great pork centre, Dumfries.

There is not a farmer in Dumfriesshire, Galloway, and a great part of Ayrshire who does not feed pigs, not for pig-racing, but solely for the curers. Carcases also come to Dumfries from Annan, Fifeshire, Stirlingshire, and Perthshire. Cumberland feeds many more pigs than it used to do, especially in the east; and its Brown and Watson boars have done much towards keeping up its bacon charter. Dumfriesshire and the Stewartry have a never-failing supply; but in Ayrshire the pigs get so much milk that they grow beyond "Cumberland Bacon" size, and are consumed round Glasgow. The skins are taken off, and the bones taken out, and, after being a few days in brine, they are sold as salt pork or ham, and eaten in the coal mines or the jerry-shops. The Ayrshire people have an eye to the hide market in feeding them so large, as every inch above four feet considerably advances the price. Small pigs from the lower parts of Ayrshire meet with a good sale, if they can weigh-in at from 9st to 14st of 14lbs. Once 500 or 600 pigs were bought out of the town of Dumfries, but none are allowed in it now. Some farmers in the Stewartry feed sixty, and nearly every cottar keeps one or two. The curers' agents go about and buy them up everywhere, and send them to the depôt either alive or with their head and feet off, and unskinned, which is contrary to the Belfast fashion. Very little is done in " Bath chaps," as farmers keep them for home consumption, especially when meat is so dear. The pigs are from six to twelve months old ; and although Irish bacon is sometimes in the market two or three weeks after the cure, genuine ham and bacon cannot be made under three to eight months.

The bacon term opens on Nov. 22nd, curiously enough when the cheese one closes, and then the curers are in full work, both in the workshops and the markets, till the second week in April. On Wednesday they will be at Dumfries, on Monday at Lochmaben, and at Lockerby once a fortnight on Thursdays. Copeland of New Abbey, Provost Bell of Dumfries, and Maclaren of Dalbeattie, are large curers, especially the latter, who throws out his hooks all over Galloway.

Provost Steel and Son, W. and R. Graham, W. A.
Roxburgh of Annan, and Sibson and Irvine of Mary-
port, are also leading men in this line at the Dum-
fries markets. Annan has a good market every
Thursday, and so has Carlisle on Saturday, but the
Scottish dealers are seldom found on its "Sands."
George Graham is a very extensive curer, and Max-
well and William Bell are the largest ham and bacon
dealers in the north of England, and have large
London transactions.*

At Dumfries the market begins at six, and in a winter's morning the dealers will sometimes go to meet
the carts. They have been known to be three miles
out on the Glasgow and Galloway roads, and "a great
runner has a great chance." A large amount of the
carcases are in the hands of the jobbers, but they are
not in such request as those which come direct from the
farmers; and the " *Hae ye sold?*" is most generally
directed to him. The difficulty in the dark is to
guess the weight of the pigs, as it is no joke paying
6s. 10d. per stone for "fine light pigs," and finding
them over 7st. Hence, as people don't like "to go
back with their finger in their mouth," and as those
who have heavy pigs never know the weight, it is rather
a "pig in a poke" affair. Thirty to forty carts also
arrive filled with porkers from six weeks to two
months old, for which all prices are paid from 16s. to
25s. There is so much competition that porkers in

* At page 332, line 4, for "William Bell's" read "Maxwell's."
At page 238, line 9 (North), for "Birdcatcher" read "Emilius,"

embryo are sold off, and porkers in *esse* sold and weighed, and paid for as well, long before 12 o'clock.

At least twenty pork markets are held at Dumfries during the season. We find from *The Dumfries Courier* that the quantity and value of pork sold during the Dumfriesshire and Galloway season of 1864-65 was, as nearly as could be ascertained, 22,050 carcases, or 313,002 imperial stones of the value of £108,321 1s. Compared with the previous year, this shows a decrease of 1,715 carcases, or 37,505 stones of pork, and (although prices ranged from 1½d. to 2d. per stone higher) of £7,113. There is probably no season on record during which potatoes and oatmeal have been so cheap, and yet pork so dear.

A 17-stone pig furnishes hams of from 25lbs. to 26lbs., which won't fetch the top price. From about 10st. to 13st. is the favourite size, and 16lbs. to 20lbs. is quite big enough for hams. For the London market they vary from 12lbs. to 18lbs.; but they have gone as high as 80lbs., and those of Mr. Wainman's sow Fresh Hope weighed 95lbs., and were quite "sandwich ham." During the past season, if hams were between 12lbs. and 20lbs. they made from 80s. up to 100s. a cwt., and if they were between 20lbs. and 30lbs. at least 8s. to 10s. less.

Cumberland hams between 16lbs. and 18lbs. weight have been sold at 112s. and 114s. in October. The bacon rise began in 1834, and the stone of 16lbs. increased suddenly in value from 3s. to 6s. In '35,

the 14lb. stone came in, and, beginning at 5s. 9d.
has varied ever since from 3s. 9d. to 7s. 6d. In
Dumfries, during the Peninsular war, at least 11s.
was made for the 16lb. stone; and in the season
before last such was the competition that the same
quality of pork ruled a shilling dearer there than it
did at Belfast.

Cutting up is a great science, and the flitches must
be made to fit and lie level, and then the hams are
built on them by layers of three, two, one. Lump
salt from Liverpool is chiefly used, and a great weight
of it is made on the Cheshire side of the water. The
first day they are done in salt only to extract the
water, and then in salt and salt-petre. After eight
days, they are turned again and dressed with salt
simply, and then after lying for another thirteen days
they are ready for hanging, or else they never will
be. Cumberland curers pursue the same mode, but
never allow it to lie in salt more than sixteen days.
In America they are apt to oversalt, and they cannot
help it, as they must do it immediately. The pork
corrupts in a warm season, and it stiffens in a cold.
Here the lard comes out in lumps as soon as it is
split, and is melted and put into bladders, and there
it is frozen like a board, so that they cannot get a saw
into it. Keeping off the brine insures the bacon
being mild, and ham is better after eighteen months.
To suit the London market and show its ripeness
there must be mould on it, but on a four-year-old
ham there is no profit. The hams are closed up in

the houses to keep off the fly and make mould, and
are kept dry by a current of air at the top. For
the first fortnight the heat is kept at 100 degrees to
make the salt come out of the meat. Twenty-one
days after it has been hung a good ham will dry, and
be firm in fibre, whereas a bad ham swells and feels
flabby. Some of the Scottish and Cumberland curers
smoke their hams, which the Yorkshire men rarely do.

On all hams and bacon there is a regular
allowance to the buyer of 2lbs. in every 20 stone.. In
curing there is not so much loss on bacon as on ham, as,
if the shoulder misses, the rib part generally stands.
Sometimes a considerable per-centage is lost in
warm weather; but the loss is never so great in the
country as in the town, on account of the air being
less murky. The pig most to the curer's mind is one
not fat or short or big, or over-driven, but a lengthy
one of 14½ stone of 14lbs., and generally from eight
to twelve months old, which has been fed on oatmeal
and potatoes. Ten months is the best age, and some
curers maintain that no "Perfect Cure" can be
effected sooner. There will be a difference of 5s. to 6s·
per stone in pigs according to food and age. In fact,
two hams which the salt has run through in twenty-
one days will be put to hang in the same house and
on the same tier, and both look equally well, and yet
the one has not condition to stand the fire, and will
turn "as yellow as mustard," and the other will be
"as white as snow, and all right." Movable cinder
fires in iron barrow-shaped stoves are kept in many

of the houses, which are all duly ventilated, to prevent the heat at the top acting unduly. The great ham and bacon dealers' houses are fullest in March; and in William Bell's, who sends an immense weight of bacon to Yorkshire and Newcastle, and of hams to London and Edinburgh, we have seen from 4,600 to 4,800 hanging up at one time in March, tier above tier, of which there are seven. His calculation is that a stone of lard should come out of a 14-stone pig; and sometimes he has in "a very throng time" melted 600 stone of lard a day. He cures on the average 2,500 to 3,000 pigs in the season, principally from Nichol Forest and the Longtown parts of Cumberland. Provost Steel of Annan has done more; but Beattie of Shillie Hill is generally supposed to have the largest business in Scotland.

CHAPTER XIII.

TINWALD DOWNS TO HALLHEATHS.

"Mr Kirby had an order for two cows, 'one for a nobleman, and the other for the Empress of Russia, but the imperial cow died on the passage, and the worst had to be led to the Palace for inspection. ' *Why*,' asked the Empress, ' *are three teats so large, and one so small?*' ' *It's all correct, please your Majesty,*' said the ever ready Luke Nott,' *three are for the milk, and the little one for the cream.*' ' *Indeed !*' said the Empress."

SILK AND SCARLET (p. 149).

Tinwald Downs—The New and Old Race Courses—Mr. Wilkin's Blood Stock—Stable Scenes—Jamie Heughan's Discipline—Bob Johnson's Tumble off Saucebox—Drumlanrig Castle—The Duke of Buccleuch's Stock at Holstane and Tibbers—Vendace at Lochmaben—The late Mr. Andrew Johnstone—Blood Stock at Hallheaths.

ONE road from Dumfries to Tinwald Downs lies past the station gardens, whose lavender-coloured borders, yellow calceolarias, and scarlet geraniums still attest the Scottish love of flowers in the very teeth of that arch leveller, Steam. There were plenty of " stinking violets" in the Carnsalloch woods, which furnish many a grand ring to the Dumfriesshire hounds, among their deep heather lying, and round by the Burnt Firs, a noted cub harbour, at the north end of Lochar Moss. The Moss is an eight-thousand-acre tract with twelve feet of outfall; the peats are being fast cut away, but it has held for eight-and-twenty years the *débris* of the unhappy steam plough, and not even a team of eight or ten horses doing their best could prevail to part them.* Once through the woods, and the old and new race-courses were right and left of us. In summer time the road is fragrant with sweet-brier and wild roses, to the memory of "Gilbert Glossin," who was agent from Netherby to Port Patrick, and who did not forget the wayfarers, while he was laying out his own Garden at Tinwald Downs.

The old race-course was nearly a mile round, and it was here that Charles Marquis of Queensberry trained with John Smith. It was a dead flat, and when the word was given to cross the road, 102 ploughs pronounced its doom. The somewhat imposing gates are still left to the new course, but no racer has passed through them since '47, and the Southern Meeting is ended. The tents were not pitched of yore in the plain, but confined to an eminence at the west end, and the course, which is level, with the exception of a slight dip at the far side—as useful in its day as the Cantley hill at Doncaster—measures one-and-a-half miles round. Mr. Wilkin's Leicester flock feed there now, and of course *the* blood mare and foal are as faithful to it as the Dryad to the oak grove, or the "Water Baby" to the stream. Once Mr. Wilkin determined to breed no more blood stock, and actually gave away Barbara Young out of Eryx's dam, the last of the old sort.

* I see from the *Dumfries Courier* that the dam which obstructed the flow of the Lochar to the sea has just been removed, and that "if the upper proprietors only clear and straighten the course of the stream, the present generation may yet see the wilderness converted into smiling corn and grass land."

However, Fate and the first Mrs. Fobert were against
him, and the moment the former heard what her
old friend had done, she wrote to say most decisively
that it was not to be, and that she and her husband
were so determined on that point that they were just
sending off another brood mare to him. And so Mr.
Wilkin yielded to their decree, and Merrywing by
Irish Birdcatcher came down, and in after-years a
cheque of 150 gs. was offered by Mr. Blenkiron in
vain, for this little remembrance of one of the kindest-
hearted women that ever passed to her rest. The chesnut had bolted as a two-year-old at the Carlisle turn
for home, and had been seen no more in public, and
there she was last year the dam of Merrythought
by Mandricardo, and with an Underhand filly at her
foot.

Mr. Wilkin sells some fifty shearling tups a year,
and he is satisfied if he can make £5 all round.
He brought down tups thirty years ago from the
York, Masham, and Thirsk districts, and still runs
upon the Yorkshire sheep as most "calculated to fill
a glutton's eye." He does not go for the blue heads,
and makes a great point of good hard hair on their
crowns. The open coat is most essential, as they are
used almost entirely to cast Cheviot ewes, as, in fact,
there are hardly any half-bred ones in the county.
The half-bred lambs come out at Lockerby and Carlisle in August and September, and at Penrith (or
" Peerith") as hoggs the next spring. Very few comparatively are turniped in Cumberland, but on the

dry knolls up the water of the Urr in Galloway, where forty years ago you would hardly see one Ayrshire cow or a hundred sheep in a day.

There is quite a history in connection with the hovel in the corner of the Dumfries race-course. It adjoins the little paddock into which Joe Graham jumped when his hounds were carrying a good head towards Torthorwald, and lay " due east," not exactly stretched many a rood (for there never was, and never will be, much of him) in " the heaviest fall I ever had in my life." Within those humble walls Ballochmyle by Peter Lely was foaled, and so were Modesty from Theresa and Abraham Newland from Rachel by Amadis, both of them by Malek, and in the self-same year. Idleboy by Satan was another of Rachel's, which were nearly all chesnut except Wee Willie, the first of the Liverpools. She was bought from Mr. Knapton of York, and had an endless spring of it, as when she was twenty-four she threw a colt and a filly, and excited the admiration of a visitor so much when she was in foal for the last time, that he called her " the chesnut filly in the park," and dwelt at intervals on her suitability for his carriage. Venus, the dam of Vulcan, came from " Jupiter Johnson's," with Vulcan at her foot, and bred Eryx soon after. Lord John Scott gave £100 for the old mare and her foal Wanderin' Willie when she was twenty-two; and the latter brought back the purchase-money and " something more" at Doncaster Spring. Mr. Wilkin never bred a St. Leger

winner, but Eryx and Abraham Newland, each of
which was sold for £150 and a £500 contingency,
were third and second for that race. It was only
through Young Sam Day's desperate rush on Mango,
in which, at the expense of his own boot-tops, he
"split" the Doctor and Abraham when they were
running locked together twenty yards from home,
that the chesnut failed to land it. Next year there
was, in one sense, a more memorable finish of
three, as "Abraham," Wee Willie, and Clem o' the
Cleugh, all sons of Rachel, met at Dumfries, and
racing past their little birth-place, where their dam
was shut up with her foal for the day, finished first,
second, and third; and at Manchester in '37 Wee
Willie, Modesty, a very steady enduring mare for
heats, and "Abraham" won five races between them.

For many years Tinwald Downs was the head-
quarters of the best blood sires in Dumfriesshire.
Monreith by Haphazard, own brother to Filho du
Puta, and a strong and flashy dark chesnut, who got
some of his stock a little soft, was the first arrival,
at a fifty-pound hire, from Sir William Maxwell. His
successor was Viscount by Stamford, who got good carriage horses, hunters, and hacks, and especially good
mares. The grey was the St. Leger trial-horse for
Filho, and therefore his coming to run at Dumfries,
with Croft in charge and young Bill Scott to ride
him, marked in Mr. Wilkin's mind the year
1817, when he entered on the Tinwald Downs
farm.

Peter Lely was hired from Mr. Knapton of York; he got good dark bays and browns, and, like Satan, he just stayed for one season. Satan's son Idle Boy from Rachel, with his Arab quarters and rather peacocky carriage, was kept much longer, and distinguished himself as the sire of Paphos and Urania. Corinthian by Comus was hired from the late Mr. James, M.P., who once owned Saucebox, and was a capital gentleman-rider when Sir Tatton Sykes wore the Sledmere blue and orange; but this champion chesnut of Cumberland did very little for Mr. Wilkin beyond Clem o' the Cleugh, an honest £50 Plate horse, and much beloved of Tommy Lye, when the lads had to be dodged in heats. The beautiful dark-brown Vulcan by Voltaire from Eryx's dam did long and good service, and the county was full of his daughters. Both his horses and mares were very capital and compact dark-browns or blacks, generally with a crown-piece of white on one of their heels. General Sharpe's Malek, with his big mealy chesnuts, and Mr. Johnstone's St. Martin, the sire of many a hardy, brown hunter, gave the county a great chance; but, although The Era is popular, there is not much enthusiasm for horse-breeding now, and Vulcan would have to forge on a different anvil.

It is upwards of forty years since the new race-course was opened. On the occasion of the meeting in October, the yard of Tinwald Downs as like a training stable for nearly a fortnight. Every cart-shed was boarded up and extempore stalls invented, and thanks

to spare stables and hovels, seven-and-twenty horses
stood there at one Caledonian Hunt. "The Marquis's Stable," with a racing plate nailed to the
door, and " *The Shadow—won* 57 *races*" still legible
within its circle, is now a byre with Ayrshire cows
and a tortoise-shell bull, not to mention the occa-.
sional presence of a tortoise-shell tom-cat, which was
offered by an old woman to Sir Charles Phipps for
£50, and, on the utter failure of that royal negotia-
tion, to Mr. Wilkin, junior, for one. The three-stall
stable was the stage upon which General Chassé
appeared in one of his finest sensation dramas, carrying his boy George Gilchrist about by the hand,
and shaking him, as a tiger would a Bengalee, till help
arrived and they were forced asunder at the point of
the pitchfork. The lads slept in the granary, and
Jamie Heughan, who has been forty-eight years with
Mr. Wilkin, and three with his father before him,
slept there also with a stout cudgel. He was just
the man, as they say, in Scotland to " gar kings ken
they had a lith i' their necks ;" and being " a mad
sort of body," if any lad talked at unhallowed hours
or tried to put upon him, he came down so hot and
heavy on the beds that, as Mr. Wilkin has it, " *plenty
of your eminent trainers, Derby and Leger men, will
mind Jamie as long as ever they live.*"

The principal course was " once round from the
garden gate," and year after year Mr. Wilkin might
be seen on his garden terrace with quite a troop of
friends. He was never at the St. Leger in his life,

2 z 2

and only once on the Tinwald Downs course during the running. This was when Bob Johnson had that terrible tumble off Saucebox, after which he was never quite the same man. Mr. Wilkin ran to the house for a brandy bottle, and then galloped up the road and through the gates to him. He was lying helpless and fainting in the middle of such a dense ring, that the bottle had to be passed over their heads. It fell into the hands of a thirsty cobbler, who could not resist "a wee drappie," and took a most protracted suck at it before he could be made to pass it on to poor Bob.

Lanercost was fond of this course, but, for very good reasons, he and St Martin did not meddle with each other either in the Buccleuch Plate or the Cup.* Next autumn he accommodated St. Bennett and Malvolio separately, and in 1840 he took a terrible revenge on Charles XII. for his Doncaster Cup defeat. "Charles" then walked over for and won the Cup, and with this double Goodwood Cup winner that race died out. The Caledonian Hunt Meeting was last held here in '44, when Alice Hawthorn and Brevity won nearly everything. Next year Mr. Merry swept all save the portion of The Shadow, and in '46 there were only a dozen horses. Then it sank down to six horses and one day; and old Annandale was second for the handicap to Marian Ramsay, who also won the last race, a Give-and-

---

* See "Scott and Sebright," p. 188.

Take Plate, by half-a-neck.   Oddly enough, a lad called Wilkin rode the loser, and then Mr. Wilkin's mares Rachel and Venus were left with the Leicesters in undisturbed possession.

Such were the experiences of our saunter out of Dumfries, and once more we were in the saddle, and away towards quite a different point of the compass up the Valley of the Nith.   There is very little wheat in the valley, which opens up after Auld Garth.   Dun ponies seemed to be most plentiful, and a boy informed us that "*they were a' strippit doon the back —King o' the Country always gat them that way : ye've heerd tell on him surely?*" which indeed had not.   They seemed a good sort, though perhaps not a model for the flying horse which surmounted the town cross in the centre of the long lime avenue of Thornhill.   The loam and the gravel vary all the way along the valley of the Nith; but on referring to a map at Holstane, we found that after pursuing the east side we were "in an oasis of the new red sandstone, in the midst of a huge bed of limestone extending from Port Patrick to Dunbar," and slept none the less soundly for the discovery.   The possession of the hills which began to flank us on the right, five miles out of Dumfries is pretty evenly divided between the black and "the pale faces" or the Cheviots.   The latter hold Closeburn Town Head, which dies away in that arable valley below Low Garth, where half-bred lambs are got ready for Lockerby.   Blackfaces wander over Bellybucht, which

has an old Roman road on the face of it, and they
hold "more than Roman sway" on the loftier Gar-
roch as well. From Bellybucht the range stretches
away by Scatlaw Mains, where

"Last May a braw wooer
Cam doon the lang glen,"

and past the little burial-place of the Queensberry
family, when they dwelt at Durisdeer, till it is at
last lost in the great neutral sheep heights of the
Louthers.

Drumlanrig Castle is in the valley three miles from
Thornhill, close by the burn side, and backed up
on the south by a chain of woodlands.   There is no
foxhunting here, and the cubs are strictly gathered
up for England.   The rams' horns staircases to the
entrance were in course of alteration at Drumlanrig Castle, and the gardens, over which Mr.
Macintosh (brother to the James Macintosh who
did with his pen for Scottish trees what Parson Gil-
pin did with his pencil for English) presides with a
staff of a hundred men, were of course not in their
bloom.   In fact, there were only the gravel com-
binations left, to make us realize autumn, when (as
we afterwards proved) the scene from the terrace
almost forbids a sigh after " sweet Bowhill."

The Duke of Buccleuch has 2,500 acres at Tibbers
and Holstane, under the management of his farm
steward, Mr. Johnstone. Twenty years ago, the
Galloways were the only stock on the farms; but
since then Ayrshires have been introduced, and

are kept at Holstane, where Mr. Johnstone resides. His Grace rather hangs to Galloways; but
still, he has bought a few Anguses, for the sake of
trying the cross. The young cows and heifers are
principally by Freebooter (203), and among them
were the first, second, and third in the yearling class
at Kelso. Mr. Graham of Meikleculloch bred
Freebooter, as we have already stated, and sold him
to Mr. Birrel of Guards, who sold him back after he
was second at the Carlisle Royal, and so he found
his way to Tibbers, like his nephew Knight of Liddesdale, the present chief of the black harem, and
others of the Meikleculloch cracks. The calves are
generally dropped in January and February, to be
ready for the Highland Society, and are suckled
twice or three times a-day for six months. Agnes
Waugh has led a vestal life among them for nearly
thirty years. She "*was no' at Battersea*," as she
observes, "*wi' the kye; but I wur at Kelso, and we
made grandly out wi' the heifers there.*" We had
met nothing so genuine since old Hannah at Lord
Feversham's. Second Agnes, or Agnes Lockerbie, her assistant, was quite a second edition of Ra-
venscroft's Polled Herd-Book, in a kirtle and bare
feet; and two such able field-marshals soon put the
Freebooters and all the rest of them in array
for us.

There was a curious union of Herd-Book numbers
in M'Gill by Balsalloch (92) from Halliday (92),
the second cow at Battersea, where her daughter

Miss M'Gill was the first yearling heifer. *"Come out, Small Bones!"* and out she came, true to her name, and Gordon as well, with Scroggie Hill and Beauty. *"That's Young Mary the Second, or London Mary we ca' her,"* says one of the Aggies, and so stimulated she went away at score, with the narrative of how *"Original Mary hung herself."* Still, there was an old Mary left in the land, with a good deal of shorthorn character when you stood behind her. There too were Sproat, Keir Lass from Barndannoch, and Graham, a business-like little cow, and with not more sweetness, but more Galloway character than Brown Lugs. Queen was a trifle more on leg than some of them, and Beauty of Drumlanrig. Halliday 2nd, and Agnes, all owed much of their nice forequarter and good thighs to Freebooter, Knight of Liddesdale was roaming in his paddock, and came quietly at Mr. Johnstone's call to his loose-box, with as blithe a step as the bay of thirty-two summers, who was just backing a cart on to the green manure-heap.

About fifty "bacon swine" are reared each year at Tibbers, and then finished off near the dairy at Holstane. His Grace has kept to whites, and began by crossing a white Sussex with one from Lord Sefton. With good feeding the sort would reach about 22 st. at twelve months; but of course they go off to the curers when they are much lighter weights. One boar struck us as having a peculiar head, and we found that it was only a copy of his sire's, which was embalmed in consequence at Dr. Grayson's Thornhill Museum.

About 160 Highlanders with a slight admixture of Shetlanders were grazing in the Park, and as they stood on its banks or plunged into the Nith to drink, they composed a cattle group which made us yearn, for the third and last time in Scotland, for the camera. The West Highlanders are bought up at 2½ years at the Falkirk September and October trysts, and are kept two years, and then sold at about a £10 profit at 40 to 44 stone of 14lbs. to the London and Liverpool butchers. The flock numbers 1,200 Cheviot ewes, whose annual cast is replaced by seconds at Lockerby, and crossed with a Leicester tup from Mr. Wilkin's or Mr. Beattie's, and the lambs are sold off at 22s. to 28s. Two hundred black-faced ewes are also put to the Leicester for mules, which sell well about home to the feeders at from 16s. to £1. Many of them go to be turniped in Galloway, and find customers from the South in spring.

The ewes were sharing with the Ayrshires the great 125-acre meadow by the Carron side, in front of the Holstane Mains, which lie snugly under Castle Hill, one of the green outspurs of the Louthers. It was milking-time, and the "little white ivories" were left in possession while Prince by Tower led in his fair and flecked followers. He won the gold medal at Sanquhar, and we found in him a good corrective to those shorthorn points which it had been often so difficult to shake off in Ayrshire. Among the cows, which had some trouble to follow him in his gay trot to the stalls, were Miss Harper, the blood-like Nightingale, first at Hamilton in '63; Miss Fingland, with a very engaging countenance, and second, as she well might be, at Sanquhar, in a ring where sometimes forty yearling heifers have to stand together, and fight it out upon shape alone before the vessel can prophesy of itself. Stately had a delightful vessel; Charlotte's horn and middle-piece were equally true-shaped; and Kate we remarked on more for her neat bone. Beauty's vessel has gone now, and Mr. Heslop's "brilliant ruin," who has walked out of the ring with many a card in her time, kept quite away, as if she knew that she had no part or lot with the ducal thirty-four, of which the best are occasionally shown at Sanquhar, Thornhill, and Dumfries. The Holstane dairy deserted with the times from Dunlops six years ago, and it is now making Cheddars of 56 to 60lbs., and getting 14s. the 24lbs.

It was now "Bock agin, Sandy;" but the Valley of the Nith will well bear riding twice. There was no shorter cut, and with another call at Tinwald Downs for a stirrup-cup, and a long look with young Mr. Wilkin at his capital black Spanish fowls, we set the mare's head over the hill for Annandale. We had to skirt Lochar Moss, and pass Torthorwald Tower of murderous "*I'll mak siccar* (sure)" fame. Then King Robert de Brus's castle, and "*the Castle Lochs and a' the lochs—nine of 'em,"* glistened before us, and transformed Lochmaben, which we had only thought of as a pig market, into quite a fair "City of the Waters." Herons from Hallheaths and wild-ducks pause there in their flight to the Solway, and pikes and vendace seem to be the fish tenants in common. These vendace are said to have been originally brought from Italy by the monks. They are less than three ounces, and have a black heart-shaped transparency at the back of their heads, through which the brain may be seen. Thus they keep their hearts not "for daws to peck at," but for the Vendace Club, when they meet at Lochmaben early in August, to fish and dine together, with Sir William Jardine in the chair. Fried in bread-crumbs they are quite the white-bait of the North, and a ten-dozen basket is a good day's sport.

A half-bred Arab by Minuet from a Telemachus mare, in the breaking bits, showed that we were approaching a spot where other "good things have been landed." In a few minutes the clock cupola rose above the thick laurel approaches to Hallheaths, once the home of the owner of Charles the Twelfth. St. Martin, Annandale, Verulam, Mentor, and Telemachus have all been stabled under that cupola since the late Mr. Andrew Johnstone came back from China, great in the faith of a blood horse,* and, curiously enough, the two last died from broken legs, caused by the kick of a mare. St. Martin has also

---

* See "Scott and Sebright," pp. 171-72.

been dead for some years, but his name endures with the Dumfriesshire Hunt. The grass here is three weeks later than it is at Sheffield Lane; but the few yearlings that go up to join the "Lane lot" at Doncaster can hold their own in the average. Old Nugget by Melbourne is in residence, and she sent up Emigrant (410 gs.) last year; and Vagary by Voltigeur and Jungfrau roam in the holme by the Annan side with their foals. The Derby was denied to Annandale, horse and district, as the St. Leger was to Nithsdale with Abraham Newland, and in both instances by South Country riders and outsiders. Old Annandale looked well, but his back was beginning to sink beneath the burden of three-and-twenty summers. Still, that tough old boy "Terrona" looked at his grand ends when he met Defiance at Lockerby that spring for the £40 Hunt Prize. In vain did his colleagues on the bench ask him to let it be a unanimous decision in favour of the younger bay; but "*Unanimous! no, never!*" was all they could extract from such an emphatic Andrew Marvel. This was the third year of the struggle, and Houlakin and The Era had won it before, and in his turn Defiance has had to yield to a younger horse, Warmanby by Mountain Deer. Mr. Andrew Johnstone loved Annandale next to Touchstone, and felt sure at one time, that whenever the old horse died, his blood combined with that of Alice Hawthorne's dam must bring his son to the front. With Clydesdale it once seemed as if it was to be, but his legs gave way before the Derby. Still, Balrownie, Johnny Armstrong, and One Act are something for one horse, and the dams of Stampedo and Haddington are also by him. It is now four or five years since he left Sheffield Lane, and he has scarcely seen two blood mares a season since.

The three white legs of his hardy little chum Minuet have done good service in India. He belonged to Mr. Smollett, M.P. (then of the Madras Civil Service), and so did The Child of the Islands, who was faster, but rather delicate. When "The Child" went wrong, Minuet took his place as second horse, and (as there was no Merry Monarch to drop from the clouds) he won the Calcutta Derby of 7,000 rupees for three, four, and five year old maidens, "pegging away in his old cricket-ball style from end to end." Ridden by the lanky John Hall, he carried off the Civilians' Cup at Madras, and as it was a 2½ miles handicap against all comers, it may be said of him, as Lord Westbury did from his marble chair of the proposed rifle match between Lords and Commons, that he "would meet" the Arabs "at any place and with any weapon." He was brought over in '50 along with the famous Elepoo, who was 15h. 0¾ inches, or just an inch beyond his own standard. Minuet has carried his owner, who rides over 13 stone, to the finish in a capital run with Sir Watkin, and as he can screw and creep or have a fence any way, he has been used to hunting mares in the district. The stock have been generally bold wide jumpers, but a little hot, and one of them, a four-year-old from a St. Martin mare, won the Hunt prize of £10 for the best four-year-old colt or filly at Lockerby. Hence the late Mr. Tattersall, whose grandfather's most successful blood-stock venture was his trip to buy an Earl of Eglinton's brood mares, proved a little out when he joked Mr. Johnstone and said he " might do to get mules with."

Mr. John Johnstone followed the horses from India. As the portrait and memoir in the Calcutta *Sporting Magazine* prove, he was a mighty hog hunter in his day, and, as " Josto King of Spears," he was known "in the field of Kushnaghur," as well as in the Calcutta Tent Club. For two seasons he hunted the Calcutta Hounds, which ran the jackal, in default of foxes. They had a supply of draft fox-hounds out each year from England, and generally thirty-five couple in kennel. Throwing off in the grey dawn, and finding in a dry nullah or a grass jungle was very different to a climb up Rammer-scales hill, or a fast thing from the Duke's cover to Castle Milk; but Joe Graham is " Josto" now, and, as Joe says, " Mr. Johnstone's a clipping secretary, and one of our first flight." The J's, to wit the Jardines, the Johnstones, and Joe, keep the game well alive in Annandale.

Hallheaths is not occupied at present, but there are vestiges of the quiet, earnest sportsman who died there in '57. Herring, senior, came here with his son Charles to paint hunters, and we also found

his masterly hand in Charles XII., Beeswing, the
Arabs, Eleppoo, Minuet, and Telemachus, a very
neatly-moulded horse, and all shot with grey hairs.
The mare with her sweet form and light blood-like
neck carries her ears well forward, while the mighty
Charles's are screwed back as if he would like right
well to have a nip at somebody. Amid all his re-
verses when his back had become quite hollow and
his tail was cut, he retained some faded notions of
royalty, and he would not pass through Balby toll-
gates, the southern portal to the scene of his St.
Leger, and Cup victory against Lanercost, Beeswing,
and Compensation, till both the gates were opened.
When he got there, Tom Dawson, who had trained
him when he left John Scott's, did not know him in
the sale ring, and, although he was the sire of some
capital hunters, no one would venture on him at
" a pony." He went to Ireland after that, and was
eventually put down at Sheffield, when quite a shadow
of his old self, and a carving-knife and fork were
made from his cannon bones.

Mr. Andrew Johnstone began breeding at Hallheaths with Theresa Panza by Wagtail, Proserpine by
Rhadamanthus, Marchioness by Velocipede, Morsel
by Mulatto (the dam of The Cure), and Grimston by
Verulam, and eventually a Goodwood Cup winner,
was the first foal he bred. For a time he stuck to
Verulam, a fine crested horse, who spread many rich,
bold-fencing bays over the Yorkshire hunting fields.
He commenced training with Ralph Scott from Tom

Dawson's, in the big field in front of the house at Hallheaths, and by dipping into the holme, and so back again into the park, they made a very good 1½ miles out of it. There was also a gallop for hard weather on Thorniethwaite Moor, where he used to freshen up the decayed thoroughbreds, which Tom Dawson picked up for him, when he horsed the mail between Hanginshaw and Gretna. One of the best and fastest wheelers he ever used was by an Arab he bought at Tattersall's. He was always at the great race meetings, and no one delighted more in seeing the early gallops at Chester, or, if it was wet, watching them from his window in Paradise Row. Goodwood was his delight, and we used to see him pacing slowly up and down the esplanade, with his hands behind his back, considering whether "Charles" and the "crimson, and green cap" would win the Cup next day. Young Job Marson had already confounded Newcastle by just beating Beeswing with the long striding brown over their own Town Moor; but it was not until he beat Frank Butler a head on Hyllus over Goodwood, after a tremendous finish in which "the maiden bay" tried to savage Charles, that he fairly won his spurs with the public. He was up again the next year, in the thousand-guinea-aside match, and Robinson, who had a hundred-guinea retainer, rode Hyllus. Nothing could alter the '41 form, and Job was mortified enough when the first call of Lord Westminster for Sleight of Hand forced him to give up his cup mount to

"Our Jim" on the Thursday.   Mr. Johnstone never
had a great horse again, but he stuck faithfully by
Touchstone when his own sires failed him, and not
only bred Lord of the Isles, but a 1,800-guinea yearling, Lord of the Hills, by him.   Three colts were the
produce of the four mares which he sent to him
in his very last season.   About two years before his
own death, Mr. Johnstone talked of clearing out all
his sires, and bidding for Stockwell at Lord Exeter's
sale, as the legitimate successor of the "Eaton
Brown;" but he changed his mind, and did not live
long enough to regret it.

It was no slight difficulty crossing the ford to
Broadholm; but Mr. John Johnstone on Queensberry,
the winner of a Dumfriesshire steeple-chase, was
quite a Trinity House pilot, and we got well across
near a weir, which Robinson Carr and "Sandy" had
done their very best to pull down, to get at an otter.
Arabs have quite a colony here.   We had left a Minuet
over the water at the foot of a hunting mare, as well
as a yearling in a shed; and here the cross was taken
the opposite way, and a grey Arab mare had an Era
foal, which was to be entered in the Oaks.   Two
half-Arab ponies were also trotting away to Lockerby
station, on their road to Mortlake, and Mr. Johnstone changed Queensberry in the evening for a
grey of the same cross.   Shorthorns are a new
love; but he was not off with the old greyhound one,
and among a leash of seniors there were saplings by
Canaradzo and puppies by Master Blue Hat.   But

we could not linger long to run over the "coltish chronicle," in that little office where *Racing Calendars* are the ledgers, and Oppressor, Gretna, Caterer, and all the other Sheffield Lane winners, were named before the fatal second Tuesday in July; and "Forward to The Shaw!" was the watchword of the night.

CHAPTER XIV.

LOCKERBY TO MOODLAW.

"Ca' the yowes to the knowes,
Ca' them where the heather grows,
Ca' them where the burnie rows—
My bonnie dearie!

"Hark the mavis' evening sang
Sounding Cluden's woods amang!
Then a faulding let us gang,
My bonnie dearie."

BURNS.

The Churchyard of Old Drumgre—Lockerby Lamb Fair—Breeding in Dumfriesshire—Sale of the Moodlaw Tups at Beattock—Ericstane—The Shaw—Eskdale Muir—A Day at Moodlaw—Annals of the Moodlaw Flock.

OUR remembrances of Annandale are very mixed ones, and drawn from visits at two or three different periods of the year. We had the finest view of it from the hill above "Hebbie Renwick's," where there is a shepherd's burial-ground in connection with the churchyard of old Dumgre. "The graves are the graves of our ain folk" in that lofty solitude, and the sheep browse over them at will; and when you have scraped away the moss from one deep sunken stone, you read the proud epitaph, "*Here lys the corps of ane honest man.*" "Oh! what a beautiful clearing it would make," said an Australian, as he looked down on that vale, so thickly wooded that we tried in vain to trace out our route —where we had seen Bonnie Dundee snorting round his paddock at The Heuk, and stretching his battered old legs for another hunting season, and where the fallow deer had flitted across the road, as we came back at dark from Raehills.

We caught the same dale from a different point when we looked over it from Lockerby hill at the time of the great August lamb fair. Dreary little places often have the magnetic power of becoming a great fair focus, and so it is with Lockerby. "The Ewe and Lamb" sign tells its simple story. August brings the lamb fair; September creeps up with Galloway cattle and cast ewes, and "fetches the greatest weight of money with it;" and tail lambs, cast ewes, and store cattle conclude the year in October and November. There is also the show of Galloway bulls, fat cattle, and hoggs, in April, when the Dumfries Hunt give blood-sire and hunter prizes; and in September the local show extends its favours even to Savoy cabbages and canaries.

The town was full of holiday lads and lasses; and " *Are ye gan up the hill?* " was the challenge of the hour. The lads sometimes fail to climb that hill quite peaceably, with their ladye loves on their arm. One had a fit of heroics half-way up, and was going to " smash " somebody, but the crowd gathered round, with the cooling query, " *What ails 'um?* " and his Phillis hung on to him, and implored him, for her sake, not to do a deed—which he had no intention of doing. Of course we stopped at the foot, to hear the prospects of the leather plating, next day, from the clerk of the course, a most communicative black-smith. " *There will be three fra Peerith,*" said he, "*one or two fra the Langholm, and Joe Graham's tied to have yen in.*" The sheep Nestors ascended the hill soon after day-break. In the very first group we hailed there were Graham of The Shaw, " Moodlaw," Tom Welsh, and our active-minded friend John Irving, who had laid aside his Municipal, Silloth, and True Blue cares for the day, and, being no sheep among men, had arrived from Carlisle to be a man among sheep. Upper and Mid Annandale were all in that hill landscape. We looked across, with Mr. Graham as our geographical guide, to Torthorwald and Rammerscales hills, and traced the Annan as it wound along from Moffat, bear-ing four or five " waters" in its bosom.

The sheep are in different divisions on the hill. Blackfaced and cross-bred lambs are on the west side ; Cheviot lambs in separate ewe and wedder lots on the north ; and half-breds on the south. Pens are still the exception, and the lots are of all sizes from three to twenty score. No picking is allowed, and a lot must be run off by the crook with a steady hand and a straight eye. It is a great art to swirl them round, so as to mix up tops and seconds, and then to make a steady cut; and it is given to few men to count off a lot on the spur of the moment, as they scour past six or seven thick. Generally three or four buyers club together, and take a lot subject to the ruling price of the day, and, in case of a dispute, a referee settles it by a trial lot. Some wretched half-bred queys were the beef accessories, along with a few Irish and Ayrshire; and there were gipsies in abundance at the edge of the hill, and cheap jacks, who would fit you up with a coat and vest of Tweed, " all wool," in the twinkling of an eye. The number of lambs was by no means up to our hopes. More than a third are picked up every year, and never reach the hill at all; as dealers come about ten days or a fortnight before Langholm fair, which was once the main market of the country. It is said that 52,000 lambs, " be the same more or less," have been pitched at Lockerby, and that the proportion of Cheviots to half-breds is fully three to one.

Still the half-breds are spreading fast over all the arable lands of Dumfriesshire. There is little wheat or barley in the county, and oats out of lea, turnips or potatoes, oats or barley, grass seeds and rye-grass, is the rotation, and the latter pastured or cut for hay is most valuable for half-bred lambs. The Moffat and Langholm road is the half-bred boundary; and the Roxburghshire plan of putting half-bred ewes to a Leicester tup* is never followed. The breeders will have

* The following, which arrived too late for insertion in its proper place, is the pedigree of one of the rams (which girthed upwards of 5 feet, and measured 15 inches from the back of the head to the setting on of the tail, when he was shown at Kelso) that Lord Polwarth has used a good deal of late.

very open wool, and large masculine heads very clear
of wool on their Leicester tups, so as to keep up the
half-bred character as much as possible in the lambs.
The mules, too, with their grey faces and grey legs,
are gradually coming into favour. In early maturity
they hardly touch the half-breds, and their wool is
coarser, but they clip quite as heavily. Crossing blackfaces with the Cheviot tup to produce them has been
tried, but has never yet brought a profit. The prejudice against Cotswolds has always been strong, as the
lambs were thought to be too coarse. Some tups
were brought to Moffat in 1850, and were led out in
halters like ponies, and sold for £6 or £7 each, but
they have not been tried since. The Leicester holds
his own for crossing, and a great many Dumfriesshire farmers buy five and six year old Cheviot and
blackface ewes at Falkirk October, and send them
as " grit ewes" to stock turnip land in Galloway, and

His sire was bred by Mr Cockburn of Sisterpath,†
  g s — Mr Cockburn of Sisterpath,‡
  g g. s. — Mr. Taylor of Presson,
  g. g. g. s. — Lord Polwarth,
  g g. g. g. s. — Lord Polwarth,
  g g. g. g. g. s (4th Prince Albert) — Lord Polwarth,
  g g. g g g. g. s. (3rd Prince Albert) — Mr. Thomson of Haymount,
  g g g. g. g. g. g s. (2nd Prince Albert) — Lord Polwarth,
  g g g g g g g g s (1st Prince Albert||) — Lord Polwarth,
  g. g. g. g. g. g. g. g. s. (Taylor's big sheep) — Mr. Taylor of Presson,
  g g g g g g. g. g g g. s. — Mr Taylor of Presson,
  g g g. g g g g g. g. g. s (out of a ewe got by a Compton sheep) —
    Lord Polwarth,
  g g g g g. g. g. g. g. g. g. s — Lord Polwarth,
  g g. g g. g g g. g g. g. g. g s — Mr. Jobson of Hezelrif

  † First-prize ram at Edinburgh, 1858, and bought by Lord Polwarth for
35 guineas.

  ‡ First-prize shearling and two shear at Kelso in 1855-56, and taken by Lord
Polwarth, for the season of 1855, for 25 guineas.

  || Got by Mr Taylor's champion sheep, which beat eleven of the same age
at the first Northumberland Show.

then sell them at the House of Muir and elsewhere in February.

Moffat fair, at which about one thousand rams, three-fourths of them Cheviot and the rest Leicester and blackfaces, are annually sold, clashed with the Kelso ram sale; but "Moodlaw's" sale came off on the day before it. For a long time this sale and "Kirkhill's" have been on alternate years. The old inn hard by the bridge which spans the Evan Water looked quite bright that day, with tables spread in the coach-houses, and union-jacks floating from the hay-loft. "Ericstane" was in the chair; and as visitors dropped in, table after table was added, till at last the coach-house "threw out skirmishers" with knife and fork, half-way across the yard. There was no music save the drone of a bagpipe in the distance, and no blackface on the field save a negro who sold sweetmeats, and treated each Cheviot breeding sahib to a most reverent salaam. Fully a hundred shepherd-dogs lay about or under the platforms, and amid the plaided crowd there walked an Edinburgh horse-dealer with his hands in his pockets, and trying hard to appreciate that cock of the lug and glint of the eye for which the Moodlaw flock is so famed. All the tups had been collected two or three days before at Mr. Brydon's farm, Kinnel Head, and therefore most of the breeders knew them by heart. "Skelf Hill" and the sheep men from the Hawick side mustered strong; and while the young Brydons, in the absence of their

father, marshalled the tups outside the ring, the
lusty manhood of Tom Welsh was master of the cere-
monies within.   There, too, sat Linhope, with his
catalogue clasped to his breast, as he eyed the first
lot, and the still more portly form of " Baitlaws" in
his brown gaiters, with his two hands resting on his
stick—as moderators of that Cheviot assembly.

Then "Linhope" broke silence. " Old Duke, what
age is he ?"   " Five shear," says Mr. Oliver ; " he
won at Perth, Battersea, Langholm, and Thornhill."
However, his age was against him, and 22 gs. was the
figure.   "Thorley by The Earl by The Duke by
Old Palley—who'll give twenty guineas ?"   "Twelve,"
says the cautious Baitlaws.   " Fifteen—twenty,"
says Tom Welsh ; and away they went, Moffat of
Craig going to the cry, and full of drive.   At fifty
there was a pause, and Tom Welsh "was in."
Then " Linhope," Moffat, and Archibald ran to
head once more.   " Linhope" was in at sixty, and
again at sixty-two ; but he would have no more of it,
and Archibald received the Oliverian benediction,
" You'll get into a good stock."   Ben Lomond then
gave us a turn.   He trotted round the ring, made
for a bolt-hole, and in an instant our form was tilted
up, and ourselves and a companion bit the sod.   Loud
and long was the laugh against us, and there was
nothing for it but to move mentally that his " name
be taken down," and into our note-book it went.
We did not wait long for revenge.   With a rigid
impartiality beyond all praise, The Idiot flew at

higher game; and just missing Tom Welsh, and all but scattering Mr. Oliver, he made straight to the judgment-seat, and in an instant "Linhope" and "Baitlaws" were flying heels upwards; and ere they "rose to order," he had found a bolt-hole near "Skelf Hill" (who was enjoying the scene most cruelly), and was off with Mr. Graham's £30 on his head. Going to The Shaw, he jumped the dykes like a wild goat, and took a world of driving, but proved well the next lambing "for a' that and a' that." The spirit was not knocked out of the seniors by their downfall, as one bought Jonathan for 32 gs., and the other a horned one for 34 gs., after a jocular complaint that "a guinea had been missed," which only made the hearers bid harder. It was a great day for the Old Hornie blood, as 52 three-shears averaged £9 13s.

"The Devil's Beef Tub," that strange mountain hollow, at the head of which the old mail-road used to run, took us slightly north again from Moffat. The name of "Beef Tub" is a delusion and a snare, and we fell back on Mr. Tom Welsh's snug steading of Ericstane, two miles away. Here the Cheviot and Ayrshire elements blend most harmoniously. In the entrance there hangs the fine Roman head of Brydon's Wellington; and a bower in his blue blouse was hard at cheese work, with his wife and family, behind. The Ayrshire idea has been spreading eastward apace during the last ten years, and Dutch barns with metal pillars have spread with it.

Mr. Jameson of Kirkbank an Ayrshire man, first
started it in Dumfriesshire, and in 1835 he was followed up by Mr. Miller at Balgray. The Dumfriesshire supplies of kye come from the Biggar and
Ayrshire districts. They buy them principally in
April, to calve at three on the grass. Dalziel of
Whitcastle and Stoddart of Boreland are among the
largest dairymen, and do it on their own account
with about seventy cows each; and Miss Hope
Johnstone (who took the second prize for yearling
heifers in a class of twenty at Kelso) has also a model
dairy.

From Martinmas to Whitsuntide the milk and
cream are generally sent separately to Edinburgh, all
along the Caledonian line. Each day's produce goes
on the following, but at no period is more than 8d.
a gallon got, the consignee paying the carriage.
The majority of the Dumfriesshire dairies are
managed by bowers, and the average rent is £8
to £9 10s. a cow, except in Nithsdale, where they
generally adopt the Ayrshire mode of working by the
stone. They have many intricate bargains—so many
acres of turnips for so many cows, and so many queys
to bring up, &c. In another dairy it will be reckoned
by so many cartloads of turnips to each cow, and the
bowers to pull them with the shaws; or so many
acres of turnips and tares and a ton of bean-meal
may be items in the account.

The Liddesdale hounds never get as far, and at
times they are sorely needed. Black Hope up

Moffat Water was once a great foxhold, and on regular field days the shepherds turn out with carbines. Once thirty-two couple of Mr. Murray of Broughton's hounds were over the scaur, and only one was killed; and a farmer spoke of it to us as his special crown of rejoicing that he was held over that scaur by his heels to keep him steady, and pelted the fox off his half-way house ledge at last.

Moffat Water and Whamphray Water are both crossed; and the steep brow near the little church of Whamphray, with the pillar which speaks to the memory of Carruthers of Kirkhill, is scaled at last, and we are once more back at The Shaw. It had its small pack of harriers in the late Mr. Graham's time, but his son has no divided love except between Galloways and half-bred lambs. The house lies on a little eminence on the high road from Lockerby to Langholm, and the waters of the Caudle burn and the Dryfe flow down the pleasant glade.

Mr. Graham's Galloway herd is never large, as he sells both bulls and females; and his principal strains are from the Blind Bull (brother to Black Jock and Moss Trooper), who was bred by the late George Graham of Riggfoot, and was first at Edinburgh in '48. The present bull is from Mr. Halliday's of Molock. His Cheviot ewes, whose cast is replaced annually with second ewe lambs from the adjacent flockmasters, are put to Leicester tups, either of his own breeding, Mr. Bell Irving's of Whitehill, or Yorkshire ones at a pinch, and the top lambs go off

about the time of Lockerby fair, while the seconds
with a month's more keep bring nearly as much.

Our onward route was past Boreland, where Mr.
Stoddart has his dairy, through large sheep parks, and
so over Eskdale Muir, where the Cheviot and curlew
are monopolists. The homestead of " Twiglees" own
brother to " Terrona," and a great Highland Society
winner at one time, is a little to the left, and at last
a turn and a dip in the road reveal Eskdale church.
Young Thomas Brydon was laid there soon after.
He was in a very failing state at the last Beattock
sale, and a winter spent, with a very devoted friend,
between France and Torquay quite failed to restore
him. Few young men gave higher promise as a
flockmaster, and his death was a very deep sorrow
to those who knew him best. There, too, stands a
pillar to the memory of the Rev. Dr. Brown, who
laboured summer and winter for forty years in that
quiet spot, where " the pedlar was murdered down
yonder," and where the shepherds still assemble in
a " Cameronian meeting-house."

A ford has to be crossed, and then in the distance
beneath the fir-capped scaur we catch our first
glimpse of Moodlaw. Three counties meet just above
the steading at Cracksmuir Hill; but really, what
with eternal heather and sheep parks, we had long
since lost all county distinctions. Mr. Brydon has
four farms in all, two of them in Selkirkshire; and
Moodlaw, with its moor, moss, bog, and lea, is about
the best pasture in the south of Scotland. Eskdale

Muir belongs principally to the Duke of Buccleuch, and is rented at 7s. to 9s. 6d. per sheep. The best land is clay, with mossy bogs, and black at the bottom. The drains are eighteen inches deep, and placed eight to ten yards apart, and renewed every four or five years at the tenant's expense. Where the pick does not "come in to pick your pocket," the making generally costs about nine shillings per hundred rods of eighteen feet. As for the old "penny pie concern," of twelve to thirty yards apart, it has gone quite out.

The Mawkey ewe was in the paddock near the house with her twelfth set of lambs; and two fawn greyhounds, coupled to keep them out of mischief, were the first to give us greeting. The flock has been in the family for nearly eighty years, and the Cheviot pedigree goes back for fully half that time; but save an occasional grey-leg, no trace of the primitive blackface comes out. Mr. Brydon's uncle showed sheep at Stirling about 1830, and won a tea service for the best Cheviot; and in 1840 Mr. Brydon came to Moodlaw.

His great object has been to get them shorter and thicker, especially above the knee, or "the butcher's grip," wide between the forelegs, with hard white hair on the crown, deep in the girth, well-woolled below and on the arms and thighs, with a fine park-ranging neck, light and clefty in the bone, white on the legs, and black on the nose. A flat crown and too pointed ears are points he has always struggled against; and a fine Roman head, with a full and daring eye, is quite his coat of arms. He also prefers the coat rather open, as the closely-planted ones are disposed to shed their wool in the spring when the new and the old coats separate. The wool calculation is five fleeces of ewes and hoggs, and three of hill-ranging tups to the 24lb. stone. If a ewe nurses two lambs, she has one-third less wool, and if she is in the cast she is generally among the shots. From Martinmas until the beginning of April, about 3,000 brats are used for the ewe hoggs, as the woollen cloth prevents the wet from settling on the fleece. This is, however, a plan which few, except Mr. Brydon, observe, and he does not recognise the objection that it prevents the wool from rising properly. There are eight thousand ewes in the flock, which have generally five crops of lambs, and the cast has gone for years to farmers in the district. The wedder lambs are all sold in August, and 120 tups are kept each year. Eight sales have been held so far, with about nine score in each of them, and, as a general rule, the two-shears sell best.

Since Mr. Brydon succeeded to the flock, he has been a steady shower, both at the Highland Society, Moffat, Thirlstane, Langholm, Dumfries, and Thornhill. Old Stirling won eleven prizes. He was a sheep of grand style, and sported a 13lb. coat as a four-shear. Old Palley was also "all gaiety and life," with a very special coat and a head which was thought worthy of stuffing. Roughie was of the

Sampson kind, and a very useful sheep, but Sampson himself was "not of an off-hand show appearance." He was the largest Mr. Brydon ever bred, and weighed nearly 19½ st. of 14lbs. even when his season had sunk him 5 or 6 stone. As a ewe-getter, there was none to compare with "The Rigglin," for which Mr. Borthwick of Hopesrigg gave £100. Robson, from whom many of the best ewes are descended, was a horned one, and for staple and quality of wool he was unequalled among the tups, aud brought £75 at Beattock. Horned Cheviots are generally more hardy and coarser in the coat, but Robson's was a complete contradiction of the rule. Hornie was sold for 55 gs. to Mr. Patterson of Twiglees, and Mr. Elliot of Hindhope got his sire, who, like Old Tom, was more of a ewe getter. The Captain (95 gs.) by Old Palley went as a three-shear to Mr. Borthwick; and Mr. Graham of The Shaw had the remains of " Heb" in a present, when he had been used for five seasons.

The old Mawkey ewe thrice shared first-prize honours in a pen of five ewes, and gimmers, and she had twins every year but two. Out of her twenty-two lambs, one of them was Lord Clyde (the winner of 8 prizes) by The Duke, and another Sir Colin by Heb, who won five prizes. But as we were pondering over this Eskdale matron, the rain came down in such torrents, and swelled the brook to such an extent, that further progress was impossible. There was no Langholm that night, and we resigned ourselves to a most pleasant captivity.

CHAPTER XV.

MOODLAW TO ARKLETON.

"O yes! and that's e'e time, O yes! and that's twa times, O yes! and that's thend and last time· All manner of pearson and pearsons whatso-e'er let 'um draw near, and I shall let 'em kenn that their is a fair to be held ττ the muckle toune of Langholm for the space of aught days, wherein if any Hustrin, Custrin, Land-couper, Dub-skimper, or Gang-the-gate-swinger shall head any Urdain, Durdain, Rebblement, Brebblement, or Squebblement, he shall have his lugs tecked to the muckle Trone with a nail of twal-a-penny until he be doun of his hobshanks and up with his muckle doups, and pray to Hea'n neen times, God bless the King, and thrice the muckle Laird of Relton, paying a groat to me, Jamie Ferguson, Baily of the aforesaid Manor So you've heerd my proclamation, and now I'll awa' haam to my danner."

GENTLEMAN'S MAGAZINE.

From Moodlaw to Langholm—The late Sir Frederick Johnstone—Langholm and its Bye-laws—Langholm Lodge and its Bard—Hunting—The late Lord John Scott, his Racing Stud—A Crack with Terrona on Cumberland Border Sires—Terrona's Poet—Mr. John Jardine and his Greyhounds.

THE Esk was down again by noon, and, crossing it once more, we followed it on the south side as far as Langholm. There is more bent, and therefore less feeding quality, on the hills beneath which it flows than at Moodlaw; and the valley, which occasionally opens out into a series of holmes, is fringed with plantations of beech, oak, and fir, which steal at intervals almost to the hill tops. With the exception of a few West Highlanders and Galloways, we saw nothing but the shorthorn once more. Many of them were Irish-bred stirks, which are gradually driving out the blacks. Bilham, the farm of one of "Christopher North's" sons, lies in a hollow to our right, and we pass close by the steading of Borthwick of Hopesrigg, who has fought and won at the Highland Society, and sells forty to fifty of his tups at Hawick each September. The spur and wings on a sign tell that Westerhall is nigh; and tying our mare to the gate, we saunter up the plantation walk leading to the pillar which was erected to the memory of Sir Frederick Johnstone.

"Waterford," "Greene," "Moore," "Musgrave," "Macdonald," and many an associate of his merry Melton days have gone, like him, to the land of shadows. The villagers told us, in their simple way, what a man he was, and, with an emphasis that three-and-twenty years had not deadened one whit, that he was "sair likit in the country-side"—"like a galloping horse with his harriers;" how he ran on foot, and hunted all Eskdale, Ewesdale, and Annandale as well, and how he used to van the pack from Westerhall to the meet, before he got the Falford kennels. The evening sun was just lighting up the shadows on Whita, the hill of the monument, as we emerged from quite a shady alcove on to the "muckle toune" of Langholm, or rather of Malcolm Brothers. The statue of Sir John, one of the foremost minds in the Indian Council, looks down its greeting from the bleak hill above to Sir Pulteney in the market place. They were honoured with high confidence from strictly opposite quarters. The one was the trusted friend of Wellington, and the other had, on the authority of Napoleon, " the true face of an Englishman." Hard by him there hangs the most Draconic code of bye-laws on the clock-house that ever town-clerk penned or provost pondered.   Swine-scalding, bull and "furious animal driving," carpet-beating, water across foot-paths, ashes, cart driving, are all regulated by it.   If your chimney is on fire you're fined, and if you're a parent you're answerable for your child, and for each offence you may be fined 20s., or have twenty-four hours in quod.   The spirit of Jamie Ferguson's "proclamation" does, indeed, linger in that terrible edict.   Before we had been there two minutes, we had all but broken a bye-law, as you "mayn't attach your animal to a house," and we had hung ours for a minute on the statue-rails, so we thought it high time to decamp down Ewesdale, and consult " Terrona" as to the consequences.

Had it been race-time, the Langholm Lodge meadow would have been a sure find for him, either at the cords or the wrestling-ring.   Tom Sayers came there to watch the science of the " Cumberland chip," with a view to its use in his own more bloody fray with Heenan, and received divers attentions from his newly-found " Uncle."   Scott, Ivison, Ben Cooper, and Dick Wright have all been champions on this velvet sward.   It is said that in the New Forest the married women play the lasses at cricket, and deliver " shooters" and " run like mad" between the wickets to the shout of " Well hit, mo-

ther!" from the lads; but Langholm saw another
sight, when a Cumbrian mother arrived to see her
lad wrestle, and not only laid odds on him, but exhorted him to "*tak a good hold*," with other scientific and strictly local directions. All descriptions of
Langholm Lodge pale before "Old Davy the Mins-
trel's." It is now fifty years or more since he went about
with a cuddy, and not only ground knives, but composed verses, which he recited on the smallest provo-
cation, and with extra emphasis for ale or a bit of
baccy. A call for "your verses on Langholm Lodge,
Davy," was answered on this wise, and if the bard
was on the cuddy at the moment they were thought
to be all the more impressive:

> "Oh! Langholm, thou art beautiful,
> Where three fine waters meet,*
> In view of a large country hall,
> A great lord's country-seat,
> Which he hath called after thee,
> For to augment thy fame,
> And in record will stand and be
> The Langholm Lodge by name."

Decidedly the finest Langholm minstrels of the
present age are the scratch pack which are hunted
by the Duke's gamekeeper. Sometimes they join
the Liddesdale, with whom Ballantyne of Shaws,
Graham of Broadlee, Elliot of Twisselhope, Kei
of Whitehaugh, and Jamie Smith of Harwood
Mill are the Hard-riding Dicks. Jamie is "tar-
rible keen," and when he is not foxhunting with
Ballantyne, he may be seen following his two foxhound bitches (either *solus* or with quite a large field),

---

* Ewes, Esk, and Wauchope.

and a straight-backed Liddesdale hare in front of them. On one occasion Lord John Scott brought Williamson and the hounds, and they drew towards Cannobie. Will didn't care for such house-side hills, and Lord John was always for getting him into the flows. However, he knew what they were up to, and escaped their wiles pretty well, and delivered himself pretty smartly when he was safe back at St. Boswell's : " *Good my lud, did ye ever ken the like o' that ?—men and muirs a' alike. I've been in the flows, and they've never been in bed—they're fou yet ; there's something else than a fox in their 'ee.*" Lord John loved this wild Langholm hunting, and spared himself no fatigue. He once rode some thirty miles to Langholm the day before a hunt, from Spottiswoode, and found at Cannobie, through the Wauchope country and over Eskdale and back to Langholm, and then to Thirlstane Castle, forty miles away in the heart of Berwickshire. The quiet dalesman might well run out to look, as he swept past like the storm, catching up his hacks of yesterday at points on the road.

It was well said of him that he was a " Scotch-man of the Scotch," and that " in the days of Border chivalry he would have been the hero of many a ballad." He leistered about the Ettrick and the Tweed, and he and the Duke of Athole vied with each other, in their otter-hunting bouts, who should tunnel farthest into the fortress when it had gone right under the bank, and who should come out from

helping the terriers with most sand in his hair.
He had a racehorse or two in Scotland, but never
regularly settled to the sport till he had purchased
Phryne and hired Pantaloon; and engaged Mat
Dawson in '48 to train for him, first at Newmarket,
and then at Compton.   He sold Elthiron, the first
of "the PP stock," to Lord Eglinton, to his own
sorrow, for 250 gs.; and he stuck to the remainder,
except when the £6,500 for Hobbie Noble tempted
him.   His sister Miserrima was then tried high
enough to have won five out of six Oaks; but Frank
Butler, on the roaring Iris, waited and outstrode her.
George Whitehouse, a very quick man at a T.Y.C.
post, and then Marlow, rode for the stable.   Hobbie
Noble was a slug in his work, and The Reiver very
awkward to do with in the stable; and Cannobie was,
perhaps, the best horse his lordship ever had.   He
gave up racing a few years before his death, as his
health was not strong enough to bear the excitement.
Mr. Merry took the stud in a lump at last, and
had two foals from Phryne.   The old mare died at
Hasketon, very near her time of foaling a colt by
Alice Hawthorne's son Oulston, to whom she had
been sent for the sake of getting collaterally at
another Thormanby.*

Lord John, who named a race-horse after him, and
British Yeoman, are ever on old "Terrona's" lips.
He was quite in his glory when he repaired to the

* For a further account of Lord John's Cawston stud, see "SCOTT AND
SEBRIGHT,' pp 222—226.

field near the house, with the hound "Yeoman" at his heels, to show us the Giraffe mare with the last drop of the old horse at her foot. It had been duly named "Terrona," and bids fair to be a Border gallant in days to come. With a view to showing its paces he rattled on his hat like a tambourine, and then called up the rest of the Yeomans from the long meadows with quite the chest-notes of a Mario. The Cheviot gimmers which came second to the Moodlaw pen at Kelso were in the field, but his son John looks to them. " Terrona's" heart is in the horse-ring and the saddle; and, as he observes with much seeming satisfaction, he has "been left twenty-two times for dead with strange horses." Being once safely beyond the clad score, it seems quite reasonable that he should now "put in for two dozen."

Somehow, he always recovers in a most marvellous manner; and his reel with the late Marquis of Queensberry at "The Crown"—when Joe Graham was quite the Beau Nash of the evening, and in that capacity kept the two fiddlers so ably up to the mark that they played " Bonny Dundee" one-and-thirty times—is talked of yet in Langholm. His spirits never flag, and a peep at his face when a blood-horse is the theme is like a sunbeam on a frosty day. What a crack we had that night of every Cumberland or Border horse we had ever heard of or seen going down Stanwix brow each Saturday in our schoolboy days. He gave us them all, from Bang-

tail down to Laughing Stock, intermingling his dis-
course with Yeoman elegiacs.

First it was blood-horses; and "first and foremost
came Bangtail, with his dark whole-coloured stock.
He ran some four-mile heats with Pleader, and each
won a heat, and then they had a dead heat.   Outcry
by Camillus got great and good horses, roarer as he
was.   Mr. Blamire, the member, brought Gregson
and Grand Turk the coacher into the country from
Tommy Swan of Bedale's.   Gregson got great, fine
greys, when to own a grey was to have £10 extra in
your pocket.   Ben Ledi had good action, but curby
hocks.   The Corinthians had all bad tempers, and
light back ribs; and Royalist was a cock-thropple-
necked horse, short and sound, but with no action or
power. The Earl was a little curby, and had an ugly
head; but he got sound, good stock, and not very
handsome.   Grey carriage-horses were Grey Wigan-
thorpe's *forte*.   Mr. Ferguson wanted a grey, but Sir
Tatton couldn't sell him one under four hundred, so
he dealt with Mr. Garforth.   They were good carriage horses, but, like him, they were short of speed.
Phœnix was quite unsound when he raced, just like
all the Cobwebs.   He was an elegant horse, of a su-
perb colour, but he wanted bone and fore-feet, and
the stock put out curbs perpetually.   The Yeoman
(and here he was most emphatic) has done a deal in
sixteen years; three-fourths of his foals were colts.
There are some rare mares by him; and Charley
Boy, that was a high lifter and slapping character

of a horse. The Yeoman nearly always got bays
and browns, and generally whole-coloured, if he did
get a chesnut even off a brown mare with not a speck
of white on her, it would have stockings up to the
knees and hocks, and it was generally a good 'un. If
The Yeoman had a fault, I grant you, it was rather
light fore-legs. The Galaors were a bit long in the
back, and short in the quarters. Mr. Ferguson
never had a better; great, fine, slapping weight car-
riers, there are some grand mares by him, generally
browns, and speedy too. The Ravenhills had much
better forelegs than he had himself, and he got them
good dark browns, but a trifle high-tempered.

"Candidate was not thorough-bred; his mares threw
good hunters, and he crossed remarkably well with
the Clydesdales. He was the first that came to
Harker Lodge. Lord Selkirk imported him when he
was four years old from Yorkshire for his Kirkcudbright tenants; and then Mr. Ferguson and Mr.
Fawcett of Scaleby and one or two others bought
him. He had navicular disease and contracted feet,
but still his stock were pretty sound, and had grand
action. Grand Turk had rare ribs and quarters; he was
a rich bay with no white hairs, and got as good, in
fact better, mares than Candidate. He was a flashy-
looking horse, and got them all bays, but "somehow
he didn't put his rib on them." "The Turk mares"
were terribly run upon, as their action was so showy;
he laid a great foundation for carriage-horse bays.
Bay Chilton was no use to him in the show-yard.

Nimrôd was by Muley out of a "Turk mare," and had all the family action. Monarch was a great bay horse, far too big, and put them all unsound in the Penrith district.

"There have been a great many good cart-sires. Young Clyde had fine action, and a light middle. Blythe did wonders. He had won at the Highland Society and at a great many other places, and they picked him up to go South. He was kept there three or four years, and then they said he was too big, and exchanged him with Mr. Fawcett of Scaleby for a coacher. Then Wilson of Burgh got him, and he made him pretty well. He had him more than eight years, and he took the Carlisle prize five years running. The Stitchers were the old sort, bays with short legs, and wide and sound. Mr. Ellis of Netherby brought Stitcher to the Bush Inn, and began the new sort forty years ago. Scotch Miracle was one of his sons, and Young Clyde was off that tribe. The Scotch Miracles were square, well-set horses, great at a dead weight or on a farm. Mr. Borthwick's horse was a thick one by Stitcher; and Glancer was smaller than some of them, but very good in action and everything else."

The Terrona, or rather the Flask Wood pheasant covers, stretch down the Ewesdale valley, which we had now entered again on the south side, after riding nearly three hundred miles across and down Scotland from Hawick. We found disease busy among the larches, first attacking those between ten and thirty, and then their seniors. Rising above Flask Wood is the rich green of Arkleton Crag, the hill which separates the Ewes, and the little stream of

> " Tarrass for the good bull trout,
> If it be ta'en in time."

Carlisle may be seen from the Crag on a clear summer day, but the rival hills above Muckledale are a more lofty theme for " Terrona." We cannot say that he loves the Muses, but we do know that he gave Lady Florence Cust a lead after the Eskdale fox hounds down a brae which no woman's steed had ever trodden before. He vowed on the spot that he would " commemorate the deed for ages yet unborn," and looked up a poet from the dales, who did his spiriting well. The stone was inscribed and conveyed on a sledge, and duly toasted in whisky; and there it stands, with this inscription, in fulfilment of the vow—

> " Reared by a veteran sportsman's hand,
> In sunshine and in mist I stand,
> To tell the time and mark the place
> Where high-bred beauty led the chase,
> And gentle lady's graceful steed
> Gained from the field its hard-earned meed:—
> I mark the spot on this wild fell,
> That fathers to their sons may tell
> How once a youthful English bride
> Taught the rough Borderers to ride."

A ford to the right, a little farther on, leads to Arkleton past the gardens, which are Mr. John Jardine's delight. The bowling-green and everything about the house, which overlooks a little wooded burn flowing down from the hills above, are alike trim and tasteful, and the painted glass windows and

the statues are true to the love of the leash. Mr.
Jardine has a flock of about 1,400 ewes and ewe
hoggs, and uses Aitchison, Brydon, and Borthwick
tups. After the fourth crop of lambs, they are
brought from the heights on to the improved pasture
for a crop of half-bred lambs, which feed far quicker
than the Cheviot, although all have not the rich
grazing of Minsca and Torbeck Hill. The half-bred
system begins at Burnfoot, and branches when it
reaches Langholm, not only six miles down Ewesdale, where it stops and is resumed again nearer Hawick, but away by Cannobie, one of the five kirks of
Eskdale, into Cumberland. The Cheviot wedder
lambs are sold at Carlisle, and the seconds and the
shots of the ewe lambs go to Lockerby and Melrose
fairs, to be used as dams of half-breds in flocks where
not a Cheviot is bred.

We had to sit a short time, waiting for the greyhounds; but with the help of a telescope we sighted
Willie Keddie coming down from the Crag, with
the short-tempered Owersby following meekly at
heels. Willie was once a shepherd with Mr. Elliot
of Hindhope. He was quite a noted sheep-clipper,
and in the greyhound training profession of later
years he has clipped the wings of a few when they
least looked for it. There was quite a troop behind
him that morning, and among them "Fly" or Old
Border Union by Jeffrey from Ladylike, "a good
steady one, who placed herself well to the game like
her dam, but was short of pace for the flat."

Sam and Tollwife's picture hangs in the drawing-room, and, as Mr. Jardine says, "they began me." She was by King Cob, and had three successive litters to Sam. Miss Hannah, who was never beaten in her puppy season, was one of five with Marmora. Toll-wife's dam was Matilda Gillespie, who was slow, and, like Tollwife, could live a long time. Mr. Nightingale begged Mr. Jardine to send Matilda Gillespie to King Cob, as his stock ran so stout and kept their heads so well down. Motley, the sire of David, was an own brother to Marmora and Miss Hannah, and a first-class dog at Amesbury, Ashdown, and Market Weighton. He was a fast-driving dog, and, *per* Mr. Nightingale, "he could use a hare fastest, and put in more work than any greyhound of his day." This Willie Keddie cordially endorses with "*he could strip 'em up without bending in Lid-desdale.*"

The Tollwife stamina has never been lost in this kennel; and be it at Ridgway, Biggar, Kelso, Teviot-side, Coquetdale, Broughton, Brampton, Brougham, or the Waterloo, "if the Jardine dogs live through the middle of the course they live to the finish." They are always kept well all summer—a great secret of success in coursing—for there is no more determined man than their owner, or one who succeeds better in everything he takes in hand. The Baron by Kentish Fire from Linnet, "a strong, steady dog," is peculiarly associated with his name, and showed what he was made of by beating Scot-

land Yet at Carstairs, after an undecided course.
The hare durst not take her fence, and swerved
down the brae, and the dog rushed in and used
the point. It was in a sixty-four dog stake, and
Scotland Yet's merits in the middle of the course
wiped off the first and last work, and brought
out the red and white flags. His daughter, Ladylike, was one of a litter from Bella. She was a
good winner at Brampton and Lowther, and very
clever about not going too far downhill, which gave
her a great pull on the steep ground at Biggar.
At the stud she made a hit with Barrator, and one of
the litter was Selby, whose Waterloo honours were
shared by Clive, another of Mr. Jardine's breeding,
by Judge out of Moeris, and of the same litter as
Jeffrey.

There were six of them; and Mr. Majori-
banks's trainer, who had his choice, left Jeffrey
and Clive, the latter on account, as he said, of her
white feet, but really because she was the worst
looking puppy. There were two dogs and two
bitches among the four he selected, one of which
was for Lord Stradbroke, but none of them were
good. Mr. Jardine had always a great love for
Jeffrey; he sent Ladylike to him when he was sold,
and Faldonside, Crerer, Ingomar, and Border Union
confirmed this choice. " Selby," says Mr. Nightingale, " was not handsome, but with great power and
bone, always stealing away up to his game. He was
rather leggy for his length, clever, and turned well

for a big dog, and always ran with•fire. He fairly
galloped over and ran down Portsea in the last
course but one for the Waterloo Cup, for which
Mr. Hedley, a relation of Mr. Jardine's, trained
him. Clive had not his brilliant dash. She was a
low-running bitch, and went clean away from
Antipas in the fourth ties for the Waterloo."

In a private trial before the Cup, Selby beat her, and
carried the money of the party. Clive only lost one
course out of twenty-two, and that was with Mr.
Gibson's Lassie in the Caledonian St. Leger. She
was very easily prepared, and ran at 59lbs.; and at
Biggar she divided the St. Leger with Mr. Borron's
Black Knight, who got the bye when she met Cardinal York. This was once a great stake with Mr.
Jardine, as his dog Terrona* divided it the next
year with Canaradzo; then his Faldonside and Crerer
divided; and on the following year his Otterburn
was beaten in his fourth course by Sea Foam. Mr.
Jardine has been a courser for twenty years, and
yet he was never near a Waterloo Cup except when
he divided it with one of his own breeding. Since
then he has been second for the Plate with Faldonside and Owersby, and his Miss Hannah won it for
Mr. Marjoribanks.

And so we hied on our way back through Ewesdale, viewed "Terrona" once more at the distance
as happy as a cricket among his mares and foals, and

* This dog was lent to Mr Jardine by Lord John Scott when he ran at
Biggar, and his lordship left especial directions before his death that Mr.
Jardine should keep him.

got safely through Langholm without violating a single bye-law. The road from there to Cannobie—with thick nut-copses on one side, the Esk murmuring over rock and chasm on the other, and the deep, silent shade over head—is one of the sweetest summer rides in Scotland, and not a cheerless one in winter. The " Cross Keys" Hotel seemed almost on English ground ; a chesnut, with a species of " Happy Tom" on a donkey at his side; called up " Terrona's" lecture of the overnight ; and the long green Lomax holme across the river " marched with Cumberland" at last.

CHAPTER XVI.

CANNOBIE TO KENSINGTON.

"If you will pass your life with birds and flowers, try to raise the finest turnips and breed the largest fowls."

DR. JOHNSON.

Woodhouselees—The late Miss Rachel Bell—Ecelefechan—A Day at Knockhill; its Horses and Greyhounds—Hoddom Castle—Hunting Recollections of Joe Graham—The Dumfriesshire Kennels—Blood Royal in his Barn—Mr Beattie and his Stake Nets—The Solway Flow—The Red Kirk Herd—From Holme Eden to Kensington

WE stopped short of those double turnpikes on each side of the Border boundary, which try the traveller's patience so sorely, and renewed our acquaintance with Woodhouselees. The farm, which belongs to the Duke of Buccleuch, has been occupied by successive generations of the Bell family since 1707. With the century the present Mr. James Bell's father entered on it. He was a leading agriculturist in his day, and an active director of the Highland Society for several years. After his death in 1832, his son George held the farm for four years, and then transferred it to his sister Rebecca, who inherited all the country tastes of the family, and who occupied it until her death in July, '61.

James Little, the grieve, who has been nearly forty

2 c c

years about the place, and "took Miss Rebecca in tow" when her father died, was in the road listening to the rambling recital of a Cumberland cart-sire man —how " we worn't beaten but we wor cheaten" in the ring at Carlisle—and then dismissing him in our favour, with the comforting but rather general assurance that his horse was " a weell-comed 'un." He quite waked up when we reminded him of his dear old mistress's times, and asked after the mares which had such choice foals by Ravenhill and British Yeoman. We remembered how she would be about everywhere with her blue sun-bonnet, and with her egg basket on her arm, now snipping off the dead roses in her dainty flower-garden, now sallying into the pastures to have a look at the last fall of half-bred lambs, or " a word with James" at the head of the turnip-hoers, and then joining her sister Isabella at their own girls' school, which many a village lass has had good reason to bless.

There never was a more spirited disciple of Ceres and Christian Curwen, but her heart lay more in the farmyard than the arable land. Her small pure whites and middles, with their strong dash of Brandsby blood, used to go off ten in a cart, three times in the season, to the Annan pig market. She crossed her Ayrshires with shorthorns, and made Dunlop cheese. The prize rosettes were to be found on her pens of Dorkings, Spanish, Golden Spangles, Bramah Pootras, and Hamburghs at Edinburgh, Glasgow, Manchester, and Liverpool; she

could command ten guineas for her prize pens of
Rouens, from such judges as Mrs. Ferguson Blair
and Mr. Gibson of Woolmet, and as much for her
Aylesburys; but as James says, "We never fashed
the turkeys." Both Leicester and Lincoln rams were
used to the Cheviot ewes, and the latter answered
well. Half-breds abound all the way from Langholm,
but they are not bred on "the flying stock" or cast
Cheviot ewe principle, and "middle" Cheviot lambs
are bought to keep up the ewe stock. James often
tells, in connexion with these purchases, of the
astonished look of a Southron visitor, who heard
him say to his mistress, "If nine score lambs be o'er
mony, we can just *shoot* a few on 'em." Things go
on under the management of Mr. James Bell (who
spends his time between Liverpool and Cannobie) quite
in the good old way. It is a six-course rotation,
oats, turnips, oats sown down to pasture, and three
years' grass, and now fully 100 pigs are fed off each
year.

From Cannobie we cast back once more past Gil-
nockie and one or two more Border towers, and by
rather a dreary cross route to Ecclefechan, that wonderful little town which prides itself on its manners,
and requests all those who are short of that article to
come for "half a Saturday" when soap-suds are rife.
It has always been impressed on our minds from
Sylvanus Urban's story of the lady near there, who
used to ride round and round her barn on a sheltie as
she read novels, and declare that it was the only

2 c c 2

mode of enjoying a circulating library. Burnswark or those two hills united by a rampart, and Woodcockair were our beacons, and on we went past the little church where one of the monuments seemed to have made itself legs and walked clean out of the wall, and where a husband, who had not been burdened with "my spouse Nancy," writes: " And to be short to her praise, she was the wife Solomon speaks of." Despite this hint, celibacy still exists about here to very great extent.

Old Pallinsburn looked well as we met him in sheets for a morning's walk, and everything was thriving at Knockhill. The swallow had come back and built in the porch once more; the brood mares were all in-foal, the spotted sheep were all in-lamb, and the burning of Aurora in her stable, which happened the only year the swallow was away, seemed in a fair way of being forgotten at last. Birkie's bark was heard of course, as we rode up, and so was Will's reproving voice to her and half-a-dozen more behind. The Ayrshires, with one or two beauties among them, were having their morning's run in the sloping meadow. The black ducks were on the pond, and the white crow on the tree; the Dorkings were strolling in and out of the laurels, or standing on one leg under the Irish yews; and an aviary was full of the choicest fancy pigeons, principally blues and purples. There had been American turkeys, but they were no sooner let out of their hamper than they winged their flight straight to Woodcockair, and Will and Bob, like Lord Ullin, were "left lamenting" for nearly a fortnight.

Inside the house there is the same ever fresh variety. The late General Sharpe's grey mare hangs near "Uphorn," the Ayrshire; and Hughie Graham shares his canvas with Maid of Islay, both of them "family fawns." Myrrha by Malek is there with "a frame like a cart-horse;" and there too, from Robert Harrington's hand, is Leda with her pistol tail, and "Simmy" on Philip—a pair, as the Ayrshire lasses used to say, "*worth all the men and horses to look at.*"

Lord Wemyss hated waiting, and if "Simmy" said to him, "We've won one heat, my lord—let them have the next to themselves," he shook his head, and wouldn't have it. Lamps were tied to the posts when Leda ran her five two-mile heats, with all the endurance which the Voltigeurs (when they can undergo a strong preparation) inherit from her and Mulatto; and "Simmy" and she might have brought it off if she had not hugged the bank and lost two lengths by slipping. The darkness also told on Mr. Sharpe, as he had his pocket picked during the fourth heat, for the only time in his life. Leda was by Filho da Puta (who walked from Newmarket to Monreith when he was five weeks old) out of Treasure by Camillus. For fifteen years Mr. Sharpe never visited Doncaster without buying a horse from the Houldsworths or Sammy King, and he got her for £50, because her hip was down. She first ran at Dumfries, and cut up so badly that she was put into a straw yard, and the farmer's sons rode her to school. After that, she won two fifties in Lord Elcho's name, and Sir James Boswell offered £250 for her, but Mr. Sharpe did not care to part with her, and said "A thousand or nothing." To use his own expression, "I was crazy on Mulatto;" but it proved very methodical madness, as her produce Martha Lynn became the dam of Voltigeur. All the old mare's stock found a purchaser in Mr. Ramsay, the colts at £100 and the fillies at £80, and soon after Martha had been swapped away to Mr. Stephenson, Leda herself died while foaling a colt to The Doctor. Hazard by Black- lock was another of Mr. Sharpe's Doncaster pur- chases, and so was Dan by Catton. To win the Maiden Plates at Edinburgh was his great aim, and when he was confederate with Lord Wemyss (then Lord Elcho) in Philip, Brunswick, and Gondolier, his sphere was considerably extended. Beagle by Whalebone was his first stallion ; and Brunswick, whom he bought more out of charity than fancy at Perth, because the party had lost every half-penny, and did not know how to get home, was his second. Sister to Jerry was also in his hands when her black brother won the St. Leger, and she died visiting Brunswick.*

Of later years, hunters have been a great point with him. Knockhill, the present crack of Lord Wemyss's stable, was by Turnus out of a roan mare,

* See "Scott and Sebright," pp. 152 and 234.

A GLIMPSE OF KNOCKMILL, 1864.

whose dam did credit to her Tam O'Shanter trotting blood, in Mr. Sharpe's brother-in-law's Sir Thomas Kirkpatrick of Closeburn's drag, and then ran in the "Defiance," and finally in an Edinburgh cab. His half-brothers Tom Linne and The Friar both followed Knockhill after a Derby and St. Leger forfeit had been paid for Tom, and two more own brothers joined them at four years old. Gubaroo, bought from his breeder, Captain Archdale, was another of Mr. Sharpe's selling, and, great as he was at stone walls, he nearly killed himself over one in Amisfield Park. Mr. Tinning of Tinwald owned Dumfries, and when Mr. Sharpe sent for the horse, who was on sale, and bid Bob Carlyle get on him near Repentance Tower, Bob never repented more.

Our stroll round the house was soon over, but the outlyers had to be seen. The old Ayrshire cow Meg is fully sixteen years old, and still milking superbly, She was a model in early life, when she won four prizes, and there are scarcely any marks of age on her now, except the prodigious length (15 inches) of her horns. The brood mares and sheep were sharing the cattle-field pasture. There roamed Johanna Wagner, who had won two or three things in her day, with a foal, Ravenshoe, by Mr. Sharpe's own horse Mandricardo of Mr. Greville's breeding, Cora Linne, a full sister to Montrose, who belongs to Will and Bob, and was due, like Trip the Daisy (Butterfly's own sister), to Chevalier d'Industrie. Both Trip and Cora were winners; Trip scored the

Cumberland Plate and sundries, but Cora beat her easily in a trial at Airdrie. The latter was tried to be better than the Heir of Linne, but before the money could be got on for the Goodwood Nursery the secret got wind, and the market was forestalled. The ewe flock, which all wear bells, began from some spotted Cheviot ewes, with a touch of Shetland in them, and they have been crossed with a Leicester and a Southdown. Still, the primitive magpie colours come out, and only grow a little lighter with exposure to the weather. It wants no dyeing, and some of the lads have had coats made from it. Carle Time and Tak Tent were at the kennels, and so were Cut and Dry (" one of the old style who never leaves his hare"), Fly with her sweet head, Black Agnes and her Carl Time puppies, and What Care I, the dam of Cut and Dry. Mr. Sharpe runs very little in public, except there is a meeting in the neighbourhood, and, unlike their forefathers, who were stripped at Malleny and the Roman Camp in the brave days of old, his greyhounds are not named after the heroes of the Border minstrelsy.

Monarch, by Mr. (now Lord) Gibson Craig's Count from Lord Torphichen's Fly, was Mr. Sharpe's first great dog, and he it was who began "the family fawn." " He was square and thick, and with less fire to his game than either Hughie Graham or Mercury." His blood is in all the Scottish kennels, as it goes through Driver to Drift, the second for the Caledonian Picture, and, curiously enough, Violet, the winner's dam, was from a daughter of Monarch, which Mr. Sharpe gave away. His grandson Jason also took the blood South. The most beautiful he ever got was Mr. Sharpe's own What from Captain Wyndham's Whisk. Monarch won three times at the Roman Camp, and Mercury four times. The brothers were widely different in their styles, as Mercury was "a desperate rusher, very clever with his teeth, but not very fond of a young fence which required a double effort." It was in one of these fences at the Roman Camp that Hughie Graham got stuck. "Hughie" was by Liddesdale, a son of Bowhill (who was bred at the Duke of Buccleuch's) from Queen of the May. There were four dogs and two bitches in the litter, with Bell the Cat and Bonnie Scotland amongst them, and Mr. Sharpe challenged the Wiltshire men in vain to run five puppies of one litter for £50 the course and £500 the main. Queen of the May had black hairs in her fawn, and so Mr. Daintree hated her. He had got some puppies from Lord Stradbroke for the use of King Cob, and as he wanted the Minerva black, he sold "The Queen" for 25 gs. at Aldridge's. Like all the King Cobs, she "ran heads down and backs up, as they ought to run," and when Mr. Nightingale saw her style at the Mid-Lothian Meeting, he said at night that until she was fairly in her stride he did not believe that there was a King Cob in all . Scotland.

Bell the Cat was "a flying rusher," and Bonnie .

Scotland "had not the pluck of Hughie when he got to his game; he had too many hares in his youth, and let them live too long." Still, he was third in the North *v.* South match at Amesbury when Welcome ran up to Mocking Bird. As ill luck would have it, he had a "No go" both with Mocking Bird and Wicked Eye, and beat the latter with only one eye. Despite this drawback, Mr. Nightingale considers his course with Wicked Eye "one of the finest I ever saw; he beat her in working, and went so straight and just from his turns; it was so true worked; each dog had her in turn." Dalton was the dog who gave Hughie Graham most trouble, and they divided the Broughton Cup after two no-goes. He won the Plate the year Hughie Graham won the Waterloo Cup as a puppy. War Eagle (who broke running down with Wee Wee), Mocking Bird, Japhet, Staymaker, and Cerito were among the Cup thirty-two; and "Hughie" killed all his hares except the first. He never ran after his second Waterloo Cup, in which he won one course with Cricketer the Plate winner. "Hughie had great pace, and was very close in his work; he could drive and command himself, fairly smother his hare, and frighten her to death."

He never "hit" well with anything of Mr. Sharpe's, but Wicked Eye, and their son Norman Hunter divided the Cup at Lytham, but Mr. Blanchard's Baffle was by him out of Wild Duck. However, he did his duty, as he won £700 in all.

About the end of his fourth season, he was brought
out of his kennel up to the house to pay his respects
to Mr. Nightingale, and in the course of his gambols
he dashed up against a tree and broke his thigh, and
was put down not long after. Will and Bob buried
him in old Mercury's grave, close by the spot where
he met with his accident. He began the Waterloo
Cup luck of Dumfriesshire, which has now won two
and divided another with Selby. King Lear, the
other winner, was a "flying, merry dog, and won
—the first year it was a sixty four dog stake—solely
on his merits." Mr. Knowles had seen him win at
Abington, and got a good stake on when others
looked elsewhere

Some Fazzoletto two-year-olds were in the paddock, and Pam's Mixture and Pallinsburn in their
sheets were the last stable features in the landscape,
as we looked back to Knockhill. We crossed the
bridge where Sandy and the Carlisle pack swam
an otter for three hours last summer before they
killed it, and so up the long avenue of Hoddom
Castle. It is now twenty years since the General
died, and it has had no inhabitant save the stalwart
keeper, who looks after the pheasants. On a summer's evening, when beech and laurel are in all their
glory below, there is no pleasanter watch-tower. The
Annan winds round the holme below the terrace,
and Mr. Sharpe's horses have a gallop of fully a mile
and a quarter along the river side, and across the
turfed bridge, and a good sobbing finish up Re-

pentance Hill. The course is nearly the same as the
General had when he trained Perlet, and Messalina
from old Myrrha. He also kept beagles and harriers, and sold the latter to Mr. Ramsay, along with
Myrrha, who was heavy in-foal with Midlothian,
for £300. The cream of the Dumfriesshire country
can be seen from here, and our companion indicated
the geography of a great run, how they found at
Castle Milk, came over Bar Hill through the Duke's
cover and Brown Moor, and how he died honourably
in the meadow below the castle. Repentance Tower
to the right, and built by an ancient lord of Hoddom,
to atone for the souls he had sunk in the Solway,
almost flings its shadow over the birth-place of
Thomas Carlyle; and farther on is

> "That wooded hill
> Far kenned as Woodcockair"

It has always been a great harbour for foxes, and it
is recorded that after the Revolution the Hoddom
men ran their curate, Timothy Thomlinson, to ground
or to tree in it, across the Annan, and never heard
of him more.

Mr. Sharpe's hares were trotting about near the
March fence betwixt the lairds of "Hoddom" and
"Dormont," on Ronald's Hill, above the Dumfriesshire kennels. Joe Graham put on his Cumberland clogs, and came with us as guide; but scenery
was as nothing to him, unless "the noble science"
was blended with it. He had no eyes from that
coign of vantage for the silver line of the Solway and

the breakers at the mouth of the Nith, but he could tell of the Kinmount Woods. If your eye came to slow hunting over the Vale of the Annan, he lifted you at once to Castle Milk, and told how "the Duke" and the Jardines were "the soul of the hunting." "Castle Milk's our meet," he says; "most like an English meet of any—regular Badminton-lawn business, and everything for all. Lockerby side," he added, "is muirland and the best scent, and here we can always run with an east wind, "which they cannot in some countries."

Mr. Hay of Dunse Castle hunted the country before Mr. Murray of Broughton, and then Major Colomb came from the Inglewood, and kept it for a season or two, with Joe Hogg as his huntsman. There was then a long dreary blank, until Joe appeared upon the scene in 1848. He is the son of a farmer at Newtown, near Carlisle, and "still fond of a bit of hunting from a lad." The taste in his case seems to have become chronic, as he indulged it first with the Carlisle foulmart hounds, and then with the harriers, and he was finally gazetted to be first whip under Bob Cowen of the Inglewood. The kennels were at Tarn Wadlin, and Sampson was the head of the pack. They took out the old dog merely to find for them, as he knew every inch of the biggest covers, and was never known to leave a fox behind. He was a very mute hound himself, after he had once flung his deep-finding note, and yet his best son Cumberland lost his life in a very curious way, for "*making an oration.*" Mr. Boag succeeded Bob Cowen, and then the Inglewood were broken up, and Joe was engaged to go under the late Charles Treadwell to the Berwickshire. However, he was taken ill, and never went, and settled near Holm Hill, to hunt stag for Mr. Salkeld, with fif-teen to twenty couple of the Inglewood. For the first year Cowen hunted them, and Joe only rode to save the stag, and then he took the horn, and has never been without it for five-and-twenty sea-sons.

Lord Galloway did the leading stag business, and like her Majesty's The Doctor, who always runs to Wind-sor, he might be turned out at Rosley Hill, or Penrith, or Warwick, but go he would to visit the county member at Barrock Lodge. In fact, Joe was kept so hard at work among the Barrock shrubberies, hour after hour, that his knowledge of plants grew perfectly Paxtonian. His lordship lived a curious life. Once he crossed an arm of the sea, and was never found till they slotted him a week after among some tur-nips at Burnfoot, and took him finally at Annan. Then Cumlogan was mislaid at Lowther for a time, and when he was brought back he kicked out the side of his car, to Joe's amazement, on Broadfield, and there was another bye day for him. One way or another, they had a deal of sport, and Lord Galloway was still so full of pluck when Mr. Salkeld gave up and sent him to Baron Rothschild's, that he lay out all night in the South after an excellent run, and, according to Joe's Southern correspondent, "the Master of the Queen's Buckhounds asked if they could get him any of the sort."

About the close of Mr. Salkeld's season (1847-48), the Dumfries men got so weary of their winter idleness, and missed the good old days of Mr. Murray so sorely, that they begged the loan of the hounds for a week. Accordingly Joe came over, and had three capital days, and finished up with a clinker to Castle Milk. The fox, the hounds, and three of the hardest riders were all in the river together below Rockhall; but they unfortunately changed in the whins, and the rear men met the run fox stealing back. There was of course a great dinner that night at Lockerby to wind up the week, and in his speech after dinner Joe proposed to devote himself and his sixteen couple to the country two days a week at £240 for the first year. His visit had lessened the foxes by a brace. A third of the few which were in the country were at Kinmount, and Mr. Johnstone* and some of the Jardines were still in India and China. Matters progressed very well, although the Blue Bell Yard at Lockerby was the most primitive of kennels; but the Marquis of Queensberry took the command next season, the subscriptions were doubled, kennels were built at Seafield, and the hunting was increased to five days a fortnight.

Besides the covers we have mentioned, they sometimes go to Waterhead, an outside cover on the

---

* The late Mr Andrew Johnstone's first blood mares are not stated correctly at page 351. For "Theresa by Wagtail" read "Theresa Panza by Cervantes, Wagtail by Whisker," and add "Royalty by Emilius."

moors near the Moffat hills, for a day, and find
most capital foxes. Tinwald Downs, Cumlogan,
Brown Moor, and Wamphray are always good for
cubs, but they don't place much reliance on litters.
"As for the fences," says Joe, "there are not two of
them alike, banks and timber, and walls and ditches.
The Marquis was a terrible loss; he was always at
the head of his column and never looking for weak
places." His cheery "*Hark to Pallafox!*" his fa-
ourite hound, as he rammed the spurs into Little
John or Bonnie Dundee (so called in honour of the
fiddlers' feat), and came crashing out of cover for
a start, seems to ring in their ears yet. He had a
wonderful voice; they could hear his halloo any distance down wind, and Woodcockair used to ring
again when he tallyhoed him away for Kinmount.
He liked the wildest hunting, and a day on Criffell
pleased him beyond measure. "*Joe,*" he used to
say, "*if I could only get some of the Melton men up
here, we'd give them a dusting!*" and then away he
went, among bogs and sheep-drains, and perhaps six
or seven foxes "cooring" along the walls together.
For three seasons he opened the hunting with a week
at Langholm, and, what with hunting by day and
fiddles by night, the little town had quite a convivial
week of it. It may be that some enthusiast kept it as
a memento; but it is certain that Joe lost his cap on
one occasion, and returned gracefully at the head of
his hounds, in a straw hat borrowed for the occasion.
He was much worse off on another occasion, as he and

the Marquis lost the hounds entirely. The find was at the Bar Hill, and they saw the last of them near Thornhill. The kennel door was left open, and some stragglers arrived on the second night, and the remainder in a third-class carriage of which the Marquis and Joe guarded the doors.

On the death of Lord Queensberry, Mr. Carruthers of Dormont came to the front at the request of the members of the Hunt, who increased the subscription. He at once built new kennels, and has gone on steadily improving the hounds which belong to the Hunt. Perhaps the best run yet was on the last day of his first season. After drawing all the best covers blank, the hounds were going home at half-past three over Rockhall Moor, when a travelling fox was viewed, and the scent proving something wonderful, they regularly raced the fox over Hartwood, Thorniethwaite, Ryemuir, Skipmire, Shaw Hill, through the holding cover of Dalfibble, where he disdained to hang, and over the wild Kirkland Hill, Glenkiln, and on to Burance, where Joe Graham, Mr. John Johnstone, and Jack Roberts, the whip, the only ones up, saw the fox and hounds all on the side of a hill. The ground was so soft, and intersected with moss bogs, and the horses so well pumped that the riders had to get off, and giving theirs into Roberts' charge, Joe Graham and Mr. Johnstone footed the fox and hounds over the snow on the top of Queensberry, where they separated after a serious consultation, Joe to follow the traces of the hounds, and Mr. Johnstone to find a shepherd to give Jack a line to follow Joe. The distance gone over was not less than twenty-six miles. All the people in the fields shouted as they passed, "*Go on; the fox is no a hundred yards aheed.*" Well might Joe vow, when he parted with Mr. Johnstone, "*I never want to see another fox like this.*" But for a little whisky which he begged at a shepherd's hut, Joe would never have got to Thornhill at all, but he reached it in his boots with a few tail hounds, while the rest went on with their fox to a strong breeding place, near Dame's Deer, and cast up again in twenty-four hours. There was another grand run last season from Brown Moor to Wester Hall, where they killed.

'When old Jolly Boy and all the Cumberland hounds were worked out, the Atherstone, Rufford, Durham County, and Rhûg drafts came in. Monitor, with his serious features, and Matchless, his sister, are the pick of the pack, and of the Rhûg sort, a great many of which come white like Marshal, and old Malakhoff, whose low-scented qualities convinced Joe that he would be "quite a waterman" for Dr. Grant, when he grew too slow for the Castle Milk business. Talisman and Touchstone are the only ones left by him. There are also one or two black and tans throwing back, like Mr. Baker's, to the bloodhound. Myrtle and Triumph have always a good word from Joe; "little Rally is as good a one as ever ran before a stern—the best I ever bred in

Cumberland or Dumfriesshire;" and Damsel and Daphne are his delight. The former gravely gave him a paw, in testimony of their eight seasons together. "She never ran a hare in her life, and when the young'uns are taking a tour, she sits down and lets them rattle away." Merrylass, sister to Malakhoff and dam of Matchless, had been down south to Mr. Parry's Sultan, but had only whelped a contribution of a couple towards the twenty couple which are sent out annually among the Marquis of Queensberry's, Mr. Hope Johnstone's, and other walks.

Joe's horse Captain came with him from Cumberland, and lasted for six or seven seasons. Horses do last with him, and they say in the county that he picked up one for 7s. 6d., and that it was seen ridging up turnips on his farm six years afterwards. His mind must be quite torn between the advantages of artificial manures and sheep dips, and their effect upon scent, as he has five hundred acres in hand, and twenty score of sheep, as well as four ploughs going. He also kills some twenty pigs a year, and was therefore fully qualified to ride in the farmers' race at Ayr. Ever since he was at Tarn Wadlin he has had a fancy for leather flapping, and his white jacket and black cap, and his small 9st. 5lb. figure inside them, have been seen blazing away at Hawick, Langholm, Lockerby, Whitehaven, Paisley, Blaydon, and sometimes at Carlisle, where he won the Citizens' Cup on Lizzy of Brampton.

The Fawn was in the hunting stable, and so was The Veteran by Rataplan; but we had to toil over the fallow to see Blood Royal, his winner of the last Caledonian Cup. He was in a barn, and guarded, as far as we could see, by a game-cock. The brown was bred at Hallheaths, but Mr. Johnstone thought he showed the white feather, and got rid of him. At first it seemed no catch, as he hit his leg, and was fired and stopped in his work for nearly a year and a half.

With care and patience he was got fit enough in Hoddom Holme to come out at Carlisle, and Joe scored his first legitimate race. He ran again next day, and showed the most sovereign disregard of posts, and was, in fact, all over the course the moment he was "pinched" at the river turn. At Ayr he turned sulky, and could hardly be got on to the ground until Joe mounted him; and Skipjack's party, seeing the humour he was in, sent their horse along the three miles to break his heart. However, the lad obeyed Joe's orders not to hustle Blood Royal, and to catch them up the straight, which he did cleverly enough. And so the Caledonian Cup winner returned into barn residence for the winter and spring, and then perhaps, after another year's retirement, he may go flapping again. As Joe says, "*It's something to look at a Caledonian Cup winner; but he's got no heart in him for all that.*"

The shore of the Solway became a reality at last, and when we reached what was once the sea-side home of Mosstrooper 3rd, we found that Mr. Beattie was almost off with his old love, and in a most spirited attitude of defiance on the subject of salmon. From a mound near his house you see seven counties and and seven miles of salmon nets. He considers this shore "the mother of trap or stake nets," and he is lessee of the coast from Lochar Foot to about three-quarters of a mile east of Annan. He defies Parliament, the *Carlisle Journal*, and every other "proud invader"; and leans his back, like a man and a Briton, against his "chartered rights of fishing beyond time immemorial"

Get him on that subject, and he is as diffuse as a Blue Book. At all events, he still holds his trap nets against the world, as he told us he should, and so far he is the winner. The best fish come up with the tide and the south-west breeze. They feed along the beach in warm and cloudy days, and then return into the deep beyond Robin Rigg. In fact, "the speckled monarch of the tide" now reigns supreme at Newbie. Still, the greyhound, Baron Solway, once a great favourite on the Border, and the winner of £144, runs about the yard; the shorthorn cow, Roan Cherry by Booth's Cardigan, was in the stalls with Captain Marshall from the Howes; Belted Will, one of the last of the "black Brunswickers," was on the ruined keep near the old castle garden, and Bridesmaid and Bridal Bed had not yet quitted the spot.

As a Galloway winner at the Highland Society
Mr. Beattie has had few marrows, and many photographed prize-winners hang on his parlour walls.   It
was with Palmer's old cow that he first began; but
his great hit was with Mosstrooper (296), whom he
purchased at six years old, from Gibbons of Mossband.   He won fifteen first prizes, and was never
beaten, but he had an accident on board ship, that
fearful night (when Mr. Douglas was within an ace
of being washed overboard) as he returned from the
Paris Show, and was sold to the butcher when they
reached the London Docks.   He left a very good one
behind him in Mosstrooper 3rd, who was first at the
Highland Society in '60, and first at Battersea as
well.   At Dumfries he beat all the polls for the gold
medal, and Messrs. Hugh Watson and Graham reported him to the Royal English Society's Journal as
" a bull first-rate of his kind, who gained the first
prize against three good animals."   He was out of
Lady, bred by Mr. Beattie from Lady Keir of Mr.
Keir's breed at Potholm   His daughter Bridesmaid
was also first in the cow class, beating the Duke of
Buccleuch's M'Gill, and she can be traced back
through two generations to the Palmer cow.   Mr.
Beattie is still well known as a tup breeder, and keeps
from five to six score of ewes, and sells his tups privately into Ireland, Cheshire, Lancashire, and Cumberland, as well as in Dumfriesshire.   He has used
Polwarth rams, and a half-brother to Mr. Sanday's
first prize at Carlisle did a great deal for him.

It was not the market day, and Annan had no interest for us save what centred in its old church. When we had last ridden through its streets one-and-thirty years before, men were still talking of Edward Irving's protest before the ministers and elders of the Presbytery, and telling how in the twilight of that March night he "went forth from the church, where he had been baptised and ordained—from the Church of Scotland, the Sanctuary of his fathers—never more to enter within walls dedicated to her worship, till he entered in silent pomp to await the resurrection and advent of his Lord."

Redkirk* was not very far from Gretna, and a few miles from it on the left of our route was the scene seventy years ago of the great Solway Flow. The moss rose and floated a mile or more over road and field on the north side of the Esk, and according to the *Shepherd's Calendar* it smothered in its course "2 men, 1 woman, 1,840 sheep, 9 cattle, 3 horses, 4 dogs, and 180 hares," and it took three or four summers to put matters at all right again.

* Mr Syme has a three-hundred-acre farm at Redkirk, about two miles from Gretna Green. About a fourth of it is bad moss, and the rest very adhesive clay, and good free land. He has farmed for nine-and-twenty years on his own account, and kept pure shorthorns nearly all that time. Forcing for shows has not been his object, and in fact he has hardly exhibited above a dozen times, and always been first or second. When the Highland Society came to Dumfries in 1845, he was second both with a cow and a heifer. His herd has generally numbered from forty to fifty, and he has had a regular trade for them with Messrs. Miller, Armstrong, and others, near Toronto, Canada West, where they have been remarkably successful in taking prizes. Some of his bulls have also gone to Australia, and one to Singapore, to cross with the native heifers. Mr Stirling, M P, has had a few of his blood, and Rosy did good service at the last Keir roup. The Canadian market was virtually closed to him three years ago, and this led to the sale of his herd by Messrs Wetherall in May last. He, however, retains two old cows and two heifer-calves as the germ of a new one.

We should have liked to linger on the Border, but the Waterloo was at hand, and we had a sovereign even with "Stonehenge" that we would have the patience to ride from Carlisle to Kensington. Taking Knells, Holme Eden, and Corby Castle on our way, we rattled along in a hard frost up the Vale of the Eden, and over Shap Fells at night, with nothing but the dreary whistling of the wind through the telegraph wires to bear us company. The lights at Kendal were a pleasant beacon at last; and Settle, Skipton, and Skibeden was our line of country next morning. Had we read Admiral Fitzroy more closely, we might have avoided that heavy storm which swept down the valley for nearly an hour between Skipton and Burnley. There was no friendly Horse or Lion, Red, White, or Blue, which abound in those parts, to receive us; and there was nothing for it but to fight it out, get on with the mare's head at an angle of 90 degrees when she would go, and get to leeward of a hedge when she wouldn't.

The Towneley roan and chesnut, Royal Butterfly and Kettledrum were duly visited, and the last we saw of our Scottish friends was at the Waterloo, where "Dalgig" and Mr. A. Graham were very sweet after two courses upon King Death. It was all mud next day beyond Stockport, and hard frost at Buxton, mist and rain at Ashbourne, and snow at Derby. Then we passed through Quorn, and into the heart of Mr. Tailby's country, and bent away through the big Pytchley pastures to Fawsley. Another hard day, and the towers of St. Albans were in view at last, looking down on "The Jolly Maltsters," "The Post Boys," and "The Trumpet" signs, which still linger in its streets. On we went the last eighteen miles, with sleet and snow for our portion as the lights of the great city began to glimmer through the mist, and the thoughts of how to deal with bacon, wool, and cheese, those triple Furies of our note-book life, pursuing us grimly to

The End.

Printed by Rogerson and Tuxford, 246, Strand, London.

Printed in Great Britain
by Amazon